For my friends who died of breast cancer.

May your voices be heard and the truth prevail.

'… some of us will always have rotten bad luck and carry on and the disease will develop, that is going to happen, but rotten bad luck is easier to live with than the thought that your surgeon may have damaged you … You have this gnawing suspicion that maybe if you had woken up with a nice flat chest wall the day after the operation, maybe you would be feeling well now, but I'm never going to know.'

Shena Mason, 1938–2014

The Cost of
TRUST

The Cost of
TRUST

The Butcher Surgeon
and the Scandal that
Shamed British Medicine

DEBORAH DOUGLAS

Mudlark
HarperCollins*Publishers*
1 London Bridge Street
London SE1 9GF

www.harpercollins.co.uk

HarperCollins*Publishers*
Macken House, 39/40 Mayor Street Upper
Dublin 1, D01 C9W8, Ireland

First published by Mudlark 2026

1 3 5 7 9 10 8 6 4 2

A catalogue record of this book is
available from the British Library

ISBN 978-0-00-871293-8

Printed and bound in the UK using 100%
renewable electricity at CPI Group (UK) Ltd

Prologue

The renowned surgeon smiled as he stepped back from the podium, and we broke into applause. I stared up at him gratefully, full of hope after his rallying speech to a room of over a hundred enraptured women. It was 2009, and I was six years into my treatment for breast cancer.

Growing up in a working-class family, I wasn't someone who would have paid for private healthcare out of my own pocket, but my job came with insurance, and as my GP had said – if you have it, use it. That's what it's there for. It gave me immediate access to the best breast cancer surgeon in the Midlands – perhaps even the country – and those of us whose lives he had saved through surgery considered him our personal god. The difference between private and NHS medical care had been immediately apparent to me. No health concern went unchecked, and my surgeon would refer me for tests and scans constantly, which were all covered by my insurance. This was healthcare as it was supposed to be, and he exemplified the best of patient care.

He was an ordinary-looking man, middle-aged and balding, a little overweight, but he had a sort of rockstar effect. His demeanour was one of eminence. An expert, an angel, a life-saver. He enjoyed his reputation, and being centre stage. The audience was a mix of NHS and private patients, brought together by our membership of a local charity support group where experts could come and address us on everything from surgery and chemotherapy to wigs and aromatherapy.

Solihull had a higher rate of breast cancer than average, and this particular surgeon's talks were the most popular. I had seen him address an audience many times since I'd first become his patient and joined the support group. On one occasion I was asked to give him a vote of thanks after his talk, so I made a short speech about our gratitude for his hard work and support, and presented him with a bottle of wine.

He was always accompanied by his right-hand woman, a breast cancer nurse to many of the patients in the room. It had been her idea to start the support group in the first place, and while she was only the nurse for the private patients, everyone knew her. She supported NHS patients who wanted to transition to private, giving them advice and the promise of faster, more attentive treatment. At the charity's biennial 'pink ball' – a black-tie fundraising event – he was always the guest of honour, and one year she arranged for a bagpipe player to 'pipe' him in as he walked on stage, in a nod of respect to his Scottish heritage. They were a team, my team. There's nothing about luck when it comes to cancer, but I did feel lucky to have Ian Paterson on my side. He was the best doctor that money could buy.

Seven years later I sat in a different sort of auditorium – the viewing gallery of Nottingham Crown Court – and watched Ian Paterson stand trial for crimes so horrific they would make the front page of national newspapers, destroy the health of hundreds, and change my life for ever.

My name is Deborah Douglas. I'm the chair of the support group Breast Friends Solihull, a retired Rolls-Royce aerospace professional, a wife, mother and grandmother – and a former breast cancer patient. Between 2003 and 2011 I trusted Ian Paterson over and over when he told me I needed a mastectomy, breast reconstruction, seven months of chemotherapy and an operation to remove gallstones. My body was left scarred from shoulder to hip, but I lived in gratitude that I had been treated by such a great man.

In 2013, it all fell apart in what would become one of the biggest scandals in British medical history. I've spent more than a decade since then campaigning for justice for everyone affected, and to change the culture in medicine that allowed him and others like him to thrive. This is my story.

1

In my campaigning work I am often asked about resiliency, bravery and what it takes to stand up to authority in the face of injustice. In my fight against Ian Paterson, the medical establishment and the government, I often drew on skills I gained during my aerospace career, but my working life does not tell the whole story. I have always been a fighter.

The notorious back-to-back houses of Birmingham are now mostly gone, designated 'slums' in the twentieth century and consigned to demolition. The testaments to their existence are photographs, stories and a set of refurbished dwellings in the city centre that function as a museum and living history.

Our council-owned Victorian terrace in Nechells was a one-up-two-down with an outdoor toilet shared by other houses. We moved there in 1959, when I was almost one. Mum was pregnant with my brother John. Her two younger brothers, my uncles Joe and Norman, had been taken into care when their father left, so Mum, who had also been in care, decided to bring them to live with us. She was just twenty, now with three children to look after and a baby on the way. My parents had the bedroom, while the rest of us shared the attic. Joe and Norm had single beds while John and I slept in a dilapidated double bed with a dip in the middle which we'd roll into every night. We called it 'the sink hole'. Downstairs was a small living room, a cupboard-sized area for the kitchen, with a cooker and sink, and a dark, damp, coal cellar illuminated by a single electric bulb. In the shared yard was a small metal grating that could be opened for coal to be delivered straight into the cellar.

Mum was always running around cleaning and cooking for everyone, while Dad was a disciplinarian. He had had no real parenting role models, and his style of fathering was, 'When I say jump, you say, how high?'

The tiny house was crowded and chaotic. Eventually, Joe got married and moved out, while Norm joined the army, but they would often bring their friends back to our house and stay over. Mum would welcome and feed them all, even if it meant giving up her own dinner.

Mum was the heart and soul of the family, perhaps because she had been missing those things in her own life. She was born in Birmingham to a Brummie mother and Belfast father. Her mother Rose was a heavy drinker who spent her days in the pub drowning her sorrows after her husband left her to marry bigamously in Wales. When Mum was eight, Rose got a job and left her daughter to take care of her younger siblings, Maureen, Joe and Norm. Inevitably, an accident happened. Joe scalded himself with boiling water and the authorities descended, first sending the family to the workhouse and then splitting up the children. Joe and Norm went to Erdington Cottage Homes and Mum and Maureen were sent to a home run by a Catholic charity. Thereafter, Mum would sleep with her sheets and blankets tucked tightly around her and wouldn't move a muscle in bed. If I ever shared a bed with her she would say, 'don't move, I can't stand people moving in bed'. Eventually, she told me that the nuns and priests would put their hands inside the sheets. If she wet the bed the sheet would be pulled from under her and she'd be forced into a freezing-cold bath. Other than that, she never talked about the trauma that she and other children suffered there, but decades later when that same charity hit the headlines for historic abuse, I was not surprised at the details.

Mum's hard upbringing shaped her character. Photos of her as a child show her 'hungry poor', skinny and underdeveloped for her age. After she aged out of care at sixteen, she was isolated and had no support network, so she went to the Isle of Man for the summer to work as a chambermaid. She returned well fed and with a few bob in her pocket for new clothes. She would attend the local dance in Summer Lane – a notoriously hard area of Birmingham, but one that was held in affection by anyone who lived there, for its sense of community and large Irish population. This is where she met John Maher, my dad.

While Mum always used words to stand up for herself, Dad preferred his fists. At fourteen he had been sent to Birmingham from Ireland with his father, Jack, who was looking for work. Dad spent his final year of schooling at St Chad's Catholic School, where he stood out for having the 'wrong' clothes. He fought the four boys who picked on him and they became friends for life. After leaving school, he got a job in Ansells Brewery, met my mum, and two years later she fell pregnant. At the time she was living as an 'unpaid skivvy' with a woman who convinced her to handle her pregnancy with a hot bath and a bottle of gin, but baby Deborah was going nowhere.

Mum was nineteen when I was born, Dad just eighteen. Still kids themselves, they had no one to turn to for advice. When I was a teenager, I found a copy of their marriage certificate. The date of their wedding was 23 May 1958, four months before my birthday. I shouted out, 'Hey Mum, did you have to get married with me?', waving the certificate around with a big grin on my face. She looked mortified and said, 'I never wanted to tell you in case you made the same mistake as me.' Her advice to me as my girlhood advanced was, 'keep your hand on your halfpenny'.

Still, they made do, and I was welcomed and loved.

Our lifestyle in the back-to-back was as Victorian as the house itself. Going to the toilet in the night meant either going on a potty, which was usually kept under the bed, or sitting over a tin bucket. The rest of the time we had to go outside to the yard where the shared toilet was located. There was very rarely toilet paper, but sheets of newspaper ripped into squares and hung off a nail on the wall. Next to the toilet was the 'brewhouse', where Mum did the weekly wash in a tub. There was a mangle for squeezing the water out of wet clothes – a trap for inquisitive little fingers. To wash her children on a Sunday evening, Mum would fill a tin bath with water from a small portable boiler or saucepans from the stove and place it in front of the coal fire. That fire was fascinating to me. Someone told me my nightie was 'inflammable', so I decided to see what would happen if I put a corner of the hem into the flame, then pulled away quickly as the material began to shrivel. I was left with a crunchy hole in my nightclothes and a sense of a narrow escape.

Not every child was so lucky, and our tenure at the back-to-back came to an end following a tragedy; the death by fire of a local mother and daughter. Afterwards, our neighbour, Pauline, presented a petition to the council. She was accompanied by protestors with children, carrying placards that said 'Pull Down These Death Traps'. Many of the old houses had no fire escape at all.

It was a relief all round when, in 1967, Birmingham Council cleared the slums and relocated us to a house in Kitts Green, around five miles from the city centre and a significant upgrade for us. We had an indoor bathroom, hot water and a garden. Finally, at age eight, I had my own bedroom, and I could begin to figure out what sort of life I wanted.

We were Brummies, but I knew we were also Irish. Not just from my Dad's accent and stories, but from our social lives, church and my schooling. I had attended St Vincent's RC

Primary School and had Holy Communion in a beautiful white dress, my parents proud and beaming. Birmingham had a significant Irish population, which had only been a positive thing in my childhood, but the beginning of what became known as the Troubles in Northern Ireland caused a significant shift in attitudes towards us. In 1969, when I was just starting senior school, daily scenes on TV of rioting and bombings changed the British people's perception of the Irish and they started to see us as a threat. I'd hear people saying 'Irish bastards' when talking about what had happened on the news.

In 1972, following the Bloody Sunday shooting on 30 January of twenty-six unarmed civilians by the British Army, the Provisional IRA extended its campaign to mainland Britain. Over the next few years, attacks or attempted attacks took place every few days, and a great fear set in. Adverts on TV and at bus and railway stations warned us to be vigilant and report unattended packages, which only reinforced the fear. I was told by my parents to stay away from the city centre, and it became almost a weekly occurrence that someone would call in a hoax bomb threat at my school. We'd be evacuated onto the school field and usually sent home.

Two years later, nine off-duty soldiers, as well as an army wife and her two children, aged five and two, were killed in the bombing of a coach on the M62 by the IRA, leading to new anti-terrorism laws targeting suspected IRA members. It felt like everyone was under suspicion, and the laws meant detention and deportation could happen to any member of our community at any time. Our anxieties were heightened by the July 1974 explosions in Birmingham, including one at the Rotunda, the city centre's iconic high-rise office block. But we tried to continue our everyday lives as normally as we could.

It was impossible to fully avoid the city centre (or 'town' as we called it), and at sixteen years old I was keen to get out and enjoy myself, as any teenager would. On Thursday 21 November 1974, I got home from school to be greeted by Dad asking if my brother John and I wanted to go to the pictures to see the new sequel to *Planet of the Apes*. We didn't hesitate to say yes, and, as usual, it became a community event. John's friend Gary came along, as did Mark, the fourteen-year-old son of one of Dad's friends, who we collected before jumping on the number 53 bus to town.

The Odeon cinema in Birmingham city centre was next to a pub named The Tavern in the Town. Also nearby was the Rotunda, which housed a pub named The Mulberry Bush on its bottom two floors. Both pubs were full of patrons as we arrived at the cinema, settled into the middle seats of our screen, and began to watch the film. At around the same time, the newspaper the *Birmingham Post* received a phone call saying a bomb had been planted in the Rotunda, but not on which floor. It was in a bag near the rear entrance of The Mulberry Bush and, six minutes later, it exploded.

Inside the cinema, we heard a noise unlike any bang I'd heard before. It was more like a boom, a great rumble. We all jolted upright in our seats. I instantly knew it was a bomb. Dad told us to stay calm and not move as the cinema manager appeared and reassured the audience that everything was all right and the film could continue. Ten minutes later, there was an obvious restlessness in the auditorium, and several people got up and started to leave. As they did so, a second explosion rocked the building. The screen went black. Dust blew in from the side of the stage where the building had been damaged, and panic set in. A few people were screaming, and everyone rushed to get out.

The second bomb was at The Tavern in the Town, next door.

Dad told us once again to stay calm. We waited for what seemed an eternity, then he asked us to hold hands and not let go as he led us into the aisle and out through the exit, which was being lit by someone's torch.

Outside in the cold November air we stood away from the cinema on the other side of the street and looked at the scene.

There was glass and rubble in the road from the pub next door. The air was smoky and smelled strange. People were dazed, some bleeding, including people from the cinema who had left after hearing the first blast and had been met with flying debris from the second just a couple of minutes later. We could hear sirens. Still holding our hands, Dad shouted for us to stay in the middle of the road and away from buildings as we walked steadily down New Street, onto the High Street and then right onto Carrs Lane in the hopes of catching a bus home.

As we waited, I saw a classmate, Lucy. She was in shock and shaking all over. 'It's Yvonne, she's in there, they won't let me near!' Her sister Yvonne was in The Tavern in the Town, where Lucy and her boyfriend Jimmy were planning to meet her to celebrate a friend's birthday. Although we were all underage, it was normal for us to drink in pubs. Lucy and Jimmy had just seen another friend, Les, who was covered in white dust, the skin on his face and hands injured. He could barely talk or hear from the impact of the blast but had managed to tell them that Yvonne was in the pub. Lucy and Jimmy ran to the pub, but the police wouldn't let them near, instead telling them to go home and check to see if Yvonne was there.

Miraculously, some buses were still running, so we all went home. I tried to reassure Lucy on the way. She later told me she ran all the way down her road and burst in the back door to the kitchen where her sister Bernadette was washing her hair ready to join her sisters at the pub. Lucy screamed to her dad, 'There's been a bomb in town, Yvonne's in there', as the newsflash hit the TV screen that many people were dead or injured.

We carried on our own bus journey and got off a couple of stops after Lucy to drop Mark home and use his landline to call Mum and tell her we were safe and would be home soon.

Lucy's family didn't have a phone. Her dad went into town on the bus in search of Yvonne, but by then New Street had been cordoned off so he couldn't get near. All he could do was turn around and go home. Her mum rang all the hospitals from the nearest phone box, but there was no sign of her daughter. Hours later, the police came to the door and told them Yvonne was alive and in hospital. Initially the police were sympathetic, but Lucy said that as soon as they heard her dad's Irish accent, their attitude changed and they refused to take them to the hospital.

Yvonne survived. She had been pulled from the pub through a hole that had been blown in the wall and taken to hospital by one of the many local TOA black cab drivers who acted as emergency ambulances that night. She was badly burned and spent weeks in hospital, but she was one of the luckier victims; 21 people died and 220 were injured.

The events of that night changed us all. The next day I went into school and the class was in disarray. Two girls were crying while other classmates tried to console them. They thought that because Lucy had been going to the Tavern and was not in school, she had died. Another girl was furious on behalf of the victims, as her mother was a nurse who had treated the wounded. She said she was going to beat up another girl, Margaret Kelly, because she was Irish. I said, 'If you pick on her you'll have to fight me first. I'm also Irish.'

None of us were the same after that. That Saturday I went to work at my job at Saltley Market and experienced what I now know is called a flashback. A lorry loudly rumbled past and I froze, my heart pounding as I believed in that moment it was another bomb and I would surely die. There was no escape to be had. The bombings were met with outrage and the Irish community bore the brunt. Windows were smashed in, people were beaten up, workers at the Rover car factory were dragged off the track and assaulted. Dad started acting strangely. Whenever the phone rang he wouldn't let us answer it, telling us to leave it to him. I later learned he was getting death threats against him and his family from an anonymous caller.

My friends and I were robbed of the innocence of our teen-age years. We grew up overnight, and we learned that many people believed that being Irish meant you were guilty. One of the worst terrorist attacks on British soil also led to one of the worst miscarriages of justice, as the men known as the Birmingham Six were wrongly arrested, beaten and imprisoned for the bombing. In 1991, after years of legal battles and un-wavering support from journalists and campaigners, they were finally released and compensated. To this day the fight goes on to bring someone to justice for the massacre carried out that night.

2

What little I know about Ian Stuart Paterson's childhood suggests it was not much like mine. He was born in Glasgow in 1957, but at some point in his childhood his father, a civil engineer, relocated the family to Bangor, County Down. The young Paterson had what appeared to be a privileged education, attending Connor House, a private 'preparatory' school that served as a pipeline to Bangor Grammar School, which he attended from 1966. When researching these schools to gain some insight into Paterson's early life, I discovered that former Bangor Grammar teacher Dr Lindsay Brown was convicted of sex offences against young male pupils between 1968 and 1982, dying in February 2024 before additional cases dating back to the 1970s could be prosecuted.

There's no suggestion that Paterson was a victim of this man, but I found the culture of the school at the time worryingly familiar. Victims and concerned parents had campaigned for an independent inquiry into Brown's crimes, which was eventually granted and published in July 1998. The report was kept under wraps, but it was finally declassified in 2018 at the Public Record Office in Belfast under the twenty-year rule, and it makes for chilling reading. I recognised all the same key issues that would later cause me to become a campaigner: management minimising or ignoring complaints, a lack of protocol for dealing with incidents, the alleged offender being allowed to remain in place during investigation, and a climate of fear by colleagues that giving evidence would jeopardise their careers. One former pupil even mentioned the 'old boy's club' nature of the place, a phrase that increasingly seems to mean 'untouchable'. Whether it's education, healthcare or any other sector, the fact that one man with such power over vulnerable individuals could be allowed to get away with crimes for so long is a disgrace. And yet, I do not find it surprising at all.

Ian Paterson left Bangor Grammar to attend the University of Bristol, from where he graduated in 1981 with a degree in medicine in his early twenties. He was a keen rugby player, representing Bristol University and Sale. He claims he was capped for Ireland.

In 1984 Paterson moved to Manchester to train as a general surgeon at Stepping Hill Hospital. There, he had exposure to multiple specialties including plastic surgery, bowel and breast surgery, and vascular surgery. He chose to specialise in the latter, a career detail that will become very relevant later. That same year he married Louise, a physiotherapist, and they honeymooned in Barbados.

He claims he was then seconded to Harvard Medical School for a two-year research placement (Harvard did not respond to a request for confirmation) before returning to England in 1991, which is when he moved to Birmingham. I have been told that he never quite fitted into the upper echelons of medical society. His former nurse, Bethan Lloyd Owen, once told me, 'he didn't come from the same background' as his colleagues. Medicine is an elite and privileged profession, and also the one most likely to be 'inherited' (something that dates back to medieval guilds). As the son of a blue-collar engineer rather than a surgeon, perhaps Paterson had something like imposter syndrome. By 1994, his career had progressed and he was offered a role as a consultant vascular surgeon at Good Hope Hospital, an NHS hospital in Sutton Coldfield, Birmingham.

Gill Dallow was thirty-three years old when she attended Good Hope Hospital for what should have been a routine laparoscopy. The operation changed her life for ever. Her surgeon cut into her so aggressively, his scalpel hit her spine and severed major blood vessels. Gill lost eleven pints of blood and was left fighting for her life in intensive care.

'I had massive internal bleeding and they had to open me up and repair everything,' she said in a BBC interview. Her heart had been massaged by hand on the operating table in order to save her life. 'If it hadn't been for the theatre staff next door who came in, I wouldn't be here.' In 2001, Gill was awarded £40,000 in damages but was left with permanent physical and psychological scars. 'It's knocked my confidence. I don't really have any friends. I don't go out. I had to stop work. I used to be a registered childminder at the time and had to stop that because I just couldn't cope.'

No amount of compensation can make up for lost potential, a life thrown off track by the actions of a reckless surgeon. But at the very least, patients should be able to know that it will not happen again to someone else. Gill Dallow's near-fatal operation was in 1996, and her surgeon was Ian Paterson. She was his first victim.

All surgeons make mistakes, sometimes with fatal consequences. It's part of having one of the world's riskiest, most difficult jobs. What makes Ian Paterson different is how easily he lied to cover it up. As so many of his later victims would report, at first he presented himself as a saviour. He told Gill there had been an equipment malfunction and he'd fought to save her life. He might have got away with the lie, and the almost-lethal incompetence, had a brave colleague not blown the whistle. A local newspaper received an anonymous letter that said Paterson was at fault, not the equipment. Gill said in her eyes he went from 'God to the devil in one fell swoop'.

'If something had been done then, when this happened, none of the other women would have suffered,' said Gill. 'That's what hurts me the most.' She is quoted as saying he should have been struck off the medical register there and then for lying.

But instead, he got a slap on the wrist. A review was commissioned by the Royal College of Surgeons, which recommended that Paterson should undergo a period of supervised practice for a few months. When this was completed, he was free to carry out unsupervised laparoscopic surgery again. The lying was never addressed.

Paterson did not have a good relationship with colleagues at Good Hope Hospital. He had a reputation for being difficult, and would openly argue with co-workers. But he remained charming and popular with patients, a classic Jekyll and Hyde. Of course, had they been aware he had almost killed a woman and then lied to cover his back, they would perhaps not have agreed to be operated on by him, but there was no way of them knowing.

Although Paterson had trained as a general surgeon, in 1998 (two years after the Gill Dallow incident), he applied to work at Solihull Hospital, specialising in vascular surgery. The medical director there was Mark Goldman.

Goldman offered Paterson the job. Once he had accepted the post at Solihull his already fractious relationship with Good Hope Hospital deteriorated further and he was asked to leave by the chief executive without completing his notice period.

Francis Murray, a senior manager at Good Hope Hospital, was clearly concerned enough with the appointment that he phoned Rowland Hopkinson, one of the directors of the Birmingham Heartlands and Solihull Trust, to alert him of the fact that Paterson had been the subject of an investigation in 1996. It has never been clear whether this information was ever shared more widely with those responsible for appointing him. Andy Stockdale, the oncologist and Paterson whistleblower, said, 'It's always a surprise to us why they took him on when they knew he was trouble.'

One explanation is that the Trust was desperate. There was a backlog of operations, new government targets meant that patient referrals had to be seen within ten days, and there was an issue in recruiting surgeons. Paterson was able to turn on his charisma, and he soon found favour with patients and some of the nurses who worked with him, which in turn made him popular with the management. Despite the Gill Dallow case (or perhaps because it was not widely known), he was seen as a technically able surgeon who would help the Trust deliver targets.

Not everyone liked him, though. One surgical nurse who worked with him told me she took an instant dislike to him because he came into theatre arrogant and dismissive of her skills. He was seen by other specialists as being autocratic, ignoring the opinions of others, always wanting to have his own way and using bullying tactics if he didn't get what he demanded. The vascular surgery department had been working well, with meaningful multidisciplinary team meetings (MDTs), but these soon fell apart as Paterson refused to attend and was disrespectful towards his colleagues.

Soon after joining Solihull Hospital, he made a sideways move from vascular surgery to breast surgery. The hospital only employed one other breast surgeon, John Taylor, and demand was high. Paterson's attitude did not change. It was his way or the highway, and he didn't want to work with anyone who stood up to him. A third breast surgeon was recruited, but she left within a year because she found it increasingly difficult to work with Paterson.

When considering applying for the role she had vacated, a consultant surgeon named Hemant Ingle got in touch. 'I called her,' he said. 'She informed me that Ian Paterson was the breast lead during her time at Solihull and he did not treat her well; he wanted to control the whole unit. Her words were, "If you want to ruin your career you can apply for that job." I was taken aback and asked her why she was saying this. She said, "Well, as long as Ian Paterson is in that job you will never be able to do anything that you want to do."' She explained to him that when she joined she had a horrible time for six months. She was never given clinics, so she therefore had none of her own patients, just follow-up clinics. She was never given a theatre list, either. When she complained to management, nothing changed. They said, 'Mr Paterson is the breast lead and he should sort things out.' Despite this warning, Ingle applied for the job.

John Taylor also departed, leaving Paterson in charge of the department. Later on, in court, Paterson would claim he had built up the breast care clinic at Solihull, modernising the department and bringing his expertise to help many of his patients. In practice, this meant that between 1998 and 2007, he could simply do what he wanted.

3

My career started on a market stall. I had attended a secondary modern school and, having shown an aptitude for art, completed my A level in one year. Encouraged by my art teacher, I was accepted onto a pre-diploma course in Art and Design at Birmingham Polytechnic. I was the youngest student, surrounded by kids who, unlike me, had money. The tutor there told me I should apply to Central Saint Martins College of Art, in London, where I would 'lose my working-class accent'. That confirmed that it wasn't for me, and I couldn't see how I was meant to pay for it without the resources that my classmates seemed to have, so I dropped out of college and started working. I eventually got a position in the Lucas Aerospace factory that later became Rolls-Royce Control Systems, and worked my way up.

In 1978 I met a handsome man named Bob Douglas at The Bell pub in Birmingham, and promptly married him. We bought a house and had three kids, during which time I took a career break and worked night shifts cleaning buses while Bob worked as a bus driver. When the kids started school I went back to my career, and I was eventually promoted to a managerial role. By late 1999 we were doing well: a happy, hardworking family and a far cry from the life my parents had started with. That year they moved to a house nearer to me, Bob and our three teenage children. We celebrated the millennium together, and the year 2000 felt like the beginning of a great new chapter for the Douglas family. But life – and cancer – had other plans.

Mum was sixty-two years old, and until then she had never been ill. When she wasn't being a wife and mother, she worked as a canteen assistant for West Midlands Travel, where she was popular with everyone. When I was a teenager, she and I were often mistaken for sisters. She had beautiful blue eyes, mousey hair (which for as long as I can remember she bleached blonde), a wide smile and a deep, loud voice that spoke at a rate of knots. Her accent was Brummie, but when she attended school parents' evening she would always put on a newsreader voice. I used to get embarrassed about her doing this and would say 'don't try to speak posh'. 'Well, you have to, or they won't understand you otherwise,' she'd reply. Mum was quick-witted and had a saying for every occasion, was naturally funny and interspersed her sentences with swear words. If someone mentioned her swearing, she'd say, 'it's better to hear that than be deaf'.

In the summer of 2000, we found out that Mum's brother, my uncle Joe, had throat cancer. A few days later I had just got back from an overnight flight from Greece when Dad rang.

'Hi, Fairy. When you've had a sleep come to our house, we need to talk to you about something. Have a rest first, no rush.' Of course I wasn't going to have a rest. I rang my brother to arrange to collect him on the way, and immediately set out to see my parents. Whatever was wrong, it was obviously about more than Uncle Joe.

'Your Mum's got something to tell you,' said Dad. Mum was sitting on the sofa and gave us a weak smile. We hugged her as she told us that doctors had found a lump in her oesophagus. She'd been saying for ages that when she swallowed it felt like her food was sticking, and I'd reassured her it was probably acid but she should get it checked out. Now, I tried to reassure her again by saying, 'Well, it might not be cancer, it could be benign.'

A few weeks later she went on her own for what she thought was a routine appointment with a junior doctor. He started talking about her treatment options as if she had been fully briefed on what exactly was wrong.

'Is it cancer then?' she asked, confused.

'Yes, I'm so sorry. I thought you'd been told, you have oesophageal cancer.'

Had she been told in advance, of course she wouldn't have gone alone. We were all shocked and frightened, but I also felt furious about how badly the diagnosis had already been handled.

Her next appointment was with a charismatic, confident consultant, Paul Super. I went with her, along with Dad and John. Super's lilting Scottish accent was very reassuring as he delivered the news: 'It's a big operation, Mrs Maher. We have to go in through your ribcage, but you are young enough and fit enough to get through this.' We thought she was going to be okay.

Mum was started on chemotherapy, which made her really sick. She was told her hair would fall out, so I went with her to Rackhams, one of the largest (and to us, the poshest) department stores in Birmingham. The wig department was in a corner on the fourth floor, but there was no privacy and shoppers would walk past as she tried on hairpieces. There were only a few places that accepted NHS wig vouchers, so her choice was limited. She was shown a couple of short styles that sort of matched her colour, but the woman serving wasn't very helpful and it seemed to be an effort to get the boxes down for Mum to try on more styles, so we finally settled on one that we both thought was the closest match to her own hair. I took her back home. The kids were there with Dad, so we showed them the wig, and of course everyone wanted to try it on. We were all laughing until Mum said in a loud voice, 'I'm not wearing that fucking wig.'

She did eventually wear it a few times. A few weeks later, just before she went to hospital for her operation, we went shopping for a few things. As we sat down for a hot chocolate, she said, 'Do you think I'm going to die?'

'Of course I don't think you're going to die!' I told her. 'You'll get through this and get better.' It never entered my head that there would be any other outcome. But she was scared, because her mum Rose had gone into the same hospital at the same time of year and died at age sixty-one, a year younger than Mum was now.

The day of Mum's operation I was working the late shift, so I could go to the hospital beforehand. I was there when they wheeled her trolley away to the operating theatre. She had tears in her eyes. I kissed her and said, 'You'll be alright, Mum, love you.'

I went into work but couldn't concentrate on anything. It was the most stress I had ever felt. I watched the clock; it was major surgery so she would be in theatre for hours. The time passed painfully slowly, but eventually I phoned the hospital and felt a flood of relief as I was told Mum was out of theatre and doing well. I left work early and went straight to the hospital. Mum had tubes everywhere. She looked so vulnerable. I stared at her in the bed and her eyes flickered open. She smiled.

'Alright, Mum. Well done, you got through it,' I said. I saw her daily after that and she started to improve, but she was in a lot of pain.

'The bastards have taken my rib out,' she said. 'It's part of the operation. They never said any of that to me.'

Over the next few days she got a lot better. 'If I can walk up a flight of stairs tomorrow, they're letting me out,' she said happily. 'That's great, see you tomorrow, Mum.'

But the next day she had taken a turn for the worse. Her oxygen levels were low and it was affecting her breathing. The doctors thought she might have had a virus and were running tests, but she was getting weaker by the minute. I paid careful attention to her surroundings and medical care, and during one visit I noticed there were splashes of blood on the side table and floor near her bed. The nurse said she'd lost her balance and pulled her drip out. The next day the blood was still there.

My brother John and I started taking it in turns to be with her. We had to feed her, as she was no longer strong enough to do it herself. She was confused, and thought John was the doctor. We had no idea what was happening to her, but we now know it was most likely the MRSA bug, a type of bacteria that can infect wounds and make you delirious. People in hospital, particularly the elderly and those with compromised immune systems, are very susceptible to it.

Christmas and New Year came and went. We were at the hospital every day, worried sick. On 2 January 2001, all of her friends turned up throughout the day, lifelong friends she'd known since school. Mum just lay there mostly sleeping. I stayed with her all that night; she had been moved to ICU as she wasn't getting any oxygen. A lovely nurse came to wipe Mum's face and make her comfortable, and reassured me she was in good hands. I went home for a few hours' sleep, but when I returned to the ICU ward with Dad and John, we weren't allowed in.

A nurse came out and spoke to Dad. 'Your wife has had a heart attack. She's comfortable, but we've had to intubate her, she's on a ventilator.' Eventually we were allowed in to see her, but we were warned that it might be distressing. It was. Mum was unconscious, tubes everywhere. Her face had ballooned and her eyelids were swollen. She was unrecognisable. An hour later, a nurse told us the news we had been praying not to hear. 'Her condition is deteriorating, she hasn't got long.'

I asked for the priest to be called. He came and gave Mum the last rites. We were not an overly religious family, but I think we all found comfort in praying. Nothing could have prepared me for seeing the person I loved die in front of me, and the physical pain in my heart. We stood round Mum talking to her, telling her how much we loved her. At 11.30pm the nurse told us, 'She's gone. Your mum has passed away.'

She had an extraordinary funeral. Two double-decker buses turned up at the church with all her friends from the bus garage, as well as the many lifelong friends she'd made over the years. I tried not to think about the cruelty of her death but instead to remember the gift of her life and the lessons she had taught me. Strength, resiliency, love, and to make myself heard.

4

From almost the beginning of his career, Ian Paterson supplemented his NHS salary with work in the private sector. This is common for consultants, who are lured by lucrative deals at for-profit healthcare providers. David Rowland, director of independent think tank the Centre for Health and the Public Interest (CHPI), wrote in a 2022 *Guardian* article:

'The private hospital companies have for many years clocked the need to keep NHS consultants close to them, showering them with lavish corporate hospitality and offering them financial incentives, such as share ownership schemes and joint ventures to encourage them to do work in their hospitals.

'Under such schemes, the more private work they do, the more the business benefits and the greater the dividend pot which the consultants can draw from.'

In other words, it was a nice earner for Paterson. Moonlighting was accepted as long as the consultant sought permission from their NHS employer. He began private surgery work in 1993 at what was then BUPA Little Aston. In 1998 he added BUPA Parkway to his roster and focused most of his private sector attention there (both hospitals were acquired by private equity firm Cinven in 2007 and rebranded as Spire).

Paterson's dual income made him rich. He worked hard for his expensive and privileged lifestyle. His three children attended private schools, his son later becoming a solicitor and his daughters following in Paterson's footsteps as doctors.

The family lived in a Grade II-listed Georgian house in Edgbaston, a prestigious, sought-after area of Birmingham. The house boasts eight bedrooms, four reception rooms, a wine cellar and a coach house converted to a gym. He also bought a holiday home in Florida, and reportedly invested in several buy-to-let properties in the UK. Former colleagues told me he liked to spend £500 on champagne dinners at a Michelin-starred Birmingham restaurant, and the husband of one of his patients said that Paterson had let him borrow his Aston Martin for a spin rather than fret in the waiting room.

By contrast, Bob and I were your average upwardly mobile working class. The managerial role I'd worked my way up to at the aerospace factory came with private medical insurance. This was not something I'd have paid for myself, but it was incredibly reassuring after the experience of Mum's cancer. It felt like a major safety net for my health, a 'just in case' that was there if I needed it. What could be the harm? I was a staunch supporter of the NHS, but I also thought that private medicine got you access to the very best doctors, nicer hospitals, quicker appointments and more thorough tests than the NHS could afford. If anything, it was taking some of the burden away from the NHS, I rationalised. In 2002, private health insurance was becoming increasingly normal, the sign of a good employer and a generous remuneration package. In 2024, over four million Brits had health insurance, covering over seven million people.

I hoped to never need my medical insurance and wasn't even sure what making a claim would look like. The policy booklet was stored in a drawer, and I counted my blessings that my health was good. But cancer was never far from my mind.

After Mum's death, Dad was lost. Since they were young married teenagers, he had relied on her for all things domestic while he worked as a roofer. She did the shopping, cleaning, ironing, cooking – all the traditional roles of an old-fashioned housewife, even while she too had a full-time job. After her death, he'd come to my house for dinner most nights, but he tried to gain his independence. 'How much ham do I get for one person?' he'd phone and ask. Or: 'Can you come and help me sort some bills out?'

He had always needed his family's support for paperwork, because he was functionally illiterate. He had a fierce and quick intellect but had had no schooling, was deaf in one ear from a perforated eardrum as a baby, and was finally diagnosed with dyslexia in his fifties after I persuaded him to join a course for adult literacy at a local college.

Growing up with a dad who could neither read nor write presented challenges, and as a child I had had to grow up quickly in order to fulfill the role of interpreter and communicator on his behalf. That never changed. Eventually he settled into a widower's routine, cooking for himself and going to woodwork classes. I'd pop round and would hear Mum's voice through the TV. Dad played videos of her repeatedly. I found it quite disconcerting, but he got a lot of comfort from it.

But then he seemed to get weaker. He was looking after himself but losing weight and becoming more and more breathless. I encouraged him to go to the doctor, but when he finally did he was treated for depression.

'Dad, of course you're sad. But there's something else wrong with you, you can't walk from one side of the room to the other without getting out of breath.' I kept nagging, and he finally saw a locum who sent him for a chest X-ray. A week later he was summoned by letter to ward 19 of Heartlands Hospital. My brother John and I were worried. We knew that was the cancer ward, so we insisted on attending the appointment with him.

The consultant didn't beat around the bush. 'Mr Maher, there is no good news. You have lung cancer and I'm afraid it's inoperable.'

I couldn't believe what I was hearing. But then I heard Dad ask, 'how long have I got?' in a tone that betrayed how bad his symptoms had been. He had already known there was something very wrong, and he seemed almost relieved to have it confirmed. 'We can't say,' the consultant told him, 'but we'll give you some chemo to help with the tumour.'

Dad moved in with me, Bob and the kids, who by now were seventeen, fifteen and thirteen. Bob and I took opposite shifts so one of us was always home. I was doing well in my role, but I was mourning the loss of my mother and worrying about how rapidly Dad was declining. I visited Mum's grave almost every day, trying not to think about the prospect of also losing my father.

Dad only had four sessions of chemo; the oncologist said there would be no benefit to having more. After that he wanted to move back to his own house. 'So you can get your life back,' he said. I insisted he still come round for his dinner every night. As his health declined further, he decided to travel. Joining us on our family holiday to Cyprus, he was adamant he was going to paraglide. His breathing wasn't great, but he was grinning from ear to ear as he was lifted by a parachute into the sky over Paphos Bay. We returned to Ireland, visiting New Ross where we boarded the Dunbrody, a replica of the first wooden sailing ship to cross to America during the Great Famine. We even visited Blarney Castle, in Cork, and took it in turns to lean over backwards to kiss the Blarney Stone. It was no mean feat, but Dad did it.

I hadn't really considered my own health during this period, except to briefly acknowledge the implications of both parents having had cancer, a thought I quickly dismissed as too stressful to dwell on. In February 2002, John and I took Dad to Fuerteventura for a week. On the second day, I was walking across the hotel lobby when I felt my knees buckle. Everything went hazy. I had fainted, and woke up to a very concerned John leaning over me. My arm was sprained and badly bruised, and the rest of the holiday was painful and uncomfortable. Dad wanted me to see a doctor as soon as we got home, to find out why I'd collapsed. But I was more worried about him. The flight home was rough. He had excruciating pains in his chest and I kept thinking, 'please God, get him home safe'. After we landed he seemed a lot better. His consultant said his heartbeat was irregular and the tumour was pushing against his heart. There would be no more adventure holidays.

On 6 May 2002, Dad died. I stayed with him through his last night, sitting on his bed, trying to comfort him as he gripped the headboard in pain and gasped for air. His suffering was unbearable, but he refused to go into hospital where Mum had died. In desperation, I called the Macmillan hospice. 'My dad needs help.' I couldn't manage by myself, failing to lift him when he fell trying to get to the toilet. I called John and he arrived shortly before the Macmillan ambulance, and Dad was blue-lighted to the hospice. He was given an injection, and he became peaceful. As his breathing slowed, I held his hand and felt a tiny reaction to my squeeze. A few hours later, he gently passed away surrounded by people he loved.

I had put my own health aside while dealing with Dad's illness, his death and then his funeral. I had lost both parents to cancer, and the spectre of the disease was both ever-present and the one thing I didn't want to think about. I went back to work and looked after the kids while I processed my grief and found a new normal. My knee had been giving me trouble ever since I had collapsed on holiday the year before, but I had been ignoring it. Stress seemed to seek us out; in October 2003 Bob was made redundant; I was so worried about him that when I noticed a pea-shaped lump in my breast, I ignored that, too.

It was during a chance conversation about two months later that it finally clicked. One of Mum's old work friends told me that a friend she worked with had been having problems with her knee. 'It kept giving way under her. The next thing she knew she'd been diagnosed with breast cancer.' I thought about the lump I'd found in my left breast. A lightbulb moment, except the thing it illuminated was one of my nightmares.

On Monday 3 November 2003, I went to my GP. I'd booked it a while before to discuss why I was feeling tired and disconnected at work. I had figured it was the stress of everything, but I also told her about my knees, and the lump. She examined me and said in a reassuring voice, 'I don't think it's anything to worry about, but I'm going to refer you to the hospital to get it checked.'

I wanted something to be easy for once, or at least easier than it usually was. The months-long waiting lists, the huge and busy waiting rooms, the red tape and the terrifying thought of going to the same hospital as my parents flashed into my mind. I remembered that private medical insurance document in my drawer and said the words I'd live to regret: 'I have BUPA cover with my job. I've never used it, though.'

The GP was encouraging. 'If you've got private health cover you might as well use it,' she said. I went home feeling more reassured than I might otherwise have done, and called the BUPA helpline. I was given an appointment at the hospital now known as Spire Parkway for that very Friday, 7 November 2003, with a consultant called Ian Paterson. *I thought, how great is private medicine?!*

5

I only knew Ian Paterson as his patient, and I wasn't witness to his technique, his attitude or the conversations he had with colleagues over open bodies on his operating tables. But I now know what he was like in that environment too, because of testimony from former colleagues. They describe a very different man to the charming, jocular professional I met in consultations. 'We called him "Pac-Man" because he used to gobble up all the breasts,' a former nurse told me. She described how he was nasty to colleagues, and would throw things in the operating theatre, which she described as 'a bloodbath'. His technique was messy and – as was confirmed by others – unusually fast. 'He liked to say he was the fastest surgeon around,' said Karl Fortes Mayer, a retired consultant breast surgeon who had the operating theatre next to Paterson at Spire Little Aston in the early 2000s. 'His patients would lose a lot more blood because he was rushing.' Fortes Mayer says rushed surgery is not good surgery. 'You have to take your time to do it correctly.'

One healthcare professional who worked with Paterson in the NHS said he successfully bullied a senior member of management about an issue over patient consent. 'He came in like a bull, really aggressive, threatening to sue her. "Don't you dare," absolutely intimidating her. She was relatively new in the job and I think at the end it was enough to make her back off.'

Paterson gained a reputation for disrespecting his colleagues at every level. Another NHS clinician said, 'He lacked empathy or emotion, I believe he looked at any sign of illness or emotion as weakness.' Paterson mocked this colleague for taking time off for an uncle's funeral. The colleagues of Ian Paterson are crucial to this story. Some of them were whistleblowers, critical to his eventual downfall, but others were part of his small, loyal team. Perhaps the most important of the latter was Bethan Lloyd Owen, my breast cancer nurse specialist and Paterson's right-hand woman.

Lloyd Owen was born in Wales and had, as far as I've been able to tell, a good nursing career. In 1993 she won a Nurse of the Year award, and was the recipient of a BUPA Idea of the Year award in 2003 and 2004 for her cancer self-check guidelines. In 2002, she began to specialise in breast care and continued to develop her career through additional training, including breast prosthesis fitting and patient counselling. By the time I met her, at my very first appointment with Paterson in November 2003, she had worked her way up to Consultant Breast Care Nurse, a specialist role that included leading the patient's nursing team, managing chemotherapy and other treatment, discussing treatment options and risks with the patient, and providing emotional support.

I had hardly slept the night before my appointment. Bob had taken the day off work to drive me to the hospital. I barely said a word on the journey, just stared out of the window, trying to contain my thoughts. As we pulled in, I noticed the car park was almost empty, except for a few high-end cars belonging to consultants. I looked at the building, a low, flat-roofed, red-brick and white complex that could have been an office on a business estate. It was neutral, reassuring, calm.

We walked inside the double doors and I could see the reception desk ahead. The receptionist beamed when I told her I was there to see Ian Paterson. 'You're in good hands,' she said. 'Mr Paterson is the best consultant you could have. Everyone wants to see him.' Paterson was a 'Mr' rather than a 'Dr' on account of his seniority as a consultant, although the naming convention dates back to the earliest days of medicine when surgeon and doctor were very different careers. Bob and I sat nervously in the plush waiting area for a few minutes, then I heard my name. A pleasant nurse with a reassuring Irish accent introduced herself as Mary, and took me through to a sunny and modern consulting room.

'Ian Paterson,' he shook my hand and then Bob's. He was tall, heavy-set, in his forties. His face was nice enough but bland, forgettable even. He was wearing a navy-blue suit that looked tailored, and a crisp shirt and tie. His manner was friendly and engaging as he asked us to take a seat. The blonde woman next to him introduced herself as Bethan Lloyd Owen, my breast nurse specialist.

My voice was shaking as I told them that Mum had died from oesophageal cancer and Dad from lung cancer, both aged sixty-two. Lloyd Owen interrupted to say, 'Lung cancer is very different to breast cancer, Deborah. My mum died of lung cancer.' Paterson didn't comment, he just watched me with an almost puzzled look on his face that I couldn't work out. Then he got down to business.

'Let's send you for an ultrasound scan and do some tests.' I was unused to private medicine, where tests were done there and then instead of waiting weeks for referrals. Lloyd Owen led me to the scan area and handed me over to the radiology nurse, who asked me to get undressed in a nearby cubicle and put on a hospital gown. I sat in the waiting room in my gown, looking down at my feet in ankle boots, feeling very self-conscious. Finally, I was called through to the scan.

I lay on my back on the bed and the radiologist appeared from behind a curtain. I didn't catch his name. He seemed aloof and it was clear he wanted to get on with the business in hand. He squirted lubricating gel on my left breast then proceeded to push it around using a probe which he moved over my breast and up into my left armpit, stopping occasionally to glance at the screen and click a button. He then asked me to turn onto my right side. I looked up over my shoulder at the images on the screen. I didn't know what I was looking at, I just prayed there was nothing there. The radiologist said nothing, but pulled a handful of blue paper off a roll and dropped it onto my breast. I grabbed it and wiped away the cold, sticky gel. He said I could go back to Paterson for the results, then he left the darkened room.

I asked the nurse for more blue paper as my breast was still covered in gel. I got up, my gown still clinging to my chest. Mary chatted about her recent appointment to the role as she led me to a side examination room next to Paterson's office, collecting Bob on the way, and asked me to lie on the bed. Paterson appeared from his office. My heart began to race and I thought of the worst-case scenario. Then he said, 'Debbie, I've looked at the scan. The lump has an uneven and jagged edge and flashes of colour have shown up. We're going to have to remove it.'

This was the worst-case scenario I had been praying against. Was he saying I had cancer?

'I'll need to get some cells from it,' he said.

The needle was large, long, thin and hollow. I could see it was going to be painful. Paterson swabbed my skin above the lump, then said, 'this is where you're allowed to swear.'

I closed my eyes and clenched my teeth; he stabbed the needle multiple times into the area of the lump in my breast. The pain was excruciating, like a red-hot poker over and over. Once he finished, he walked slowly back to his office and said to Bob on the way, 'She's been a very brave girl. It wasn't a very pleasant experience.'

I sat up on the bed with Mary at my side and started sobbing. I was crying because of the pain but also for my mum and dad. I thought about how I'd sat with them in consulting rooms to hear the worst news. Now it might be happening to me. I carried all the baggage from watching my parents suffer. I was overwhelmed by a feeling of déjà vu. But my surgeon was confident, professional and – as I had been assured – the very best. He was going to send off the cells from the needle biopsy, and I had a follow-up appointment for the following Monday. He had suggested the lump would need to come out, but as operations go that surely wasn't so bad. At least it wasn't the whole breast.

I lay in the bath that night, my breast still burning hot, and looked down at my chest. Your breasts are not who you are as a person, I told myself. They're just flesh. Deep down, I just knew I had cancer. But if I did, the brilliant surgeon Ian Paterson would remove the lump, and my private medical insurance would cover the cost.

The follow-up appointment on Monday 10 November 2003 coincided with Bob attending a week's training course for a new business opportunity, so I took my brother John instead. I had already warned my daughter, Jen, that I thought I might have breast cancer, but needed to tell John, too. In the car, I explained what Paterson had said, trying to prepare him for the worst. 'What are the odds?' he said. 'Not after Mum and Dad, we couldn't be that unlucky.'

Bethan Lloyd Owen met us at reception and led us through to Paterson's office. He had the same demeanour as before, professional and no-nonsense. He shook our hands and asked us to sit down. My backside had barely hit the seat when he said, 'Sorry if I misled you on Friday when I said just the lump would have to come out, but we've had the results back and you have got cancer. I will need to remove your breast.'

6

I had already convinced myself the lump was cancer, but I hadn't been prepared for Paterson telling me the whole breast would have to come off. Not just the breast but the lymph nodes under my left arm. 'Why can't you just cut the end of the breast off where the lump is?' I asked. Paterson told me it was because the lump was too near the nipple, close to connecting blood vessels. He said the cancer would spread quickly if he didn't remove the whole breast, but the plastic surgeon would be able to take muscle from my stomach and reconstruct the breast. This was technically called a transverse rectus abdominal muscle (TRAM) flap reconstruction. The surgeon would move a section of skin, muscle and fat to create a breast mound, and reroute blood vessels to supply it with blood.

I got upset and said again that both of my parents had recently died of cancer. I was so scared.

Lloyd Owen reassured me, saying, 'You have the best surgeon and the best breast care team. You will be alright.' Paterson added, 'You will go into the theatre with two boobs and come out with two boobs and a nice flat stomach.' He was good at promoting the cosmetic side of things.

It was all too surreal. My brother John was in shock, and all I could think about was how to tell the kids and Bob. I tried to hold back my tears as I made arrangements for my next appointment, but as soon as I was out of the door I started to cry. 'Come on, you'll be alright, you're not sixty-two yet,' nodding to the age of our parents when they died. His risky joke worked, I laughed, and that gave me the strength to call Bob.

'It is breast cancer,' I said quietly.

'I knew I should have been there. I haven't been able to concentrate all morning.' He told me that the Bobby Goldsboro song 'Honey' had come on the radio earlier and made him well up. It's the story of a man's love for his wife who has recently died.

And honey, I miss you and I'm bein' good
And I'd love to be with you if only I could

Bob said, 'I'm coming home.' He must have driven like a lunatic because he arrived not long after we got back from the hospital. John left us to it. I promised Bob, 'I'm going to be OK.' Then I said, 'Thank God I have private cover, or I'd still be waiting for my results.'

The double team of Paterson and Lloyd Owen became my rock. They had a fantastic rapport. I would eventually speak to many Paterson patients who thought that Lloyd Owen was an angel who had helped them through their worst times, but I've also spoken to patients who told me that if you ever challenged her or Paterson's opinion she would change dramatically, her sweet demeanour and mask slipping to reveal a red-faced, angry woman whom you dare not question.

But to me, she was everything I could want from a nurse. During my next appointment with her and Paterson on 25 November, she did everything she could to put me at ease. I was terrified my cancer had spread and I was experiencing constant intrusive thoughts about it. 'I can give you a chest X-ray and stomach X-ray if you want?' she offered. I said thank you, yes. I then stupidly worried that I hadn't shaved my legs and hoped I had nice underwear on. The radiographer was abrupt and if he noticed my legs or underwear he wasn't saying. 'Turn on your side, breathe in, and hold. Breathe normally, turn onto the other side.' I didn't want to look at the screen for fear of seeing a terrible shadow. He left the room and I was on my own for a while as he looked at the X-ray. I prayed to God that it was all clear as I returned to Paterson's room.

He was holding my X-rays up against the lightbox on the wall.

'I have some good news, your results are clear, there is no spread.'

I was so relieved. My brother shook Paterson's hand and thanked him.

I said, 'So, I am curable?'

Paterson said the words I had prayed for but barely dared hope to hear.

'Yes, you are curable.'

This cancer wasn't going to kill me like cancer had taken so many of my loved ones. This incredible surgeon before me was going to cut it out, and I could go about my life as normal.

Paterson looked at his diary and said, 'I can get you into Little Aston for your operation if you want it sooner, otherwise it'll be an extra week.' I felt safer at the more familiar Parkway, which was also closer for my family to visit. I asked if it would make any difference to my cancer if I waited an extra week, and he said no. I wanted to get everything ready for Christmas in advance, so we agreed on a surgery date of 3 December 2003.

Paterson grinned and said, 'The next time we meet will be in the operating theatre, but you'll be asleep when I get there.'

The working life of a consultant breast surgeon is as much about management as it is surgery. Paterson would carry out the actual operation, but he also had to oversee my entire treatment plan, and this was done through a multidisciplinary team (MDT). This usually worked well in the NHS, with all of the team being in the same room or online to discuss individual cases and agreeing on a treatment plan, but in the private sector it could be messy. Paterson did not always play well with others. While some private patients who had shared care with the NHS would be discussed at NHS MDTs, patients who were wholly private often had no MDT at all. In my case he unilaterally decided I would need a mastectomy and reconstructive surgery. He then dictated a letter to his secretary for distribution to the plastic surgeon Chien 'CC' Kat, the oncologist Tal Latief, and Bethan Lloyd Owen, who would convey the details to me, even discussing my reconstruction and chemotherapy before I'd met Latief or Kat in person.

Two weeks before my operation I had attended an appointment with the plastic surgeon CC Kat. Not having met a plastic surgeon before, I didn't know what to expect. I certainly hadn't imagined the business-like woman with cropped hair who stood in front of me in an immaculate tailored suit.

Kat briefly explained she would be reconstructing my left breast using tissue from my body, then asked me to undress behind a screen and sit on the side of the bed with my legs dangling over the side. She sat on a lower chair and kept staring at my breasts, her eyes going from one to the other. There is something very uncomfortable about sitting forward on the edge of a bed while someone stares closely at your naked breasts without saying anything. I felt incredibly exposed and self-conscious. She scribbled a drawing on a piece of paper, then took a measuring tape and measured the size and shape of my breasts.

She asked me to stand up and then grabbed hold of the flesh on my stomach, pinching it in her strong hands and tugging it down. She asked if I had much feeling in my nipples, then proceeded to tweak them, clinically. She noted the position of my belly button and that I had a small scar on it from a laparoscopy from a previous miscarriage.

She explained that she could take the tissue for the reconstruction from my back or my stomach. She examined my stomach muscles, then asked me to confirm I do not smoke. Paterson had already promised me 'two boobs and a nice flat stomach' so I said I'd go for it.

7

I was on my own for a few nights, as Bob was away on a training course. I hadn't been sleeping and was overtired. I lay awake in bed and found myself having a panic attack. I couldn't breathe and tried to phone Bob but couldn't get hold of him. I started crying, choking back the tears as I didn't want the kids to hear me. I called my brother John and said, 'I think I might die.' He reassured me, saying, 'You won't. You're going to be OK.' I felt calmer straight away. I think I just needed to talk to someone.

I resolved to take a practical approach. Christmas presents were bought and wrapped and I'd decided to get my hair cut short. I had been told by the breast nurse that my hospital room would be very hot so that the blood supply to my reconstructed breast would have the best chance of surviving. Cutting my hair short would keep me cool, and there wouldn't be so much to lose if I needed chemotherapy.

Sunday 23 November 2003 was my mum's birthday; she would have been sixty-five. I visited my parents' graves again to ask them to watch over me. I stood and cried. I missed them so much. That night I snuggled close to Bob, who was back from his course, and said, 'You probably ought to make the most of my boob while it's still there.' I began to cry at the realisation that my breast would be gone. The new one would probably have no feeling in it, and a blank disc for a temporary nipple. I turned to Bob and asked, 'Do you love me?' He said, 'Of course I do. I love you and nothing will change that.' We held each other in the dark.

I had lots of visitors during the few weeks before my admission to hospital. Most of them didn't really know what to say. I found I was having to comfort them and tell them everything was going to be alright.

My long-time friend Alan phoned during that week. I explained the operation and how they would take the blood supply from my stomach via a vein and route it to my left breast. I laughed when he asked, 'Does that mean when you're hungry your tit will rumble?'

One night a week before the operation I couldn't sleep, so I decided to get up and go downstairs. I sat on the sofa and suddenly realised how devastatingly lonely Dad must have felt and how scared he must have been after Mum had died and he was diagnosed with terminal cancer. His tumour had pushed into his chest, causing heart palpitations and pain. My own chest felt tight as I kept thinking how brave my parents were. They both carried on normally, at least in front of me and the family. I had read an article a few days before about breast cancer. The woman survived, but the article said she could have died, and for the first time I was hit with the full force of reality that I had a life-threatening illness. I tried to dismiss the thought and think positively. I wrote in my journal 'I WILL GET THROUGH THIS!'. I had to, for the sake of my own family. I had already broken the news to my grandmother in Ireland, who was praying for me. My kids, teenagers at the time, were looking drawn, especially my oldest son, Robert. He generally kept his feelings to himself, but his best friend's mum had recently died of breast cancer. He later told me that he had believed I was also going to die.

It's a strange thing when you're diagnosed with a potentially fatal illness. Everyone around you slightly overreacts whenever you say something mildly amusing, and I could feel people's eyes on me when they thought I wasn't looking. I remember doing the same thing to my dad, staring at him, watching his every move. I was aware that he had a terminal diagnosis and I just wanted to take in everything about him because soon he would be gone. He was aware, too. He spoke for hours about memories he had growing up in Ireland. It was important to him that he passed on as much family history as he could.

I decided to go to confession. I was baptised a Catholic but after my parents died I hadn't been able to bring myself to go to church. I'd felt angry and couldn't pray, but now I felt I needed to make my peace with God. I was half an hour early for Mass. The old church was darkly lit with just candles and a few lights, peaceful and calming. I entered the confession box, knelt, and made the sign of the cross. 'It has been years since my last confession,' I told the priest, and he said reassuringly in his Irish accent, 'take your time'. I felt myself getting upset and my voice was shaking. I told him I was going in for major surgery. 'I have cancer.' He asked what sort of cancer. I told him, and that I hadn't been attending Mass. 'God won't punish you for not going to Mass. You will be alright.' He said he would pray for my surgeons and for my operation on the day.

I had to have a lot of faith. Paterson would remove my breast and lymph nodes, and Kat would step in immediately to perform the 'TRAM flap' procedure. She would remove my belly button and replace it with a hole she'd make after my stomach had been stitched up. This incision would run horizontally from hip to hip just above my pubic bone.

On the day of my admission into hospital I was up early to make sure I had packed what I needed; I couldn't sleep anyway. I kissed my children goodbye, and Bob drove me to Spire Parkway. I registered at the admissions desk and was shown to a side room. It was quite small: white walls and a single hospital bed with white linen sheets. This was the holding room where I would spend the night before my operation.

I had hardly got off to sleep when I was woken at 7am by a knock at the door. It was Kat, who had come to mark me up for her procedure. She asked me to take my top off and pull my trousers down below my waist. I stood in front of her almost naked, and she drew around both breasts with a black marker. She made a mark on the front of my neck, drew around my belly button, then made a straight line around the middle of my torso and one around my lower waist. After she had left, I looked at myself in the mirror, feeling like a patchwork quilt. I looked at the lines and knew that after the operation I would never be the same again.

At 8.30am a nurse came in with some surgical stockings and told me to get changed. Bob arrived around 10am. By this time I was quite calm and just wanted it over with. I was told I was the second operation that day and would be taken to theatre at noon. The nurse returned and gave me a tablet to relax me. The anaesthetist, Faiz Bannourah, came to see me. Lloyd Owen had told me he had an excellent reputation, and all the nurses kept telling me how lovely he was. He looked at my wedding ring, which was very tight. I had tried and tried to remove it but it wouldn't budge. Eventually, Bannourah said it would have to be cut off, because if my hand swelled during the operation I could lose my finger. He went away and shortly after a man wearing a blue operating theatre gown came in with a cutting wheel and a pair of pliers. My finger began to get very hot as he cut through my wedding ring. Finally, he prised the ring open with the pliers. I felt quite upset and asked Bob to put the ring in a safe place so we could have it repaired later.

I was now ready for my operation. I was told by Bannourah that I needed to sign a consent form, which he waved in front of me. There was no discussion about the risks. I was signing to say I was having a left skin-sparing mastectomy with an imme-diate TRAM flap reconstruction. At 11:30am a porter came to wheel me to theatre. This was it. Bob walked alongside my trolley. When we got to the big double doors of the operating theatre the nurse told Bob, 'This is as far as you can go.' I kissed him goodbye. As soon as the door shut behind him my eyes filled with tears. Kat leaned over and said, 'You're not upset, are you? I have a hundred per cent record with the last lady and a hundred per cent with the lady before. I'm a hundred per cent sure you will be alright.'

Bannourah said hello and told me to think of something nice. I pictured the view of sunny Dublin from the top of the Guinness factory, but as I closed my eyes I saw lots of birds flying up from the green field at the front of my Nan's house in Ireland. Before I knew it, I was under.

And then, just as suddenly, I was coming around in recovery with a nurse either side of me. I was pretty out of it, and kept repeating, 'I feel sick, I feel sick.' I stared groggily at the clock on the wall. It was 5.10pm. 'When am I having my operation?' I asked the nurse confusedly. She smiled and said, 'You've had it my dear.' I was wheeled back to a room in the high depend-ency unit (HDU), where I was monitored every hour. This white-walled room was much bigger. The bedding was still the same, but there was a side table with an old-fashioned telephone on it and a window, although I couldn't sit up to see anything. The walls were white and the one opposite me had a dark brown wooden door in the middle of it, which led to an adjoining room. HDU rooms meant there was a higher ratio of nurses per patient than on a general ward, and observations were every two hours. The nurse was going between me and another patient all through the night.

When the pain finally hit, it was bad. I felt like I'd been kicked by a mule. Everything hurt. I was wearing an oxygen mask and had two drips attached to my right hand. In my body was a total of six drains, three from my abdomen and three from my left armpit, where all of my lymph nodes had been removed. I had had a catheter fitted for the toilet and an epidural drip in my back. I had intermittent pneumatic compression devices fitted around my calves; they filled with air and squeezed my leg much like a blood pressure cuff to increase the blood flow through the veins and legs to prevent blood clots. They kept tightening and relaxing and sounded like someone breathing at the foot of my bed. To top it all off, the bed itself was really uncomfortable. All I kept thinking was, *it's over, and I'm still here.*

8

We live in a society that wants women's bodies to be a certain way; to have a nice cleavage and flat stomach, to look good in a bikini. Before the operation I would look down at my cleavage and tell myself, it's not who I am as a person, it's just a piece of flesh. I'm not sure I believed that, though.

The priorities for a breast cancer operation should be safety and the best medical outcome for the patient. Cut away the cancer in such a way that – hopefully – gets rid of it for ever. The operation that Paterson sold me also prioritised looks. This seemed like a win-win. I would have scars, but Paterson's words had been a sales argument: 'You'll go in with two boobs and come out with two boobs and a nice flat stomach.'

After the operation, I drifted in and out of sleep. An Irish nurse named Peggy checked on me every hour. When I was awake, I was in agony. I looked at the monitor at the side of my bed. As I breathed out, my oxygen level started to drop to 50. I breathed in and the levels climbed again. It brought back memories of seeing my mum in intensive care, the night she died. All we did was watch the screen on the monitor for her levels to drop. I began to panic, so I told Peggy about my mum and how scared I felt. 'Stop looking at the screen,' she told me. 'If there's a problem the alarm will go off.' I wanted my mum. I asked Peggy to tuck the sheets up around my neck the way my mum used to, which she did, and I drifted painfully back into sleep.

The next morning I learned I was breathing all wrong. A physiotherapist named Karen came in to explain that I needed to breathe deeply five times an hour to make sure my ribcage expanded. This would clear the carbon monoxide out of my lungs. She checked my chest and showed me how to move my hands and feet for circulation. I did exactly what she said, wanting to get better as fast as I could.

John rang to see how I was, followed by my sister-in-law. It was kind of them but I was in too much pain and felt too nauseated and exhausted to talk. When Bob arrived, I told him I didn't want any more calls to be put through. I had had a few text messages but was in no state to answer them. I hadn't expected to feel this ill. The nurses said I would have to stay in bed for another few days. One of the breast cancer specialist nurses came to check on me. I told her everything felt tight. 'I can't breathe,' I gasped. She leaned over close to me and said, 'I have a secret. I've been through the same operation.' She reassured me I'd be okay. She seemed so fit and well, and I suddenly had hope that everything would be alright.

Day two of my recovery did not start well. The auxiliary nurses wanted to change my sheets, so they needed to manoeuvre me. I had a nurse either side of me, but instead of pulling me up the bed together, one nurse pulled the sheet down instead. I screamed; my stomach felt like it had been ripped open. They had torn the stitches around my belly scar and left a hole about the size of a ten-pence piece in my stomach. There was blood on the sheet from the epidural in my back. One of the nurses asked if I was menstruating. I was too weak to say anything other than 'no', but inside I was furious with her.

The other nurse seemed to feel bad about hurting me. 'Can I get you a bowl of ice cream?' she asked. I felt so exhausted and vulnerable I couldn't say anything. I knew my life was in their hands. I was hooked up to machines, totally reliant on these two people who couldn't even pull in the same direction. I tried to keep my mind on recovering. I had a needle in my hand hooked up to a morphine drip. It was leaking. I asked the nurses if they could please take it out as it was making me feel sick, which they did. A junior doctor prescribed me a suppository painkiller instead, which a nurse dutifully inserted. It helped the pain but, it turned out, caused incontinence. I couldn't turn my body or move at all. I cried about the indignity and said sorry to the nurses who had to clean up and change me. 'Don't worry, we've seen worse. It's what we're here to do,' they said kindly.

The next day I could finally get out of bed. The nurses sat me up, but I immediately felt sick and very hot. A nurse pressed a cold flannel to my forehead, which helped. 'Let's get you on to your feet.' I stood up slowly, feeling weak and wobbly. My stomach stitches pulled as I shuffled to the chair next to the bed. My whole body was covered in sweat and I felt horrendous, but I had done it. First milestone achieved. The nurse carefully helped me get back into bed.

On day four I was supposed to be having my drains out. The nurses who came in every few hours to check on the blood supply to the breast examined the top of my breast above the tight tape that bound it, pressing the breast tissue, looking for colour and temperature changes. They didn't wear gloves and I worried that I'd get an infection from their hands. Lloyd Owen had previously told me I should have my drains removed gradually over a few days post op. Despite that, the painful drains remained in place.

On day five, after barely eating properly since before the operation, I ordered a bacon sandwich. I was looking forward to it, but between the pain of using my arm and hand to lift it, and the nausea that followed, I couldn't eat. Paterson arrived and told me I would be 'out of here' in another four or five days. Internally, I panicked, thinking such a long stay meant I wasn't recovering well. Paterson left, and around twenty minutes later Kat arrived, checked my charts and told the nurses to remove the drains and then I could be discharged. This was both good news – I must be healing well – and bad news, as I could barely stand up or move. But I perked up at the prospect of home.

The nurses came in shortly after and proceeded to take the drains out. The drainage tube from my stomach had an air lock in it and as they were pulling it my stomach started to go into a spasm. I screamed, 'STOP! STOP!' The pain was unbearable. I was shaking and my heart was racing from the shock. The nurses gave me a break until I had recovered a little, then carefully pulled again. They took all six drainage tubes out at the same time. I felt completely exhausted, but I had to go home. I thought of Mum in hospital, thinking she could go home but never getting there. That wasn't going to be me. I called Bob, but he said he thought I wasn't well enough. 'I'll be okay,' I insisted. 'I'll stay upstairs for a few days until I'm feeling stronger.' Under duress, he agreed to pick me up later that day. I had to prove to the physiotherapist that I could get out of bed, walk down the corridor and climb a few stairs. I was determined to do it.

I went home later that day, utterly grateful to be sleeping in my own bed but still very weak. I stayed in bed for a few days, taking co-codamol (codeine and paracetamol) every four hours. Bob set me up with a portable TV then camped out in the spare room so he wouldn't disturb me at night.

Once I could get out of bed I looked in the mirror at my body, trying to find the positives among the swelling and scars. I'd lost weight anyway so a new slim me with a flat stomach was looking back. I still had a cleavage, which seemed like a good thing, although if I wore anything too low the ellipse at the top of the scar would be visible. I didn't recognise the woman staring back at me. It's just flesh, I told myself again. A few days later I ventured downstairs to discover my youngest son Will and my friend Loreta had put up the Christmas tree to welcome me. Surrounded by loved ones, the sparkling decorations and pretty lights were just what I needed to see.

9

Ten days after my operation I went back to Spire Parkway for a check-up. I got myself up and painfully into a pair of tracksuit trousers and a sweatshirt. Bob drove me to the appointment and helped me as I struggled to walk. Doubled over, my stomach as tight as a drum, I shuffled down the corridor to see Lloyd Owen and Kat.

Lloyd Owen removed the wide tape around my body, covered the scars with surgical tape, and dressed the wound in my stomach where the nurses had split my stitches. She told me I could shower, but I would have to replace the tape if it came off. This was a relief, as I wasn't allowed to use deodorant because of the scar under my armpit where Paterson had removed my lymph nodes, and I was worried I smelled bad.

The tumour, surrounding tissue and lymph nodes that Paterson had removed had been sent to Spire's pathology lab for testing. Over the next few days I tried not to think about my next appointment, at which I would get the results. Anxiety was running high, but I reassured myself and everyone else that Paterson had said my cancer was curable and that he had cut it all out.

Finally, I found myself heading back to Parkway to find out what sort of cancer I had and just how serious it was. There are three grades in breast cancer, which pathologists identify by comparing the cancer cells to normal cells. Grade three is the most serious, cells that grow quickly and have a tricky prognosis. Grade two cells look different to healthy cells but grow moderately quickly compared to grade three. Grade one is the least serious (although all cancer is serious). The cells look somewhat similar to healthy cells, grow slowly, and respond well to treatment. The next stage is what dictates the treatment itself. Cancers are classified based on the TNM (Tumour, Node, Metastasis) system. If the area of cancer is under two centimetres it is classed as small. Node is whether the cancer has spread to the nearby lymph nodes. Metastasis is whether the cancer has spread, and this has different codes depending on where cancer cells are present (blood, bone, lymph nodes that are not near the breast, etc.). M0 means there is no indication the cancer has spread. There are also other tests, including hormonal, because hormones like oestrogen can fuel cancer cell growth.

As I walked into Paterson's room at Spire Parkway, Lloyd Owen winked at me, did two thumbs up and said, 'We've been waiting all day for you. It's the best news we could have had! You've got grade one, the lowest-grade cancer and there's been no spread to your lymph nodes.' Paterson had removed nine of my lymph nodes, which he called a full node clearance. I was almost speechless with relief and gratitude. 'Thank God,' I blurted out. He told me I had oestrogen-receptive breast cancer that could be treated by a drug called tamoxifen, which worked by removing the oestrogen from my body that could feed the cells. I was over the moon. Yes, I had cancer, but the prognosis was excellent. I wasn't going to die.

A few weeks after the operation I got a seroma, which is a build-up of fluid around the site of a trauma. My stomach had distorted because it was so swollen on the side where I'd had my reconstructive surgery. It was very painful, so I called Parkway and was told to come in to have the fluid drained. It was 2 January 2004, and Lloyd Owen was on annual leave for the holidays. There were no other nurses available that had the experience to draw the fluid so Paterson said he would do it himself. I took my top off and lay on the bed in his office. He took a huge needle and pushed it into my stomach where the swelling was. It felt like he was wiggling the needle around. The pain was excruciating. I began to cry. Paterson glanced at my face and said, 'Happy New Year!'

Perhaps it was meant as a wry joke, an ironic acknowledgement of my miserable situation. He was a man who had devoted his life to helping cancer patients, maybe he had earned a warped sense of humour. But I was in so much pain, so vulnerable in his hands and so exhausted I couldn't help being angry. Bastard, I let myself think. I suspected he wouldn't have said it if we weren't alone.

A few weeks later I returned to Parkway with Bob to meet Tal Latief, an oncologist. His job was to treat my cancer going forward, to minimise the chance of it recurring based on the pathology results. An immaculately dressed older man in an expensive-looking pastel suit, he shook my hand and introduced himself.

Latief reiterated that the tumour Paterson had removed was 18 millimetres and grade one. I was hoping that meant I wouldn't need chemotherapy. I undressed and Latief examined my breasts and surgical sites and ran his hand down my spine, pressing on it as he did. I thought it was odd that he checked my spine, so I asked him why, and he just mumbled that it was to check everything was okay. I thought no more about it but read much later that the most common site for metastasis into the bones was the spine.

'You have a 6 per cent advantage if you have chemotherapy treatment,' he said. I didn't really know how to put 6 per cent into context. It didn't sound like much of an advantage. I told him how sick my mum was during her treatment and said I didn't want it. Latief looked troubled at that. I didn't know what was best.

'If it was your wife, what would you advise?' I asked. Surely no doctor would recommend treatment the patient doesn't need, let alone something as difficult as chemotherapy, but I had no way to tell if the benefit of the treatment outweighed the pain. 'I would tell her to have the chemo,' he said. 'It's belt and braces after your operation and it will improve your chance of a full recovery. But you don't need to decide now, let me know at our next appointment.'

I sat in silence next to Bob in the car on the way home, mulling over what Latief had said. I thought of my mum, how ill she was and how scared we had all been. And then I thought of my own kids, and all of a sudden I was struck with the obvious. I said to Bob, of course I had to have the chemotherapy. Even a 6 per cent advantage is an advantage. I'd got through a lot already, but I could get through a bit more. I wanted the best possible chance to stop this cancer coming back.

On 14 January 2004, just six weeks after major surgery, I started my chemotherapy, which would last until July.

Latief started me on a very strong drug called Epirubicin. The pamphlet I was given warned of side effects including hair loss, sickness, loss of appetite and taste. I was scared, but the first visit went better than I expected. I had attended a pre-assessment medical before my chemo to check my blood count, blood pressure, weight and heart rate, so that when I arrived at Parkway I would be ready to start my treatment.

I was shown to my own room, complete with TV and lunch menu – the perks of private medicine. I ordered a ham sandwich and got settled on top of the bed. I had butterflies so I switched the TV on to take my mind off things while I waited. A nurse came in and introduced herself as Claire. She was calm and professional as she explained my bloods were fine. I moved to a chair next to the bed while Claire pulled up a trolley containing a cannula, a small bottle with red liquid in it and a reel of medical tape. She checked the dosage on the bottle and my date of birth. I said it needed to go into my right arm as I had no lymph nodes in my left arm. It had been drummed into me after my operation that I should never have a needle in my left arm due to being susceptible to getting lymphoedema, a debilitating swelling. Claire carefully inserted the cannula into a vein, taping it securely in place, drew the liquid from the bottle using a large plastic syringe, then inserted it into the cannula and began pushing it very slowly through my vein. It took about fifteen minutes to empty the syringe. She told me she had to be careful of leakage out of the vein and to make sure she didn't blow my vein in the process, so she needed to take her time. I could feel a cold sensation as the liquid flowed into me, but it was bearable, and Claire said I was doing well. Afterwards, she flushed my vein with water, which was an even colder sensation in my arm. I thought, that wasn't too bad, I can cope with chemotherapy. I went home with Bob feeling positive.

The second session was two weeks later. The process was the same, but afterwards I started to feel ill. The drug was building up in my system, and very soon after the second session my hair started to fall out. I would find hair in my food, chunks of it came out when I showered, it was everywhere. Every part of my body hurt, including my scalp. It hurt to put my head on a pillow, so I asked my friend Loreta to shave my head. I pulled a dining chair up to a large mirror in my tiled hall. Loreta stood behind me with the clippers, talking about how she was used to shaving her husband's head. She started with the guard on and I could see my hair falling to the floor. When she had got rid of all the longer hair she removed the guard and started to shave my scalp. I felt my eyes well with tears and joked about it being like a scene from the Magdalene laundries.

I honestly thought I'd be fine with losing my hair. I kept thinking of my mum and 'that fucking wig'. It's just hair, I had told myself. It doesn't matter. As I looked in the mirror at my newly bald head, I fought off tears. My relationship with my body changed dramatically after that. I had pain around my breast, my arm and my stomach. One minute I'd be boiling hot, then I'd start shivering because I was so cold. I alternated between diarrhoea and constipation. I couldn't sleep. I couldn't eat properly and constantly had a nasty taste in my mouth. I was also on steroids to help with the side effects of the chemo and to reduce inflammation and pain from my surgery. I was still struggling physically from the operation. Steroids helped with fatigue, but they can also affect the metabolism and how the body holds on to fluids, so I gained a lot of weight. So much for my new slim body.

One night, I wrote a poem in my diary:

Alien
I look in the mirror, a bald alien stares back.
My head is smaller, my shoulders broader
because my thick dark head of hair is gone.
I look at my breast. It has tape around the scar,
hope my boob doesn't fall off.
I look down at my new belly button. It's slightly off centre.
My skin is stretched so tight, like a drum.
I have a scar from hip to hip around my stomach,
there's still tape on it.
I see the three deep marks where the drains went in.
I lift my arm and look at the scar running
under my armpit where my lymph nodes were removed.
I always wanted a scar when I was a kid,
I was a real tomboy.
I got a good gash on my shin when I was ten
from trying to do a trapeze act
on the door frame of the girls' toilets.
I thought
that was a good one, but this is not what I wished for. I sure
look weird.

Over the next few months I went through the same process over and over. The nurses would take my blood cell count to ensure it was high enough to accept the drugs, then find a vein to administer them. As time went on my veins started to collapse and the process got harder and harder. I would try to get into a zone and breathe through the pain of the nurses trying to find a vein. They tried to persuade me to have a Hickman line fitted, which is a surgical tube that's inserted through the chest and tunnelled under the skin directly into a vein to get the medication in at the source, so to speak. I couldn't stand the thought of the procedure on top of everything else, so I said no. Eventually, I only had two usable veins on the back of my right hand, but they held up until the end.

Later on in the treatment I would be prescribed combination chemotherapy that had the acronym CFM (cyclophosphamide, methotrexate and fluorouracil). I was assured by Latief that this was the 'gold standard' treatment for cancer patients. The side effects were much less severe and I could feel recovery was on its way, physically at least. The isolation was starting to get to me. I was still grieving my parents, and their deaths from cancer were constant reminders of how things might have gone. I wanted my mum and the sort of loving care only she provided. At this time I was almost at my lowest. But I said to myself, why do we fall over? To pick ourselves up. That's what my mum had always done and was what I was teaching my kids to do. So I focused on healing.

10

By the early 2000s, Ian Paterson and Bethan Lloyd Owen were close collaborators. When he developed his private practice at what was then BUPA Little Aston and BUPA Parkway, Lloyd Owen quit her NHS job at Good Hope Hospital in Sutton Coldfield to work alongside him in the private sector. She had helped to set up the Sutton branch of the charity Breast Friends in 1998, which offered support and resources to people with breast cancer and their families. It had been a very successful endeavour, and in 2001 Lloyd Owen wanted to set up a local branch for breast cancer patients in Solihull. She approached two of Paterson's patients, June Burton and Lesley Webb, friends who had been introduced by Paterson two years previously when they were both recovering from their operations at Parkway.

Lesley described the meeting in an article she wrote for the Breast Friends fifth-anniversary bulletin, 'Over coffee, Bethan dropped her bombshell: it was an invitation to June and me to start a similar group.' She described it as 'Bethan's cunning plan'. Paterson would be involved as much as he could, helping to fundraise and address meetings as a keynote speaker to explain various aspects of breast cancer. The charity would pay for practical help for recovering patients (NHS and private), such as house cleaning or gardening, or therapeutic care in the form of relaxation treatments. It would also raise funds for specialist medical equipment for cancer wards. It was an excellent way for breast cancer patients of any age to meet and support each other, and it was immediately popular. The charity outgrew its original meeting room and was offered a monthly meeting room in a building on the grounds of Parkway for a small fee. Lloyd Owen pointed out it would be easy for Parkway clinicians to come and address the group if it was just next door, so Breast Friends relocated.

I learned about Breast Friends from Lloyd Owen in 2004, shortly after my operation. She had already given me a voucher for a wig and another for a few sessions of a relaxation treatment. 'When you're feeling up to it,' she said, 'come along to a monthly meeting. You'll meet ladies a bit further on in their treatment, it'll help you know what to expect.' I finally went in mid-February. I'd been feeling apprehensive about it, worrying it might be a gloomy environment. I wanted to make an effort, so I put make-up on and covered my now-bald head with a little suedette cap. I wasn't yet up to driving, so my daughter Jenny came with me. By then, Lesley had decided to step down and was replaced as chair by Hilary San, a well-spoken and kind woman who stood up to address us all and introduce that month's guest speaker, a fashion expert who talked us through what colours to wear. The atmosphere wasn't at all gloomy, but it was strange being introduced to dozens of other women at various stages of their treatment. A bit like prison, 'what are you in for?', we swapped diagnoses and treatment stories. I wasn't sure if I'd return the next month, but I decided to give it another try. I was so glad I did. At my second meeting, I met a young woman who was about six weeks behind me in her treatment. Her hair had only just fallen out, so we talked about wigs. It felt good to be of some use, even if it was just offering reassurance and advice. I resolved to go back again, and Breast Friends soon became a vital part of my treatment and recovery. We would listen to the guest speaker, discuss our medical issues or any other problems, and even compare photos of our scars and reconstructed breasts. It made me feel so much less of an alien.

What I did not know was that behind-the-scenes complaints had been made about Ian Paterson. In 2002, Andrew Stockdale and Indy Fernando, oncologists in the breast care team, began to be concerned about Paterson's surgical practice. They flagged in MDTs cases where patients had consented to a mastectomy but were presenting with excessive amounts of residual breast tissue. Stockdale decided to carry out his own audit of 100 Paterson mastectomy patients. His findings showed an unusual number of patients having incomplete surgery. 'What I was seeing was out of the range of what I'd seen in my previous experience with a whole range of other breast surgeons,' he said. The Trust did not take any action. In November 2003, Stockdale had his appraisal and used this meeting to raise concerns about Ian Paterson's practice. He also set up a meeting with Fernando. Between them they explained their concerns, highlighting Paterson's unusual habit of referring patients for additional operations to remove the leftover tissue, also known as a 'shave after mastectomy'. Stockdale went to see the lead cancer clinician, Andrew Wake, who spoke to the-then medical director of surgery, Mark Gannon.

Gannon asked Wake to investigate Paterson and report back.

In January 2004, a month after my operation, Andrew Wake submitted his report. It was largely concerned with the workings of the MDT, which was not operating efficiently or effectively. Wake, perhaps looking for balance, praised the MDT in light of staffing issues (he said it was 'too strongly chaired by Ian Paterson who was too dogmatic, disregarding others'), and called the MDT's target performance 'remarkable', singling out the lead clinician (Paterson) as 'particularly to be commended'. He did then say that concerns have been raised following appraisals, noting 'particular concern over the infrequency of pre-treatment MDT discussions for new cases of breast cancer', and concerns about a lack of discussion and input from oncologists regarding women selected for immediate reconstructions. He acknowledged that patients were receiving conflicting advice over the role of chemotherapy in their treatment plan. He mentioned complaints about the dysfunctional atmosphere at the MDT; 'Some hold the view that the atmosphere is unnecessarily adversarial and insufficiently democratic. Also, that there is a lack of mutual respect shown to non-surgical members of the team and insufficient regard to other people's opinions, when these are at variance with the lead clinician.'

He briefly acknowledged that multiple members of the MDT had observed 'what they believe to be an unusually high instance of positive margins' in breast cancer patients, meaning cancerous tissue left behind, and that the MDT takes the view that Paterson's surgery is 'aesthetically pleasing' but too conservative, compromising the results and negatively impacting relapse rates. In other words, Paterson was doing what was known as 'cleavage-sparing mastectomies'. But Wake didn't make as big a deal of it as he might have, citing insufficient information. Instead, he recommended an audit be undertaken into positive margins, and the figures compared to national data to ascertain whether Paterson's patients were indeed showing too high a prevalence. The report only mentioned in passing the issue of Paterson leaving breast tissue during mastectomies, presented as an accusation by colleagues rather than a fact, which made it easier to ignore. Perhaps if this particular aspect of Paterson's wrongdoing had been properly recognised, what came later would have been avoided. The Wake Report wasn't the last investigation into Paterson, and nor was it the only one to be ignored.

A few months later, in April 2004, Dr Gill Lawrence, Director of the West Midlands Cancer Intelligence Unit, was tasked with assessing Paterson's surgical practice at NHS Solihull Hospital on behalf of the Warwickshire, Solihull and Coventry Breast Screening Service. This was a standard quality assessment visit by a department responsible for those patients whose breast lumps had been found during routine mammograms.

Lawrence is a highly qualified analyst, and her visit identified concerns around Paterson's surgical practice, including his high rates of open biopsy (a surgical technique to take a tissue sample, instead of using a needle) and the specimens he was sending to pathology. She also recommended that the hospital develop a policy around margin clearance. Like Wake, she had concerns about the MDT culture and recommended a review of its meetings. She noted that not all of Paterson's private patients were being discussed at his NHS MDT meetings.

Lawrence's recommendations were not implemented, and there was nowhere to go to ensure they were. Both 2004 reports were produced on the back of concerns raised about Paterson by colleagues, just six years after his suspension from another hospital, and both gave recommendations and opportunities to investigate Paterson. Both reports were ignored, buried for the next eight years while Paterson carried on as normal.

11

The non-medical guests at the Breast Friends meetings helped us regain confidence or feel a bit more normal. Some months it would be a motivational speaker helping us with body image issues, other times a representative from an animal charity doing a talk about cancer-detecting dogs. But the most interesting –

and popular – talks were by clinicians. The medical speakers were usually Paterson, Kat or Latief, all of whom did private work alongside their NHS work.

The more knowledge I had, the more in control I felt. It helped me to know exactly what was going on in my body and what the current science around breast cancer was.

Ian Paterson was by far the most popular of all the speakers. To the ladies of Breast Friends he was the best consultant you could wish for. Everyone knew if you were diagnosed with breast cancer then Paterson was the man to see, even if that meant finding the money to go private. Charismatic, knowledgeable, confident and very charming, he would instill trust in his patients who were told – and believed – they were being looked after by the very best.

The first time I saw him give a talk the room was packed to its sixty-person capacity of women in attendance. Lloyd Owen had been hyping the event to everyone, and I was excited. My daughter Jen and I sat near the back and watched the adoring faces as Paterson stepped up. He puffed out his chest, put his shoulders back and began his talk. This one was about the damage that breast cancer treatment can do to your body. I almost didn't want to hear it, because the treatment was damaging my body at that very moment, but I knew it was better for me to know what I was in for. He talked about bone health, how certain drugs like tamoxifen and Arimidex can weaken the bones and lead to an early menopause and increased risk of osteoporosis or other conditions, and how this could, in turn, lead to a higher risk of fractures because the bones are weaker. The medical speakers would sometimes be a bit gory in the clinical details, as though they were addressing a room full of medical students rather than patients. Paterson, in particular, liked to tell alarming and graphic stories. That night he spoke about a patient he knew whose bones were so brittle, she leaned on a counter and her arm simply broke. I felt sick. Why would he tell us that? Was that going to happen to me? But his talk, perhaps because of what looked like candidness and honesty, was well received. I mentioned to Lloyd Owen afterwards that Paterson's brittle-bone story had scared me and I didn't think it was a good idea to tell newly diagnosed patients that scenario. She tried to reassure me by saying it was a very rare instance and not to worry.

For the rest of that year, as I completed my chemotherapy, Breast Friends was a key part of my life. In practical terms, I could get help and advice for myself or give it to those further behind in their cancer journey. Emotionally, the group was an essential lifeline. We had each other's backs, a unified team who saw Lloyd Owen and Paterson as our unofficial leaders and official saviours. Physically and psychologically, I was trying to hold myself together even though I felt like I'd turned into an old woman almost overnight. The skin on the back of my hands felt like paper, my veins were starting to flatten out from the chemo, and I had a blue tinge to my right arm from all the injections. I was pale, bald and my face was lined with pain, but I'd put on some make-up and off I'd go off to the monthly support group meetings and hear everyone cheer me on.

At home I wasn't always doing so well. I was struggling with the effects of the chemo, steroids and my lack of core strength. I was frustrated and angry. I'd never had to rely on anybody for anything, but now just the simplest of tasks left my stomach cramped and sore. I'd try to find a way around my lack of stomach muscle by developing techniques. One day I wanted to get some boxes off the top of my wardrobe and was determined to do it myself. I stood on a chair, slid the box onto the top of my head, balanced it there then gave it a shove, firing the box onto my bed. Ridiculously stupid because I still had the pain in my stomach, and I also got told off by Bob for doing it. I was so frustrated at my loss of independence and my new reliance on Bob and the kids. I was impatient and would end up shouting at them when they tried to stop me being active. 'Well, I wouldn't have to do this if I didn't have to wait all day for you to do it,' I'd snap. I knew it was wrong to blame them. I wanted to be the perfect chemotherapy patient, calm and uncomplaining, but instead I was frustrated and furious.

In November 2004, I decided to do something positive and organise a fundraiser for Breast Friends. I negotiated a free room at a local Irish club and booked a Tom Jones impersonator I'd found online. I called local football clubs and businesses and got some great raffle prizes. I would be going back to work soon, and I wanted this not just to be a fundraiser for Breast Friends but my comeback party. I wanted to show everyone that I was okay, that I'd got through breast cancer, that I'd beaten it. It was a fabulous night. I called out the raffle and thanked everyone in my speech. I felt like finally I was getting back to my old self. I raised £5,000 for Breast Friends, at the time the biggest single donation they'd had. After that I was referred to as 'the lady with the Midas touch' and was asked to join the Breast Friends committee. Of course, I said yes.

I knew going back to work would help my mental health, even though I was somewhat dreading it. Before my diagnosis I was working in a demanding role as a production manager, manufacturing and testing electronic flight control units with a team of around fifty people. I didn't feel I could go back to the same role straight away, so I asked if I could work in a support role in continuous improvement – an umbrella name for a work culture and company-wide effort that is designed to achieve measurable improvements in the efficiency, effectiveness and performance of the workforce and the products and services they provide. Aerospace is a safety-critical industry, so this stuff really matters. I had been trained over the years in the techniques of problem-solving and in using the right tools to improve quality and performance. I had led a design project working with our Indianapolis facility to improve test capability and won a supplier collaboration award. The company doctor said I could start back part-time and gradually increase my hours. The HR manager wasn't happy – she thought it was too soon for me to be jumping back into such a stressful environment – but I said I needed to feel useful, so she eventually agreed.

The treatment had taken a huge toll on me, but at least my hair had grown back. It was now in a modern, short style, and I had high hopes for a sort of 'new role, new Deb' situation where I'd regain some of the confidence of my old life.

I began a new senior role in the small engines department. The first day walking back onto the factory floor was nerve-wracking, but everyone made me feel so welcome. I was greeted with hugs and handshakes, all my colleagues pleased to see me. I was back with my tribe. There was a mixture of men and women in manufacturing, plus an all-male test area and management team. They knew me and I knew them.

Initially, I struggled physically. Walking from one end of the factory floor to the other would cause my stomach to cramp, and I was absolutely shattered at the end of each day. My memory had changed, too, and I found it harder to retain new information. There is a condition known as chemo brain, a side effect from six months of chemotherapy, tamoxifen and other drugs. It had caused an early menopause, with all the side effects that entailed – brain fog, hot flushes and joint ache. I'd always carried a notebook around with me and found I relied on it more and more for the first few months back on the job. But being back in production was the best thing I could have done. My mood lifted, my fitness levels improved, and I was in a good place ready to get on with things. I wanted to put cancer in the background and live again.

Bob and I had always been adventurers but had rarely had the time or funds to fulfil our ambitions. But cancer has that way of putting things into perspective. No one knows what's around the corner, so we flew to the US for a fifteen-day motorbike tour of Route 66, covering 2,600 miles from Chicago to LA. I was seated on the back of a beautiful Harley-Davidson behind Bob as we set off with our group and a support van. Bob was worried I wasn't physically up to it, but I was determined to live my life at 100 miles an hour whenever I could. Each day was tough – not just the heat, but the cramping in my still-healing stomach and the pain in my backside. But the pain and stress melted away as I watched the incredible scenery fly by, my arms wrapped tightly around Bob.

12

In 2007, changes came for Paterson's practice. In June, private equity firm Cinven bought BUPA's twenty-five hospitals for £1.44 billion, including Parkway and Little Aston. There was a great deal of profit to be made in healthcare, and Cinven partner Simon Rowlands was quoted in the press release as saying:

'*We are pleased to have been able to acquire this leading provider of acute healthcare services. The portfolio of hospitals acquired is of a very high quality, staffed by dedicated and skilled clinicians and medical staff.*'

He went on to talk about investment, organic growth and new sources of revenue from the NHS. He did not mention his customers – the patients.

After the acquisition a new company was formed, Spire Healthcare Group plc, whose website boasts: 'Spire Healthcare is a leading independent healthcare group in the United Kingdom and the largest in terms of revenue. We deliver high standards of care, with integrity and compassion and from high-quality facilities to our insured, Self-pay and NHS patients.'

BUPA hospitals were rebranded as Spire. I hadn't paid much attention to the buyout or rebrand, as I'd been assured it wouldn't affect my care. I had spent the last year in recovery, then settled back into my career and family life. I'd become heavily involved in Breast Friends and took my role as a committee member very seriously. The group was entwined with

Paterson even while, behind the scenes, something major was unfolding.

In April 2007, another quality assurance (QA) visit took place by a team from the West Midlands Cancer Intelligence Unit, led by Gill Lawrence, who had also done the QA visit in 2004 and made recommendations about Paterson's clinical practice. She was aware of the lack of compliance since but was ultimately powerless to force Paterson to change, or to force the Heart of England NHS Foundation Trust (HEFT) to intervene. She would later say: 'My frustration is that there was nowhere you could go to actually say these really important recommendations from a series of experts have not been addressed.' But at the time, while the QA team still had issues with Paterson's surgery, their overall report was positive. Improvements were in progress, and the data they examined on Paterson was 'satisfactory'. Their visit had focused on issues like how the MDTs could use video-conferencing technology to more effectively manage themselves, given they were spread across three sites. Lawrence had not been made aware of the existence of the Wake Report, and nor did her team interview any oncologists, so she did not know there were far bigger problems than access to video conferencing.

I had heard a rumour from Bethan Lloyd Owen that a new surgeon was making life difficult for Paterson. Lloyd Owen liked to say that Paterson had come from a working-class background so there was a lot of professional jealousy and snobbery surrounding his position and the profile he had attained. This seemed plausible enough to me at the time.

Hemant Ingle had originally trained as a general surgeon in India, then specialised in breast surgery and the use of sentinel node biopsies, a surgical procedure to identify and remove one or more of the nodes (glands) from the armpit using a probe. Ingle, a short, softly spoken man, was hired by HEFT to help manage the Solihull breast cancer caseload. Paterson's behaviour and attitude had already resulted in the loss of two surgeons, with the perception being that Paterson was offputting to new recruits and didn't want to work with anyone who might stand up to him. Misra Budhoo, the clinical director of surgery, dealt with that situation by appointing Ingle while excluding Paterson from the recruitment process.

'The culture of the organisation at the relevant time was hierarchical and seen by some as oppressive,' Professor Sir Ian Kennedy would later say during an investigation into the events of 2007. 'Inappropriate behaviour by consultants went unchecked. Speaking out about concerns was not easy, particularly for younger members of staff. The Board was passive, responding to what it was told by the Executive rather than actively exercising effective governance.' It was easier for senior management to go behind Paterson's back than attempt to change his bullying behaviour. It didn't seem to occur to them that if he was so unprofessional in one aspect of his job, that might be true for his surgical practice, too. In fact, they loved him, because he was fast and cleared cases at a rate that helped HEFT meet its targets. They conveniently forgot about the 2004 Wake Report and concerns raised by quality assurance, to the point of failing to inform HEFT's board of their existence at all. 'Good news was preferred to true news,' Kennedy would later remark. The clinic's star performer was not to be criticised.

As mentioned earlier, Ingle had been warned against applying for the job by the surgeon who had recently left it but said, 'I still applied for the job because I thought I would at least get interview practice. I did nearly withdraw my application, but I had by then found out that Balapathiran Balasubramanian (commonly known as Bala) was the breast lead at Solihull and out of curiosity I called him to get more information. He informed me that Ian Paterson was no longer the breast lead. He did admit that there had been problems within the breast unit due to Ian Paterson, and therefore HEFT had been unable to appoint a suitable candidate for five years. There had been a number of locums, but they wanted someone with good surgical experience. He promised that he would support me all the way if I did get the job.'

He did get the job. While he'd heard about Paterson's bad attitude, he'd never heard of any issues with his surgical technique, and was looking forward to seeing him at work.

Paterson was not happy about the arrival of Hemant Ingle. 'I started working on 1 January 2007,' Ingle said. 'First day, in the meeting, Mr Paterson didn't even bother to look at me. When the meeting finished, I approached, put my hand out for Mr Paterson, "I'm Mr Ingle".' And his first comment was, 'You shouldn't have been appointed, we don't need you.'

It might have been a simple clash of personalities, but Ingle began to notice oddities in Paterson's work. 'So many times I felt that he was advising patients to have reconstruction surgery quite unnecessarily. Almost every MDT, we used to have a fight. One day – I remember his remark after objecting to the case where he wanted a reconstruction – I said, "No, this is not appropriate." He turned around to say, "What the bloody hell is wrong with you?" But except for me, nobody else in the MDT was objecting.'

Ingle tried to give him the benefit of the doubt, and when Paterson was due to go on annual leave and asked him to take over a mastectomy case, he thought, 'you know what? He might be a little bit of a difficult person to work with, but he's actually giving me his own theatre.' So I said, "Yeah, absolutely fine, no problem, can we just look at the histology?" At this, Paterson snapped. 'He turned around and said, "God!" He literally made a cryptic comment to say, "Huh! Wasted surgeon, wasted theatre." And I had to say, "Ian, can you just stop?"' Ingle did not proceed with the mastectomy. 'This person did not need any surgery, the histology was completely benign,' said Ingle. 'Why was somebody asking me to do surgery, when there was no cancer?' Ingle began to write letters to management about Paterson's clinical practice and bullying attitude. He averaged a letter a month, but nothing was done, and nor did management inform Lawrence and the QA team of Ingle's concerns.

This all coincided with a new crossover system introduced by HEFT that meant patients were seen by whichever doctor was in the clinic on the day, rather than the same consultant every time. As a result, Ingle began to treat more of Paterson's patients. As he examined each patient, he observed that many of the mastectomies were simply incomplete. There was breast tissue where there should not be breast tissue. If a mastectomy is not complete, the patient has a higher chance of their cancer recurring. This, alongside Ingle's other concerns, pointed to something very, very sinister.

In June 2007, Ingle wrote yet another letter to Ian Cunliffe, HEFT's medical director of surgery, to complain about Paterson's personal conduct and clinical competence. He wasn't alone in trying to raise the alarm about Paterson. Consultant oncologists Indrajit Fernando and Andrew Stockdale also wrote letters of complaint. It was Stockdale's 2003 complaint that had resulted in the Wake Report, but that had been under HEFT's medical director of surgery, Mark Gannon, who had subsequently left. His replacement, Ian Cunliffe, would later claim that Gannon had briefed him on the 2003 allegations against Paterson but had said the matter was closed.

Mark Goldman and Ian Paterson were old colleagues, their relationship dating back to at least 1993 when Paterson was Goldman's registrar, although it's not known to what degree Goldman was aware of any issues. When Paterson was appointed to HEFT in 1998 as a vascular and breast cancer surgeon, he had a reputation for being difficult to work with. A senior manager notified Rowland Hopkinson, one of the Trust's medical directors, about the Gill Dallow incident and Paterson's subsequent period of supervision, but there is no record of whether this information was shared more widely. A later investigation said:

'*Once he had accepted the appointment at the Trust, Mr Paterson's relations with his colleagues at Good Hope, which had been fractious for some time, deteriorated further. Matters came to a head and the chief executive of Good Hope Hospital asked Mr Paterson to leave without completing his notice period. In what is a small community of surgeons, it is very unlikely that this would not have been known to those in the Trust. Both Mr Goldman and Mr Gannon were also surgeons, and Mr Paterson at one time had been Mr Goldman's registrar. In addition, even though the decision to appoint had been made prior to Mr Paterson's being asked to leave Good Hope Hospital, the exercise of due diligence would have identified this fact. And, once identified, appropriate action, such as careful monitoring during a probationary period, could have been taken. Solihull was on notice that Mr Paterson's appointment was not without risk.*'

A senior radiologist later said, 'To be honest, when we heard he was coming … it was, you know, "What's gone on then?" His reputation was well known as being difficult and having open rows with a colleague at Good Hope … it's always a surprise to us why they took him on when they knew he was trouble.'

An investigation was opened, headed by Ian Cunliffe with an HR consultant named Alison Money. The decision to treat the allegations as an HR issue under the Department of Health's disciplinary procedures automatically made the whole thing confidential. HR matters were, essentially, conducted behind closed doors. Rumours started to fly among Paterson's colleagues, but no one could get or give answers, even though it clearly impacted working relationships. As for us patients, well … Did anyone consider that Paterson's patients could not possibly give informed consent to treatment by a surgeon currently and historically under investigation if we did not know it was happening?

The case investigator would be Rex Polson, a consultant physician also based at NHS and Spire private hospitals in Solihull. Although competent and qualified, he was not an independent, external advisor, but part of the same culture he was now tasked with investigating. He would eventually produce the Polson Report, which looked into allegations that Paterson was doing incomplete mastectomies, recommending patients for reconstruction surgery when it wasn't clinically appropriate, and had in one case recommended a male patient for a mastectomy inappropriately.

To properly investigate these medical claims, Cunliffe and Polson approached Hugh Bishop, a breast cancer consultant, to act as an independent reviewer. Bishop agreed, but Paterson did not. He objected to Bishop's appointment, and his opinion mattered enough for someone else to be chosen instead. The agreed replacement would be Colm Hennessy, a consultant general surgeon with a special interest in breast surgery based at North Tees and Hartlepool NHS Trust. Paterson approved of this appointment, and in late 2007 Hennessy began his review of sixty-one of Paterson's NHS patient case notes. He interviewed multiple clinicians and staff members, including the whistleblowers Fernando, Stockdale and Ingle, the plastic surgeon Kat, and, of course, Paterson himself. He also spoke to Wake, but only by telephone.

Hennessy submitted his final conclusions to Polson in January 2008, and three months later, on 29 April, the Polson Report was finished. His conclusions were mixed. On the matter of incomplete mastectomies, Polson wrote:

'All of those I spoke to were concerned about cases in which there is unexpected disease recurrence and agreed that this was more likely to occur in cases where there was more residual tissue or a tumour extending near to resection margins ... Mr Paterson argued that he was also keen to remove all breast tissue but he claims it was "perfectly possible to remove the cancer, leaving fat not breast tissue". By doing this he feels he can achieve an improved cosmetic result.'

An improved cosmetic result. This is what Paterson meant by 'you can still wear a bikini'. By leaving a certain amount of breast tissue in the right places, Paterson could give women a bit of their old identity back. I would never have consented to that. The solicitor Linda Millband later said:

'I'd seen all these terrible pictures, and I'd also had the benefit of reading the notes. And I thought, well, he hasn't consented these people at all. There was no question of consent. He didn't ever give them options … it was like he preyed on people. It was horrible.'

Breast cancer changed my relationship with my body for ever, and the scars are not just evidence that I was ill but a constant reminder that the cancer could come back. A little bit of cleavage is not worth the risk of recurrence. But Paterson was adamant he was doing it safely. The oncologists Fernando and Stockdale, and the breast consultant Ingle provided details of patients they believe had had incomplete mastectomies to Colm Hennessy, who is quoted in the Polson Report as saying:

'Mr Paterson wishes to provide the best possible cosmetic outcome from a mastectomy and clearly a tidy scar and some cleavages are popular with patients. It is obviously impossible to prove whether all residual chest wall tissue after mastectomy contains breast glandular tissue. My surgical interpretation of the imaging reports and hard copies supports the concerns raised by oncology and surgical colleagues. Not all the features of the images can be put down to postoperative scarring as suggested by Mr Paterson.'

One element of breast-conserving surgery is a procedure known as a 'shave'. This is an old technique which aims to remove the tumour while conserving as much healthy breast tissue as possible. To achieve this, surgeons might 'shave' tissue from the cavity walls in thin slices to refine the margins where the cancer cells are. This technique is sometimes used for lumpectomies, but it isn't appropriate for a mastectomy, where the priority is to remove all of the breast tissue. If this is done properly there isn't anything to shave. Hemant Ingle later said,

'I was alarmed that Mr Paterson was undertaking shaves after a mastectomy. In my book that is not possible. If a mastectomy is undertaken properly one cannot take a shave as there would not be any breast tissue remaining to allow a shave. Knowing that Mr Paterson's shaves after a mastectomy were showing breast tissue meant that the original mastectomy was not done properly. I was surprised that nobody in the MDT questioned Mr Paterson on this.'

In 1998 a plastic surgeon named Fazel Fatah operated alongside Paterson at City Hospital four times, for mastectomies with immediate reconstruction. He said that Paterson's mastectomies only took half an hour, instead of the standard two hours, and that the standard of surgery was poor.

'The way Paterson did the surgery, he used quite a large scalpel,' he said. 'So instead of actually defining the tissue layer between the skin and breast tissue, he just created a layer with the knife which meant there was no separation of the two entities to make sure the breast tissue had been removed. It was a quick sweep of the knife round the top and bottom of the breast and lifting it off the muscle.' He would also take the removed specimen with him to send to his preferred pathology lab. Fatah was concerned, so he paid particular attention during the next operation and noticed that the mastectomy was indeed incomplete. Paterson had left breast tissue that should have been removed, so Fatah removed it himself and sent it to the City Hospital pathology service. The results came back: there was cancer in the tissues Paterson had not removed. He refused to work with Paterson again.

Fatah raised concerns with Martin Lee and also John Taylor, a senior breast surgeon colleague of Paterson's at the time. Fatah claims that Taylor dismissed the concerns and Fatah's request for an audit on the grounds that Paterson was aggressive and had too much support from senior management. Fatah believed that Paterson's speed was perceived as a benefit to the Trust, 'I took it that, from a quantity point of view, he was more productive as a surgeon operating on a larger number of patients in the given time.'

A mastectomy should remove 95–97 per cent of breast tissue, and the chest wall should be flat. Ingle saw three patients who were wearing a B- to C-cup bra, and his colleagues saw similar. It was clear that Paterson was doing incomplete mastectomies.

Polson agreed. The complaint was substantiated, and the report recommended, 'The practice of shaves at mastectomy should cease. The MDT needs to be confident that a mastectomy means as close to 100 per cent as possible of the breast tissue is removed. Mr Paterson should cease sub-total mastectomy, cleavage-sparing mastectomy and shavings with mastectomy, unless previously agreed with the MDT or if clinically necessary during surgery.'

Paterson agreed to this and that an independent consultant, Martin Lee, could observe his next five mastectomies to check his technical ability. And so the matter of incomplete – or 'cleavage-sparing' – mastectomies was apparently settled. Paterson had been doing them but was going to stop, and that would be the end of that. It didn't seem to occur to anyone that he had been investigated for cleavage-sparing mastectomies by Mark Wake in 2004 and hadn't stopped then, so why would he now?

Another accusation by Stockdale, Fernando and Ingle against Paterson was that he had been recommending patients for breast reconstruction surgery when it wasn't clinically appropriate. The crux of this issue was that patients had been referred for reconstruction without the agreement of the MDT, which was supposed to discuss and concur on all matters relating to a patient's cancer treatment. Polson deferred to Hennessy's expert opinion, who agreed that had been happening, and recommended that 'reconstruction decisions be taken to the MDT'.

It was a very big deal that patients were having reconstruction surgery without the agreement of their MDT. That was one of the main reasons why MDTs existed in the first place – to confer and consolidate expertise from different specialisms in medicine. If radiotherapy or chemotherapy were more clinically appropriate than reconstruction, that is what should be recommended to the patient. Paterson's failure to consult the MDT on critical matters should have been seen as part of a pattern, a big, obvious clue that he was not a surgeon who liked oversight or rules. Polson did find this claim to be substantiated, and is clear that some of the clinicians he interviewed felt the MDT was 'dysfunctional', but he also notes that 'Mr Paterson's behaviour within the MDT had improved following earlier criticism', and that he 'continues to carry out a very substantial volume of cancer work within the unit'.

The final claim about Paterson's clinical practice was that he had tried to recommend a male patient in the private sector for an inappropriate mastectomy. This is a complicated clue in the puzzle. Like all consultants, Ingle also undertook work in the private sector alongside his NHS caseload (including at Spire). Upon seeing a letter from Paterson to the patient's GP that indicated that the patient needed urgent surgery on his breast, he examined the patient and became very concerned. 'The tone of the letter indicated he most likely had breast cancer,' said Ingle. The correct course of action should have been to perform a core biopsy on the man's breast tissue, not jump ahead to an operation, so Ingle did the biopsy and the results showed no cancer. So why was Paterson trying to operate? Paterson said he was not. Hennessy reviewed the case and said, 'The correspondence for this matter indicates that the patient was quoted a price for a mastectomy rather than proceeding to a core biopsy'. Hennessy confirms Ingle was correct in doing the biopsy, and says that Paterson's defence is one of administration error.

It was a simple typo, Paterson claimed, code B2880 instead of B2800, and eventually produced a statement from his private secretary to corroborate this explanation. Polson was also shown a letter that Ingle had not had access to, which seemed to confirm that, at the patient's request, Paterson was planning an operation to remove the breast lump but not perform a mastectomy. Polson took this at face value and rejected Ingle's complaint.

For anyone to be able to investigate further they would have had to suspect Paterson was deliberately falsifying operation billing codes or telling patients they might have cancer when they did not. No one wants to think the unthinkable, especially not of a colleague in medicine or a clinic's star surgeon. But the patterns were there if anyone in power cared to look. Ingle had raised the issue multiple times, but the situation was out of his hands. Besides, this case was in the private sector rather than the NHS, so it was a matter for Spire and separate to the issue of Paterson doing potentially lethal cleavage-sparing mastectomies on cancer patients. An audit of Spire's records would have uncovered a new horrifying truth: Ian Paterson was telling patients they had cancer when they did not, so he could sell the operation to cure them.

13

Ingle had also accused Paterson of bullying. 'While I was trying to settle in, Mr Paterson was making my life as difficult as possible. Rather than being supportive to a new colleague, he would make remarks about me at MDT meetings which were quite derogatory,' he said.

He claimed that Paterson had tried to find dirt on him, presumably to undermine Ingle's credibility with management. Paterson had even phoned former colleagues at another hospital to ask if there had ever been problems with Ingle's medical competence. There had not, but Paterson spread rumours and gossip in the MDT anyway. Polson was tasked with investigating this and he found in Ingle's favour. He wrote, 'Mr Paterson was wrong in making enquiries about Mr Ingle in the way he did and he accepts this. The Trust needs to make it clear to Mr Paterson that such behaviour is not acceptable and will not be tolerated.' Paterson formally apologised to Ingle in July 2007, but there was no trust between the two men thereafter.

Polson's report looked to be the end of the investigation into Paterson. Hennessy later said that his contribution was barely discussed with him. No debrief, no follow-ups, no further contact. The same thing happened to Polson himself. After he presented his report to the team of the chief executive, Mark Goldman, he was informed that he was surplus to requirements and would not be party to whatever the outcome was or whether his recommendations were acted on. 'I was told I didn't need to stay any longer,' he said. 'I wasn't sort of kicked out but "there is probably no need for you to stay now, Rex, that's fine." I wasn't privy to any "what shall we do now, folks?"' The report was an HR matter, and therefore confidential, which conveniently allowed the management team to keep it to themselves. They did not send a copy to the Board, and nor did they update any of Paterson's colleagues – those who had made complaints and those who had to work with him and would have benefitted from knowing what to look out for. Knowledge of the Polson Report, like the Wake Report before it, was limited to a small number of senior managers whose primary concern was to protect the reputation of the NHS Trust.

That's not to say the same senior managers could entirely ignore Polson's recommendations. One of those was to fix the 'dysfunctional relationships' in the MDT (which discussed both NHS and private patients), which Polson acknowledged was underway. Patients were, of course, not informed that their cancer management team barely functioned or had a bullying issue. We just assumed that patient care would come before any other consideration.

If patient care had been at the forefront of decision-making, perhaps Goldman, Cunliffe and the HR consultant might have decided to temporarily revoke Paterson's operating privileges while they investigated the impact of the cleavage-sparing mastectomies he had already done. At the time, Hennessy was highly critical of Paterson's surgical techniques, but in a letter to Cunliffe he stopped short of endorsing a suspension in favour of more data investigation. Others, however, did support a suspension. One of the breast surgeons at Good Hope, Alan Jewkes, said he had petitioned both Goldman and Cunliffe to limit Paterson's patient access: 'So that a full and detailed inquiry could take place, because one of the central issues, as I understood it, was about this extra breast tissue being left behind, how many patients this had affected, how much was left behind and really how long it had gone on for.'

Those were excellent questions and concerns. If it was the case that Paterson's previous cleavage-sparing mastectomy patients were at greater risk of cancer recurrence, surely the only safe and sensible decision was to not let him do any more mastectomies until there was proof one way or another. Apart from anything, how could any patient of Paterson now give proper consent? The whistleblowers had already raised questions about whether Paterson was getting proper consent for the cleavage-sparing mastectomies. Mastectomy patients believed they were getting the operation that would best limit the chances of recurrence, not the one that left tissue behind for aesthetic reasons. But, regardless of their letters and entreaties, those who had complained about Paterson were kept in the dark, and nothing seemed to be happening. Paterson carried on as normal. Some speculated that Paterson's friendship with Goldman was the reason for the secrecy, while others thought it was because Paterson was so good at clearing the waiting list. Whatever the justification, Paterson was not suspended from the NHS. He was free to continue operating on patients, none of whom had any idea that something was wrong.

Polson's key recommendations, aside from fixing the culture of the MDT, included:

- An audit of Paterson's patient notes, specifically those who had had a cleavage-sparing mastectomy or a shave-with-mastectomy (both of which Paterson had agreed to stop doing), which could include giving the patient further treatment.
- A review of mastectomy patients who had had immediate reconstructions in the last three years, as they had not all been done with the knowledge or agreement of the MDT.
- A review of the cancer recurrence rates in patients who should reasonably have expected low or no risk.

I find it hard to reconcile the obvious seriousness of these recommendations with the decision not to suspend Paterson while the audits were done. If I'd known any of this, I wouldn't have let him anywhere near me, let alone with a scalpel

Ingle had also begun to look into Paterson's behaviour at Spire, after he struggled to have private breast cancer patients allocated to him. He was told by colleagues it was because Bethan Lloyd Owen would take over the cases and assign them to Paterson. He learned that Paterson would have at least twenty patients booked in on a Friday afternoon, something that was unheard of. There shouldn't be that many cancer patients at all, let alone in the private sector. Where were they all coming from? One day, Ingle went to the operating theatre to book in a small case he had been assigned, only to be told he couldn't do the operation because the patient was on Paterson's list. Ingle looked at the list. It already had six cancer surgeries logged for that week. 'Even in the NHS, we don't get that many cancers that will operate within one week in one clinic.' A grotesque possibility was emerging, but Ingle needed proof. He began to review files.

'Every patient was an eye-opener,' said Ingle. 'Once I started reading the notes, it was a Pandora's box, and that box just kept on opening.' As well as incomplete mastectomies, Ingle had uncovered something that was almost unbelievable. 'I was very surprised that these patients would have a very small fibroadenoma, which is a benign lump in the breast. And without biopsy, they would go straight to theatre. He had coded them as cancer, but none of these cases had cancer.'

One of the more confusing aspects of the Paterson case is the crossover between NHS and private patients, but it is common for patients to have cancer treatment across both. Not least because private hospitals do not have emergency care provision, so the NHS often has to step in. If something goes wrong during a private operation, an ambulance is called and the patient is 'blue-lighted' to the nearest appropriate NHS hospital. I did not know this before I signed up for multiple operations at Spire, nor did I know that the private hospitals, which are run for profit, do not compensate the NHS for this service. Nor does the insurance of the patient. It costs the NHS around £70 million a year to treat patients who have been transferred from private hospitals.

Part of the reason patients wanted to transfer from the NHS to private was the perception of waiting lists. While it's true that breast cancer surgery waiting lists were (and still are) long, Paterson would exaggerate these waiting times to his NHS patients so they would transfer to his private practice. The NHS itself was also using Spire this way. Gill Lawrence, Director of the West Midlands Cancer Intelligence Unit, has stated that HEFT at the time was the only health authority outsourcing this type of surgery to the private sector. This in effect meant that Paterson was being paid by the NHS twice: his salary, and again when he undertook NHS-funded operations at Spire.

In 2008, Paterson was discussing the management of his private Spire patients at the HEFT MDT, but also at a Spire Little Aston MDT, with Latief providing consultant oncology input. It wasn't unusual or inappropriate for private patients to be included in NHS MDT meetings, as many were being treated by both. But it helped Paterson to cover his tracks, suggesting that, 'as he works with another oncologist privately this may have upset the [NHS] Trust oncologists, Mr Fernando and Stockdale.' It also meant that he had an excuse to remove patient notes from Spire, when they should not have left the hospital (some of these notes were later found in Paterson's house). In reality, these MDT meetings weren't subject to any oversight or peer review, which gave Paterson a convenient smokescreen. Relations in the NHS MDTs declined even further, particularly between Paterson and an increasingly worried and upset Ingle. who was being thwarted in his attempts to draw attention to what looked like wrongdoing. Ingle later told me that the situation and his treatment has affected his whole life. He was being bullied by a surgeon whose mistreatment of patients was catastrophic, and yet management kept everyone in the dark. Reluctantly, Ingle agreed that for the sake of relieving tensions in the MDT, he would leave the NHS Solihull Hospital and relocate to Good Hope Hospital.

'Another interesting development to note was that Mr Budhoo, who was supporting me, was removed from taking part in any further investigation against Mr Paterson,' said Ingle. 'It appears that Mr Paterson complained to the chief executive that Mr Budhoo had a personal vendetta against him and without checking any facts he was removed from the investigation. After this, I realised that there was nothing more I could do. Then Mr Cunliffe offered me the chance to go to Good Hope Hospital and I decided that was best for me. Being kept in the dark made me completely disillusioned with HEFT and management. I honestly felt that racism was involved here. I questioned whether this would happen if it was an Asian consultant under investigation. The fact that up until 2010 Mr Paterson was still there and I was not, spoke volumes. I heard from one of the nurses in Solihull that Mr Paterson mentioned in the clinic that he removed me from Solihull because I was a troublemaker and the unit would be better if I was not there.'

14

In 2007, Breast Friends presented a £12,000 sentinel node probe to Spire Parkway (thanks to a further donation, we were also able to fund the same machines for two NHS hospitals), in partnership with a local man who had lost his wife to breast cancer. He said his wife had received such dedicated care from the team at Spire that he wanted to give something back. None of us questioned at the time why a private hospital making millions in profit would let a local cancer charity fund vital equipment rather than just buying it themselves, but it was fantastic PR for Paterson and Bethan Lloyd Owen.

Paterson took credit for the fundraising, boasting about it on a now-deleted web page. Lloyd Owen ensured that he was front and centre in all the local press releases, accepting the equipment on behalf of the hospital. This created an image of a great benefactor and a beloved consultant going above and beyond for his patients. It is true that he would occasionally help out with fundraising, at least if it presented a photo opportunity. Every year the local Rotary Club would organise a fun run to benefit Breast Friends. One year Paterson and his wife participated dressed as Pinky and Perky, two pigs from an old children's TV show. His wife ran ahead of him while Paterson briskly walked around the course with Lloyd Owen and Gordon, her chocolate Labrador. The accompanying photo, which appeared in the Breast Friends newsletter, showed no sign of the drama unfolding behind the scenes.

But in reality Paterson was becoming increasingly isolated from his peers. Despite his press appearances and guest spots as expert speaker at Breast Friends, he did not actually have a reputation in his field as a pioneer in surgery. Professor Wishart, a consultant breast surgeon and founder of Check4Cancer, commented to a journalist that he 'had never seen Paterson at various symposiums for breast cancer consultants because he didn't keep up to date with technology and advances in breast cancer treatment because he thought he knew best.'

Nor did Paterson have a history of publishing in medical journals. During the Polson investigation, he did claim he was about to publish a paper on his cleavage-sparing technique, but as far as I can tell that was never forthcoming. There are strict procedures in place in the NHS for introducing new surgical techniques. At an absolute minimum, the new technique has to undergo assessment as part of a formal 'peer-reviewed' research process, whereby other surgeons observe and confirm the proposal is an improvement on the existing technique, and of course that it is safe. There are also clinical trials to test it before it's approved, which require the consent of the NHS Trust, an ethics committee and the patient. The patient is given an explanation of the risks and offered an alternative if they don't want to be part of the trial. Paterson did not apply for any sort of approval to test his cleavage-sparing technique.

He was adamant that it was above board, stating that it was, '… simply an intraoperative adaptation of surgical technique in order to provide a better cosmetic result for the patient. In particular, my intraoperative adaptation was in relation to flap thickness and wound closure.'

He wasn't denying he was doing it, but he was denying it was a big deal, despite patients never having consented to such an 'adaptation'.

Because none of the whistleblowers were kept informed about Hennessy and Polson's findings, Paterson could keep operating in plain sight. One of Polson's recommendations was that Paterson be observed doing five mastectomies, and in 2008, Martin Lee did exactly that. Lee is a respected surgeon who attended St John's College, Oxford, before completing his medical training at University of Birmingham Medical School in the early 1970s. He had previously been the President of the Association of Breast Surgery, so he was more than qualified to oversee Paterson's surgery. But of course that process was not neutral, because Paterson was well aware he was being scrutinised. Despite that, he still performed badly. After observing the five operations, Lee wrote a report for Cunliffe that described Paterson's surgery as 'rushed'. He tried to soften the criticism by suggesting that there is variation in the speed at which each surgeon operates, but 'a point can be reached when excessive operating speed compromises outcome'. And 'operating too rapidly may jeopardise the oncological aim of complete breast tissue removal, increase the risk of postoperative bleeding, and compromise healing'. In other words, fast surgery is very dangerous, even if it does get the waiting list down. Lee later described Paterson's surgery as 'slipshod', and said: 'Watching him operate was like a whirlwind really. He would breeze into the theatre, a sort of constant impatience with things, and just try to get on as quickly as possible, and that is something I have not seen very often ... there are some surgeons who operate slowly and some who operate more quickly, but the point is that you should do it without rush, with care and attention.'

Aside from criticisms about speed, Lee observed that Paterson's basic surgical technique had some 'technical deficits' that needed attention, including improving 'adherence to sterile technique' (a terrifying euphemism for poor hygiene) and more 'fastidious attention to haemostasis' (blood clotting). Overall, Lee reported, that 'to be assured that as complete a mastectomy as possible is achieved on every occasion, there is a need for Mr Paterson to ensure that he pays meticulous attention to the goal of removal of all breast tissue.'

He suggested, in short, that Paterson get better at the very thing he had been hired to do: mastectomies. Perhaps it did not occur to Martin Lee that if Paterson was operating like that while being supervised, what was he doing when left to his own devices?

Lee recommended Paterson be given more training and monitoring, and should be given a mentor to 'support him through a difficult professional experience'. There was no recommendation that his operating privileges be suspended in the meantime, or that his patients be informed of these ongoing issues. He later said, 'I feel that if there was information available at the time which showed increased recurrence rates as well as concerns by colleagues in the team and concerns about operative technique, then that adds up to the need to actually say that we put patients' safety first and stop him operating on breast cancer.'

But there *was* information about increased recurrence rates. Ingle and the other whistleblowers testified that they were seeing precisely that and provided proof too. That should have been enough of a risk to patient safety to suspend Paterson and instigate what is called a 'rapid review of practice'. Lee should have known the basic principle that absence of evidence is not evidence of absence. This was a life-and-death issue. If there was a chance that patients were being harmed by Paterson, he should have been stopped while more proof was gathered. But Lee had not been shown Hennessy's report, and all the other concerns were hidden behind the wall of 'HR confidentiality'. He could not make a fully informed decision.

While patients weren't being protected from Paterson's 'slipshod' techniques, trainee surgeons were. The registrar who was currently being trained by him was removed from his influence, and no further trainees were sent to Paterson's breast unit. Of course, this also meant one less witness to his wrongdoing, but at least he could no longer teach cleavage-sparing mastectomies to new surgeons.

Beyond that change, it's hard to know which of Lee's recommendations were carried out. One of the more baffling ones is the recommendation that Paterson be sent for continuing professional development training, because no such training scheme for breast surgeons existed. It took ten months for Paterson to sign off on the action plan, with seemingly no pressure from senior management for him to do so. Given that, it was pretty unlikely there would be much oversight of him actually doing what he was meant to. For example, Paterson had agreed to visit the clinic of senior surgeon Ajay Kakkar (who is now a member of the House of Lords) for mentoring but did not actually go. He did provide some paperwork for Cunliffe that seemed to satisfy him, but that work is not on public record. Otherwise, he was free to carry on his surgery as though nothing was wrong.

With seemingly nothing amiss, Lloyd Owen continued to work with Breast Friends. She got the committee to approve paying for manicures at Solihull Hospital for chemo patients, carried out by her best friend.

In November 2008, Paterson spoke to Breast Friends once again. Demand was so high, the meeting had to be moved to a larger venue at Solihull Sixth Form College. Around a hundred and twenty people came to hear him speak. On behalf of the committee I gave a speech and presented him with a bottle of wine in a gift bag from Marks & Spencer to thank him for all his work, and he seemed genuinely touched. I shudder when I think of it.

15

In 2008, I had an operation on my left shoulder. I'd banged it on an open cupboard door and went to my GP, who wrote me a request for an X-ray. I had a check-up appointment with Paterson the next day and handed the letter to him. He promptly ripped it in half and threw it in the bin, saying, 'you don't need this, I'm going to send you for a PET scan'. The scan came back clear, but I was still in a lot of pain. I called the breast care team and they arranged for the X-ray that I should have had in the first place, which showed I'd broken my collar bone at some point and it had healed and trapped a nerve. I was called back to Paterson and he arranged for a consultation with an orthopaedic surgeon at Little Aston, Brian Banerjee, who shaved the bone and released the pressure on my nerve. I hated having to have another operation, but the pain was enough to overcome my terror.

I was off work for a month. When I returned, I was given an award for a project I had led on improving safety test coverage by looking at trends and component data at early-stage testing. I was thriving in a challenging environment and was fast outgrowing my responsibilities. I took a chance and applied for a job as a supply chain engineer, and was successful. In my new role I was responsible for investigating failures of electronic parts and sub assemblies, failures that could endanger aircraft and lives if not caught early. I also trained as a Lloyds Registered Quality Auditor. My health might not have been great, but my career was going from strength to strength.

My children had grown up and I was free to travel up and down the country and abroad for work. Bob was very support-ive. He had retrained as an HGV driver, while our eldest son Robert had graduated university (the first in our family to do so) and was working for a bank. Our daughter Jenny graduated with a degree in biochemistry and got engaged to her partner, Scott. Our youngest, William, was on a foundation course at Bournville College and would go on to study fine art. My cancer had shown no sign of returning. Things were good in the Douglas family.

Things were not so good for Paterson patients. He had continued to operate in both the NHS and private sectors on women who had no idea their surgeon was not in fact the best (given his patient outcomes and how his career would eventu-ally end, he could arguably be considered the worst breast surgeon in history).

In April 2008, both HEFT and Spire Parkway received an anonymous letter. It purported to be from one of Paterson's colleagues and raised serious concerns about his surgical prac-tice, asking why he hadn't been suspended while investigations took place.

'A patient with a lump in her breast had it excised privately and carcinoma in situ (CIS) was found in the excision margins and wider excision made. This, too, had CIS in the margins and finally simple mastectomy was performed. A year later she presented with Grade 2 cancer in the remaining tissue. The surgeon was Ian Paterson. This did not sound good practice. After talking to colleagues it turns out that this surgeon is currently being investigated by the Royal College for just this and results are showing that there have been a large number of mistakes.

'I understand that these results have been suppressed. The lesson learnt from Bristol is that the normal practice in such a situation is that until the quality of the surgery is restored, the surgeon in question is suspended. After talking with colleagues, I have learnt that there have been concerns before regarding his practice with dealing with benign lumps.'

The letter was suggesting that Paterson was doing incomplete mastectomies on cancer patients and giving cancer operations to non-cancer patients. No one knows who sent the letter, and no one knows who was shown the letter by its recipients, Mark Goldman (CEO of HEFT) and Will Knights (MD of Spire Parkway), but it appears that no one informed the other Spire hospital where Paterson worked, Little Aston, nor was it raised with Paterson or the medical advisory committee (MAC). Ruth Paulin, general manager at Spire Parkway, claims she was not shown the letter.

This was just a few months after Paulin had been informed that Paterson was doing cleavage-sparing mastectomies. She did not make this information available more widely within Spire, and while Paterson did tell her he would cease that practice in the private sector, Paulin didn't do anything to check. This was later described by Spire's own investigators as 'a collective failure to manage him'. Had Paulin shared this information more widely, perhaps the 2008 anonymous letter would have had more impact.

That was also the year a woman named Marie Pinfield died, two years after undergoing surgery by Ian Paterson at Solihull Hospital. Marie served thirty years as a child protection officer with West Midlands Constabulary. She had planned to buy a campervan for her retirement and travel with her dog, a West Highland White Terrier named Annie Bear.

Marie had found cancer in her breast after experiencing pain. She was initially sent home by doctors with painkillers, but after a few weeks of no improvement she was referred for a mammogram. That same day, Ian Paterson told her bluntly that she had cancer. She was alone at the time, and immediately called her sister, Shirley. 'It's not good news, Shirl,' she said. Shirley immediately rushed to see her. 'This is going to take me down,' Marie feared. Shirley told her not to be ridiculous but promised she would go with her to every single appointment thereafter.

Marie was adamant that she wanted both breasts removed. Although the cancer was only showing in one, she was a pragmatic woman and knew the risk of spread. Paterson insisted on her having a psychological evaluation before he would remove the healthy breast, the results of which clearly demonstrated that Marie knew her own mind. Shirley was present at every interaction with Paterson, and got the impression he did not want to give Marie a full double mastectomy. 'I'm just telling you now, I want them both off,' Marie told him. 'You say that, Marie, lots of women say that, but when push comes to shove you want the breast shape to stay,' he replied.

The night before the surgery, Shirley asked Marie if she should get it in writing that she wanted both breasts off. Marie said not to be ridiculous, as Paterson was a professional and knew what he was doing. Shirley wasn't so sure, but she trusted her sister, an experienced police officer. After surgery, initially Shirley was made to wait outside the door. She could see Marie asleep in the bed, and a large mound in her chest area. At first she thought that they had just sewn her back up because the cancer was too bad to operate, but when Marie woke up they realised he had done a partial mastectomy. Shirley demanded to see Paterson. 'I pointed to Marie's chest and said, "what's this?" He said, "It's just fatty tissue. I knew you'd be trouble." He turned heel and marched out. I was floored. She had been left with at least a D cup, down from at least a G. They were smaller, but her breasts were still there.'

Marie was desperately unhappy. 'I'm neither fish nor fowl. I don't have breasts, but I have these things stuck to my body. It's not what I wanted,' she told Shirley. So together they demanded a revision operation.

'When we went to see him, he got angry, and we assumed it was just professional pride – we made excuses because everybody kept telling us he was the best,' said Shirley. But Paterson still didn't remove all the breast tissue. 'Even after the second operation, she was still a C or D cup. He still wouldn't give her a flat chest.' Shirley believes Paterson was motivated by arrogance. 'The guy had a God complex. He felt that women could only exist in this world if they had a breast-shaped body.'

After the second surgery, pathology found a 2cm tumour in the removed tissue. Marie's cancer had returned – and spread. Delays to her chemotherapy meant it was too late to treat the aggressive cancer, so she vowed to make the most of the time she had left, travelling to East Asia and the Pyrenees. On her fiftieth birthday, she and Shirley treated themselves to lunch and went to the cinema. Marie died two weeks later, in October 2008. She was forty-nine years old.

A newspaper article later claimed that Heart of England NHS Foundation Trust admitted the second operation would not have been necessary if the double mastectomy had been carried out properly. An independent report found Marie could have lived for ten more years had she received the right initial treatment.

A few months after Marie Pinfeld died, HEFT finally agreed on which of Paterson's mastectomy patients to recall for review. The recall procedure was incredibly slow to get underway.

Stockdale had been writing to Cunliffe to complain. 'Listen, I've handed you all these cases. What have you done about it?' he told Cunliffe. When the ball finally did get rolling, the process was incompetent. For a start, Paterson was still operating, something that caused incredulity in the MDT.

How could Paterson be allowed to carry out remedial surgery on patients whose problems he had caused by not operating properly in the first place? The patients were not informed of this, and had no idea whose hands their lives were in. Another bizarre decision was to closely involve Paterson in the recall process. Bizarre, because he denied leaving any breast tissue (he continued to insist he was just leaving fatty tissue) and so was of no help identifying patients most at risk of recurrence, but also because he was impossible to work with. The MDT could not possibly improve or carry out the recall properly while Paterson was involved. At one point, it was later reported, consultant breast surgeon Balapathiran Bala told him to stop defending his surgical procedure, saying, 'Enough is enough, don't you know what sort of mess the whole thing is in?'

Fernando, one of the oncologists who had complained about Paterson, said that as they couldn't tell from the medical records who had had a cleavage-sparing mastectomy or not, 'every patient needs to be recalled and they need to see somebody who's independent of Mr Paterson because Mr Paterson, in all fairness to him, cannot be relied upon to make an objective judgement on this matter. So to say that we need to discuss it with Mr Paterson and get Mr Paterson to review the patient … is totally inappropriate.'

Nonetheless, that is what happened. HEFT, in its wisdom, decided that cleavage-sparing mastectomy patients would be identified from written records and photographs, and only those patients would be recalled. The very obvious issue is that it wasn't actually possible to tell if a patient had had a cleavage-sparing mastectomy just from records: she would need to be recalled and examined. HEFT caused themselves a catch-22. A major part of the problem was that Paterson did not keep good records. The three external experts commissioned by HEFT to assist with the limited recall reported: 'Many patients are likely to have had incomplete mastectomies, but we are unable to assist in determining if this is the case in the majority … because the operation notes seldom describe the technique in sufficient detail and there is no other evidence on which to reach a conclusion.'

As early as March 2009, staff raised concerns about the potential problems. Speaking anonymously to a later investigation, they said that trying to identify cleavage-sparing mastectomy patients from written records and photos would not work, and that 'if women were going to be recalled, it should be all women, not just a few'. But HEFT did not listen and 'they just carried on anyway'. The anonymous staff member asked, 'did the organisation truly not realise the potential scale of the problems? Did they not want to? Did they think it would go away?'

I think they probably did expect it to go away, or were simply in above their heads. Whatever the justification, HEFT decided to recall just twelve patients.

16

That same month, Gill Lawrence sent Ian Cunliffe a report. In 2005, she had undertaken a major audit looking at breast cancer recurrence rates, at a time when there was no mandatory reporting of such data. Her team had examined 1,966 cases from the Royal Wolverhampton NHS Trust and found recurrence rates of 2.75 per cent for women who had undergone wide local excision (WLE) and 1.38 per cent for those who had had mastectomies.

In her 2009 detailed report to Cunliffe, Lawrence included this data and also compared Paterson's NHS and private patient breast cancer recurrence rates with those of a colleague, John Taylor, and found that Paterson's were statistically significantly higher. This couldn't be explained by the type of cancer or rates of radiotherapy but must instead mean a difference in the surgery itself. She drew particular attention to the 'worryingly high' recurrence rates of Paterson patients who had had a 'shave' mastectomy or immediate reconstruction between 1994 and 2003, stating that these patients were at significant risk and should be carefully monitored over the next few years. But rather than her report being used to inform and speed up the recall process, it was, in her words, 'disappeared ... as far as I know'. Cunliffe was an eye surgeon, not a breast surgeon, and it could reasonably be argued that the huge burden of what was unfolding should not have been his alone. One colleague suggested that he was 'heavily influenced by the Chief Executive and the wider considerations of the reputation of the Trust', but he did not share Lawrence's new report with any of Paterson's colleagues.

When the whistleblower Stockdale eventually saw that report some years later and was asked by investigator Sir Ian Kennedy if the limited recall could have been justified in light of it, he said, 'Absolutely not ... It is quite clear that there were substantial [numbers of] patients at risk and it is quite clear that the Trust choosing to believe that only twelve were at risk was at the very best naive and at the very worst totally culpable.'

The recall team, including Paterson himself, had agreed on the dozen patients in late 2008. Of course, if all of his patients had been recalled, there would have been no need to involve him at all, but he was still the surgeon clearing the waiting list at record speed, and for that he was protected and pandered to. Paterson argued that recalling patients would cause anxiety for those patients and open HEFT to litigation, so he tried to suggest that he should see them himself, in private. He could examine them without telling them they were part of a recall, he said, and only inform them if there was cause for concern.

In a rare moment of common sense, the recall team rejected this approach, but it still took them six months to contact the twelve women. There was simply no sense of urgency, even though the twelve women had been identified as 'at risk' from recurrence.

In June 2009 the patients received letters inviting them to be re-examined. In the meantime, Paterson's other breast cancer patients were attending follow-up clinics and routine appointments with no idea that anything untoward was happening. As they were examined by nurses or other clinicians it became abundantly clear that there were far, far more than twelve patients who had had incomplete mastectomies. It became necessary to introduce a protocol for such patients: in the first instance the name and patient number were passed on to senior team members, who would then send those details to Ian Cunliffe to cross-reference with the existing recall notes. If she was not already in the recall system, she should be seen immediately by the consultant, Bala, and a breast nurse.

This process was not fit for purpose, not least because Bala was a very busy man. 'It proved increasingly difficult to set up those clinics with what felt like very little administrative support,' said one staff member. A senior nurse later told investigators that she insisted to Cunliffe, 'you either call everybody or you call nobody. This just doing a bit here and a bit there is just causing a whole load of distress for patients and a whole load of distress for staff.' I feel deeply for the nurses and other staff who were working under extreme pressure to do their everyday job while being expected to manage a recall process that was badly resourced, badly run and deeply flawed. Nobody knew what was going on, but as the initial recall inevitably collapsed in the wake of floods of patients seemingly at risk of cancer recurrence, no emotional support or counselling was offered to staff or patients. Delay upon delay meant that every woman who had received a cleavage-sparing mastectomy risked not only their cancer returning, but it being too late to treat. I find that unforgivable.

In January 2009, a meeting was held at Heartlands Hospital to discuss the histopathology service provided to Mr Paterson and his breast care team. Histopathologists are scientists who study the cells in a piece of tissue that has been surgically removed, to see if cancer is present and, if so, what type. Paterson did not invite histopathologists to MDTs, but an unnamed manager at Spire Little Aston later said that they probably wouldn't have gone anyway because 'he bashed heads with so many of them'. Paterson had a history of falling out with them, and had insisted that his specimens from Spire Parkway and Little Aston be sent to Heartlands NHS hospital department, which also does private work, until he had what was described as 'a massive bust-up' with them. A later investigation reports one histopathologist refusing to work with him, saying, 'I gave him a cytology report and he said, "that's not right, I don't really care about your report anyway."' Paterson then decided to use a histopathology service in Walsall Manor NHS, which the unnamed manager from Spire claimed was 'because he had decided that a particular group of histopathologists were more willing to bend to his demands than the other group'. But what would those demands be, and to what purpose?

The first benefit to Paterson was that, under pressure from the breast care team to process pathology results in time for the patient's MDT meeting a week after surgery, the Walsall lab sometimes gave results verbally, over the phone. A sufficiently dishonest doctor could tell a patient that her histopathology results said she had cancer, and therefore needed an (expensive) operation, when in fact the histopathologist had said no cancer cells were present. It was a huge loophole in the paper-trail system, and one Paterson was easily able to exploit. It also meant he could later blame the breast care nurses for mishearing.

Another second benefit to using the Walsall lab was also about data oversight, with equally horrifying implications. JJ de Gorter, the medical director at Spire, later confirmed that the Walsall laboratory did not submit data to the West Midlands cancer registry, the body responsible for collecting and monitoring data on cancer regionally, and perhaps that was a motivation for Paterson to insist on using them, because key data showing his true recurrence rates was simply not reported. Lloyd Owen would later use these figures to convince me and the Breast Friends committee that Paterson's recurrence rates were better than his peers, when in fact they were worse.

After the initial dozen had been examined, it became clear that there was something to worry about, and another forty-eight patients were identified for recall.

Speculation and rumours had become the norm among staff, but the Trust was still not saying a word, internally or to the public, and for another year they managed to keep the whole thing under wraps.

17

The NHS recall of patients was important progress for cancer patients who had unwittingly been given a cleavage-sparing mastectomy. But what of the growing suspicion that Paterson was operating on people in the private sector who did not have cancer?

Not long before the first twelve recall letters were being sent out to HEFT patients, Bethan Lloyd Owen completed her 'audit' of Paterson's private sector breast surgery. It was as good as useless, later criticised by Spire's own investigators who said, 'the presentation fails to compare Mr Paterson's practice to other consultants and only includes basic details of the breast care service'.

At the same time, Joy Masters, matron of Spire Parkway, had undertaken an audit of Paterson's patient notes. She reported that ten sets of notes she checked had 'no entries completed adequately. He had filled out all of his consent forms, but none were fully completed'. She wrote to him saying, 'I'm sure you'll be surprised by this level of non-compliance, and I would be grateful if you could strive to achieve 100 per cent compliance in all areas.'

Given Paterson was probably disinclined to achieve any sort of compliance in any area, it was a remarkably optimistic request. What should have been immediately identified as more evidence of wrongdoing was simply dismissed with a mild rebuke.

To understand Paterson's relationship with Spire, we must understand how surgeons work in the private sector. Paterson was not a salaried employee of Spire like he was the NHS, but rather a freelancer who 'rented' facilities from them (a loophole that would become crucial later). His team, including his right-hand woman Bethan Lloyd Owen, were directly employed by Spire, but reported to Paterson. Despite not being an employee of Spire, Paterson ran the breast clinic at Parkway and Little Aston hospitals. He also carried out procedures and operations at BMI The Edgbaston and The Priory. He had a huge amount of power and very little oversight.

In 2001, Paterson made another power grab. He wrote to Ruth Paulin, general manager at Spire Parkway, to ask if he could change the way MDTs were run. Ordinarily, each member of the MDT wrote their own separate patient notes, but Paterson wanted just one set of notes per patient. This is when Paterson introduced a separate MDT meeting at Little Aston. While this might seem like an efficiency move, it could also be viewed as an attempt to remove oversight and put full control of patient files into Paterson's hands. Two years later he volunteered to join Spire's medical advisory committee. These committees are supposed to review all clinical governance issues, key performance indicators (KPIs), patient deaths and adverse events. They are also responsible for awarding practising privileges to surgeons. Around the same time, the NHS was learning about his cleavage-sparing mastectomies. Despite Paterson's private patients being discussed at the same MDTs as NHS patients, there is no record of anyone at HEFT informing Spire of the issues.

One area in which there was an attempt at oversight was annual appraisals. Surgeons, like anyone else in a professional role, have to undergo checks to ensure their performance is up to par. The General Medical Council (GMC) sets the criteria, but it's also an opportunity for the surgeon to discuss their professional development, any issues at work, that sort of thing. Having worked in a safety-critical industry, I know first-hand how important checking competency is. It shouldn't be something that any professional is resistant to, let alone a surgeon. But Paterson did not want the scrutiny. Ordinarily, the annual appraisal was carried out by the surgeon's boss within the NHS, but in theory it was also meant to include an assessment of the surgeon's private practice. In August 2003, the chairman of MAC at Spire Little Aston, John Taylor, wrote to Paterson to ask him to provide proof of his latest NHS appraisal, referring to the BUPA consultant's handbook, which outlines this responsibility. A month later, Paterson had his appraisal at HEFT. It was carried out by HEFT's clinical director, Charles Hendrickse, who by this time knew about multiple complaints against Paterson. Charles Hendrickse was chair of Spire Parkway's MAC, so part of his remit was to oversee competence and complaints.

Despite that, Hendrickse gave Paterson a satisfactory NHS appraisal, and duly sent it to Taylor. It did not, however, include an assessment of Paterson's private practice, which Taylor pointed out. But, he said, as Paterson was not aware of this requirement at the time, he would let it slide for 2003. I'm at a loss to explain why. Taylor presumably didn't suspect Paterson was up to anything criminal, but surely it was a basic part of his job and Spire's duty of care to ensure all surgeons were competent, even if they were just 'renting a room'.

Around the same time, Ruth Paulin wrote to Paterson to ask him about another matter. In the NHS, Paterson had 'practising privileges' for specific operations, namely breast surgery, vascular surgery, hernias, laparoscopic cholecystectomies and thyroids. He should not have been doing any other sort of operation, but in the private sector he was doing pretty much any operation he fancied. For example, alongside vascular surgery, lumpectomies and mastectomies, Paterson had also been doing gastroscopies, a highly invasive procedure in which a camera is inserted into a patient's throat and down to the stomach, and colonoscopies, which is a similar procedure but at the other end of the body. Paulin was not telling him to stop, but was requesting he have a separate appraisal for those procedures. Paterson did not like that. In January 2004 he replied,

'The person or persons who prompted your correspondence have given you a number of misconceptions which I hope you are now completely straight about. It is all too easy to raise the nebulous concept of clinical governance when self-serving greed is the underlying motive.'

This tactic didn't quite work. Paulin replied to reiterate that he needed to provide proof of competency for gastroscopies and colonoscopies. In April 2004, Paterson was able to provide a satisfactory appraisal for colonoscopies, undertaken by a consultant surgeon at the Royal Blackburn Hospital, but I can't find any record of an appraisal for gastroscopies.

Other than that flurry of queries, Paterson's work in the private sector apparently continued without supervision for nearly three years. Paterson and Lloyd Owen carried on running the show at the Spire breast clinics, and Paterson was paid for any operation he wanted to do. In January 2007, Paterson submitted an application to join a hospital panel at BUPA that contained a list of the separate procedures he had carried out at Parkway hospital.

There were ninety-two of them, including things like colonosco-pies and block dissections of axillary lymph nodes. That is a lot of different types of procedures, many of which were presumably outside of his practising privileges. The strangest thing is that of the ninety-two, he carried out fifty of them only once.

Was he just having a go at whatever bit of medicine he fancied? Or seeing what he could get away with charging patients for? The records do not say if this information raised any enquiries within BUPA – or even any eyebrows.

Other than the appraisals, there doesn't seem to have been much cross-communication about Paterson between the NHS and Spire. Most likely, HEFT was still trying to keep a lid on things under the guise of HR confidentiality. In June 2007, Alison Woolner, head of clinical services (matron) at Little Aston, and Joy Masters, Spire's head of clinical services, received a request from HEFT at short notice for notes about Paterson's breast cancer patients. HEFT did not say why it was needed, and so neither woman was concerned about it, duly providing the information without further question.

The NHS had known about problems with Paterson since Gill Dallow in 1996, including the complaints by plastic surgeon Fazel Fatah in 1998. Stockdale raised concerns in 2003, then again with Ingle and others a few years later. In December 2007, Stockdale wrote to Goldman, CEO of HEFT, co-signed by Fernando, Ingle, Bala, Tanchel and Fletcher:

'*Cases of concern include patients who have obvious residual breast tissue remaining following mastectomy, some of whom have gone on to have a second operation when no further surgery should have been possible. We are also aware of significant numbers of patients left with positive margins following mastectomy and immediate reconstruction for breast cancer. We believe that we have identified a number of patients who have relapsed as a consequence of inadequate surgery.*

'*Despite these serious concerns, Mr Paterson continues to operate with his usual surgical practice.*'

The letter lays out the case of a patient who had had a mastectomy and immediate reconstruction. Paterson had removed the breast in five separate pieces, against best surgical procedure. 'The cancer was in multiple fragments of tissue and extended to the resection margin,' the letter said. 'It is our belief that there may be residual breast tissue containing cancer beneath this patient's reconstruction. Unless further surgery can achieve clear surgical margins, she will be left with an increased risk of local relapse, whatever additional treatment is offered, and consequently an additional risk of dying of metastatic breast cancer.'

The authors conclude: 'We would ask you to consider in the interest of patient safety whether Mr Paterson should continue to operate on patients with breast cancer until the review report is available.'

Senior management had done their best to suppress the growing concerns, but the situation (and the whistleblowers) couldn't be contained. Following the letter, Mark Goldman finally wrote to Ruth Paulin at Spire to tell her Paterson had been carrying out subtotal or 'cleavage-sparing' mastectomies and that his practice was under review.

A few weeks later, in early January 2008, Paterson admitted to Paulin he had been doing cleavage-sparing mastectomies on private patients at Spire. He agreed to stop the practice until HEFT's review was concluded.

Paulin should have known that Paterson would never do what he promised, because she had already been trying to get him to stop doing colonoscopies. There had been a to-and-fro between Hendrickse, Paulin and Paterson over the years, and Hendrickse and Paulin more than once told Paterson to stop doing the unapproved procedure. But Paterson was going to do whatever operations he wanted – and get paid for them. While his appeal to HEFT was how quickly he could get through the waiting lists, in the private sector he was valuable for his profitability. In 2008, a colonoscopy in the private sector cost at least £1,600, and that was without consultation and follow-up fees, tests, scans or medication. Those colonoscopy patients had their operations with no idea that the surgeon wielding the knife was not authorised. They did not get what they thought they were consenting to, let alone what they paid for. One patient alone was given fourteen colonoscopies by Paterson at a cost of £22,000.

Spire already knew that Paterson was carrying out colonoscopies he did not have practising privileges for, and since December 2007 had known he was doing incomplete mastectomies. But when did they first hear that he might be doing operations on patients who did not actually need them?

In September 2008, a GP named Eli Leyton complained to Will Knights at Spire Parkway because he had discovered one of his patients was about to have an unnecessary operation. 'I ran through the case,' he later told the *Tonight* programme. 'I showed him [Knights] all the letters proving [Paterson] had lied.' Leyton claimed Knights told him that Paterson could not be suspended because he brought in too much money. Knights denied this via a spokesperson, saying he had no recollection of the comments attributed to him and was adamant he would not have said something so wholly inappropriate. Another GP, Sunil Kotecha, also complained to Spire. The doctors had heard other stories from their colleagues, enough to be worried that this was not a simple error but part of a pattern of Paterson overtreating patients. It was widely rumoured he was not adhering to the MDT process, which was meant in part to safeguard against this sort of situation, and so the GPs laid out their concerns to Knights.

Knights asked Charles Hendrickse to investigate the complaint. He had overseen Paterson in the NHS from 2003 to 2005, where he received at least two complaints.

Hendrickse seemingly did nothing except provide positive appraisals. Given his previous inaction, it's reasonable enough to think he was perhaps not the best person to also investigate claims against Paterson in the private sector.

Paterson responded with his usual deflection. He had a history of blaming nurses, receptionists or other staff less senior to him, and this time he claimed there had been a misunderstanding about the patient's histopathology results, which he blamed on the breast care nurses taking results over the phone. Hendrickse seemed to accept this.

The GPs had requested that Knights commission an independent audit conducted by a breast consultant, such was the strength of their concerns, but that never happened. Instead, Knights referred the matter to Hendrickse, who asked that the audit be carried out by the last person he should have considered: Paterson's closest associate and 'right-hand woman' at Spire, Bethan Lloyd Owen.

Paterson had promised to stop performing colonoscopies in January 2008, but a month later he tried to renege on this, suggesting in a letter to Hendrickse that he was being unfairly singled out:

'Before I honour the verbal agreement that we had to not perform any further colonoscopies I would like to discuss with you and Ruth how my plastic surgery colleagues are monitored and externally appraised and why my colonoscopy practice has become a special case.'

Spire's handbook for consultants was clear that clinicians were forbidden from treating patients if they did not have practising privileges for that procedure. To make sure this rule was followed, reviews by MAC were mandated every two years. In reality, MAC didn't pay much attention to existing clinicians, focusing instead on new ones. Joy Masters is on the record as saying MAC did not discuss renewing practising privileges at Parkway. It's no wonder Paterson was able to play the system so easily. He was first given practising privileges at Parkway in 1998, but in 2007 the 'renew every two years' rule was introduced, which should have prompted a review. It did not. Investigators in 2014 said Paterson's practising privileges file 'was poorly organised, with papers filed without any obvious rationale'. Important information was also missing from it, which had taken Spire three months to hand over. 'We were told that the file used to be fuller but that documents had been extracted.' The investigators concluded: 'There is no evidence in the file that Mr Paterson ever had a biennial review at Parkway hospital.' The minutes of Parkway MAC meetings suggests a preoccupation with new consultants, or getting rid of those who weren't bringing in business. A later chairperson said in 2014:

'It's not usually about people's abilities or their problems; it's usually about whether we need 220 anaesthetists, for example, on the book and for people who are not doing a lot of work in the hospital. It's usually between consultants but the Spire view, as with most other private hospitals, is that if somebody ticks all the boxes and they may bring some business in, then unless there is a good reason to reject somebody, they are granted privileges.'

Still, that doesn't mean Spire was happy for Paterson to do work for which he had not been granted practising privileges. Despite previously agreeing to stop, he was still doing colonoscopies. In March 2009, while the audit into Paterson's breast surgery was underway, Hendrickse, in his capacity as chairman of Parkway MAC, wrote to Paterson: 'I am disappointed that I have to write to you again concerning your colonoscopy practice at Spire Parkway Hospital.' You would think that Paterson's refusal to keep his word or stick to proper surgical boundaries over and over would be considered in the audit, but, of course, it was a whitewash. And even more obviously, if Paterson was still doing colonoscopies when he had pinky-promised not to, why would Spire management believe him when he said he would also cease performing cleavage-sparing mastectomies?

18

Towards the end of 2009 I was travelling regularly for work, including long-haul flights to the US. Part of my job entailed carrying out quality audits to ensure suppliers met with international standards for quality management. I took pride in my work and was meticulous in my organisation. I always explained to suppliers that the audit was not about catching them out or finding fault but about working together to improve processes and systems, yet I was aware that the presence of an investigator can cause defensiveness, particularly in management. If I wanted to get to the root of a problem, it was usually the operators on the factory floor who knew where the issue was coming from, rather than those in management.

I was staying in East Los Angeles on a trip to an electronics manufacturer in Culver City. Rather than hire a car I decided to get the hotel shuttle bus from the airport, remembering the nightmare drive through LA traffic at the end of our Route 66 trip. I did, however, ask the hotel receptionist if the nearest shopping mall was within walking distance for dinner, and she said yes, so I set off. In the middle of my meal, around 8pm, there was a blackout. Low-level lighting from a generator kicked in near the exit to the mall, but the restaurant was pitch black. All the street and building lights were off, and I realised I'd have to walk back to my hotel in the dark.

You bloody idiot, I muttered to myself as I tried to walk with confidence. I'd seen enough films where the stranger in town gets mugged, or worse, and felt panicky. I started to pick up my pace, half walking and now half running back to the hotel, when suddenly I felt a sharp pain in my stomach. That distracted me from the threat of potential muggers, and I got back to my hotel safely, but worried. I had recently been getting a lot of painful bloating in my stomach, which I put down to a side effect from losing my stomach muscle, perhaps exacerbated by all the travelling and disruptions to my normal diet and mealtimes. I got through my trip, but I resolved to mention the stomach problems to Paterson at my next check-up.

Back in England, I headed to my appointment at Spire Parkway. Paterson immediately seemed concerned for both my health and my career. He said, 'You don't want to be ill while you're abroad. Let's get you in for an ultrasound scan.' I once again silently thanked my private health insurance and the thoroughness of Paterson as I booked the scan for the following week.

'You have gallstones,' said Paterson, after I had had the scan. 'You need an operation.' He suggested a colleague, Paul Super, but I immediately froze. Super was the surgeon who had operated on my mother, and while there's no suggestion that his treatment was related to her subsequent death from MRSA, I absolutely couldn't face the painful memories and fear. I told Paterson and he immediately offered to do the operation instead.

Gallstones don't always cause symptoms. They are nuggets of hardened cholesterol that form in the gallbladder, and can just sit there unnoticed, but sometimes they get stuck in the bile duct and cause pain. I hadn't realised I had them, but I was very upset to learn they were serious enough to warrant an operation. Still, Paterson knew his business. Unaware he did not actually have practising privileges for a cholecystectomy (removal of the gallbladder), I agreed. I later spoke to Lloyd Owen and told her I was surprised to hear he did gallbladder operations. 'Oh yes,' she replied, 'he's a general surgeon, he's done lots of them.' I kept thinking about what Paterson said about the dangers of becoming ill while abroad, so I booked my operation for as soon as possible, in early January 2009.

My veins had collapsed from the chemo in my right hand and because of the risk of lymphoedema in my left arm due to having my nodes removed, so I dreaded them trying to find a good vein for the anaesthetic. I was also extremely nervous about the anaesthetic and how painful recovery might be, but Paterson's travel warning echoed in my head. I could see Bob was concerned too; he said he hated the thought of me going through something else, and the kids' faces told the same story when they kissed me goodbye to get into the car to the hospital.

On the day of the operation, I was checked into Spire Parkway and shown into a private room. I was sitting on the bed when there was a knock on the door and Lloyd Owen entered, smiling serenely. 'Just popping in to see how you are.' She once again reassured me about being 'in good hands with Mr Paterson'. I was asked to change into my gown by a theatre nurse and then Paterson came in. In his beautifully-tailored navy blue suit he stood at the foot of my bed and said, 'This might be a difficult operation because of your scar tissue and the mesh from your breast reconstruction.'

That didn't make me feel any better. I was quite justifiably terrified; my breast cancer surgery and chemo had taken a severe toll, physically and psychologically. The last place I ever wanted to be again was in an operating theatre. But I was getting a lot of fuss and attention from Lloyd Owen and the nurses, who made me feel very special. I was wheeled to theatre for the operation, whispering to myself, please God let me be okay.

The next thing I knew I was coming round in recovery, from where I was moved back to my room. I had an oxygen mask on. A nurse wanted to take it off me, but I was scared and clung on to it. I had a phobia about dying because of lack of oxygen. I explained to the nurse how I watched my mum die, but she was firm and said, 'Deborah, you can't be reliant on this. Give me the mask.' I let her take it away.

Paterson came back into my room wearing his blue scrubs and said confidently, 'We did the right thing, Deborah. Your gallbladder was diseased.'

He triumphantly held up a clear plastic tub containing two evenly sized light-brown stones, like a show-and-tell. He was clearly pleased with himself. 'Here are your gallstones,' he said, putting the tub down next to my bed. I was too worried about the news of disease to pay much attention to them. 'What do I need to do now? Will I have to be on a special diet?'

'No,' he said, smiling, 'I've removed your gallbladder. You're completely cured, you can have a nice big fry-up tomorrow morning.'

I was released the same day. As I was getting my things together I looked at the tub containing my gallstones, which Paterson had left on the nightstand. 'Can I take these?' I asked the nurse. 'Sorry, no,' she replied. 'It's health and safety.' Well, it sounded like Paterson had given them to me as a souvenir, so when the nurse left me to get dressed I slipped the tub into my bag.

The next morning I was hungry, and, thinking of Paterson's words about a full English, ate the lovely cooked breakfast that Bob made me, then promptly threw my guts up. But at least I was home in my own bed and could sit and recover in comfort. I felt sore and my stomach was still bloated from the air they pumped into me to access my gallbladder through keyhole surgery. There were three incisions just over three inches apart that were really tender and I had pain in my shoulders from the anaesthetic. I couldn't drive or do anything strenuous for a couple of weeks. I wasn't used to sitting still. I'd got a self-funded trip to Australia planned on 21 March with fourteen other women and some of our partners to climb the Sydney Harbour Bridge to raise funds for Breast Friends and was worried I wouldn't recover in time. When I lay on my right side it felt like acid was being poured into my stomach. Neither Paterson nor Lloyd Owen had prepared me for the side effects of the gallbladder operation. Paterson had mentioned that he may not be able to access my gallbladder because of the scar tissue from my reconstruction and the surgical mesh that had been implanted. I was worried he'd damaged it somehow. I felt a bit down and teary but I knew that was probably just the pain and the effects of medication. I'd be okay. I'd got through having my breast removed, I was sure I could live without a gallbladder too.

One of my hobbies is art, something I'd kept up since dropping out of college after being told to lose my working-class accent. Our household had always been a creative one (my youngest son, Will, would go on to become a professional artist under the name Tat Vision, without having to change his Birmingham accent). While I was at home recovering from the gallbladder operation, I made a start on some paintings I'd been asked to create for the new mammography unit at Solihull Hospital. The sister there had asked for four large canvases, and my recovery sped along nicely as I had a project to immerse myself in.

I was incredibly proud when the paintings were hung in the hospital. I thought they looked great. I had a routine appointment with Paterson not long after that. As I walked into his office, he said, 'Who's a clever girl then?' I looked puzzled. 'Bethan tells me you've done some artwork for the unit at Solihull.' I beamed, said thanks, and offered to do a painting for his office. He declined.

19

Amanda Lowe was one of the first friends I made when I joined the committee of Breast Friends. We shared the same sense of humour and hit it off straight away. We were a similar age. She was artistic, and had studied graphic design at college before working in advertising and then HR.

Amanda was a beautiful person, and an inspiration. She had climbed Machu Picchu in Southern Peru to raise money for Breast Friends and really wanted to do the Sydney Harbour Bridge climb, but in 2008 her cancer returned. She died in

September 2009, aged fifty. I was devastated, for the loss of my friend and for her family, and was determined to do the bridge climb in her memory.

On Sunday 21 March 2010, with temperatures reaching 31 degrees Celsius, the women of Breast Friends scaled the heights of the Sydney Harbour Bridge to raise funds for our cause in partnership with Pittwater Pinks, a Sydney-based breast cancer charity. I wasn't afraid of heights as my dad had been a roofer and had taken me and my brother to work with him in the summer holidays, and although we didn't go anywhere near hot bitumen, we were used to climbing up and down ladders. Growing up, we would clamber over roofs and derelict buildings, running wild on the building sites and 'bomb pecks' around our slum housing. While in school, I had the opportunity to learn abseiling on an outward-bound course in Snowdonia, which more than prepared me for the bridge climb.

Aged fifty-one, attached to a harness, I ascended the bridge with the help of our guides. We had headsets on to take instructions and keep in contact, and I could hear various choice swear words and the occasional scream of 'oh lord!' from some of the other climbers, but we made it to the platform at the top, 134 metres above the sea. The views over Sydney Harbour were incredible.

Someone said a few words about Amanda, how she would have loved the view and the achievement. It was an incredible moment of solidarity and remembrance, all the women on that bridge thinking in unison about the disease we shared, and those of us that it had taken.

On my return to Birmingham, life and work carried on as before. It was hectic as I juggled my job, my family, my duty as a Breast Friends committee member and my physical recovery. I'd been largely ignoring the mental health impact of everything. Too much to do. I'd been attending night school to gain my Chartered Quality Institute Diploma, and in April 2010, I graduated at a ceremony at Birmingham Symphony Hall.

I also had something wonderful to look forward to: the wedding of my daughter Jen to her fiancé, Scott. They were married in July 2010 at Our Lady of Lourdes, the local Catholic church. Jenny looked radiant as she walked down the aisle to the Beatles' song 'All You Need is Love' with her beaming dad by her side. My sons Robert and Will were ushers, and I was the proud mother-of-the-bride. I made cake toppers, one showing the bride in an Aston Villa scarf and the other of the groom in a Birmingham City FC scarf. Friends and family had all chipped in to make the day perfect, and as Bob escorted our beautiful daughter down the aisle I wiped away tears of joy. At the reception and party afterwards, everyone ate and drank and danced together into the early hours, celebrating a new era for both families. It was just what we all needed, and for a time I forgot all about my medical worries.

But I should have known something was going on with Paterson. In September 2010, we had our annual Breast Friends fun run. Costumes were a big part of what made it enjoyable, and in previous years Paterson and his wife had joined in enthusiastically. This year, I had customised a foam Guinness top hat which I stitched to a black bra so it looked like I had a pint of Guinness on each boob. Our co-chairperson Claire Hicks wore a bra over her T-shirt to which she'd attached two fabric fried eggs, and various others had decorated theirs with sequins, feathers and jewellery. The weather was good as we assembled at the five-kilometre track at Norman Green Athletics Centre in Solihull. The race officials sent the fastest, more professional runners off first, after which those of us who weren't so fit jogged and walked the route until we were in sight of the finishing line, at which point we broke into a run, laughing and cheering at our achievement.

As in previous years, Bethan Lloyd Owen was there, wearing her pink wig and a pink bra over the top of her clothes. Her black labrador Gordon was by her side. But this year, no Paterson or his wife. I asked Lloyd Owen where he was and she said the bra decoration theme didn't really suit him.

I didn't see him again until October 2010. He was the guest speaker at the Breast Friends monthly meeting, where he talked about advances in treatment of breast cancer, but his speech had none of the hallmarks of confidence we were used to. In previous years we'd had to have a bigger venue to accommodate the larger audience he attracted, but this time that wasn't needed, and the atmosphere was muted. I was asked to give the vote of thanks on behalf of our group, something we do at all of our meetings. I stood up and thanked him for his presentation and for sharing the latest advances in breast cancer treatment. As I handed him a gift bag containing our usual bottle of M&S wine he seemed emotional, off kilter. Rumours had been flying, but it would be another few weeks until we discovered what was going on.

On 4 November 2010, Alison Dayani of the *Birmingham Mail* was the first journalist to report on the unfolding Paterson story:

PATIENTS RECALLED IN SURGEON PROBE
SIXTY breast cancer patients have been given special health checks at a Midland hospital after a top surgeon's procedures were called into question.

The examinations follow concerns raised over mastectomy surgery carried out by Ian Paterson at Solihull Hospital, part of the Heart of England NHS Foundation Trust.

It is understood that issues raised by a fellow surgeon sparked an investigation at the health unit, which discovered that Mr Paterson was leaving a small amount of breast tissue around the cleavage, for cosmetic reasons, on some patients. Most surgeons follow national guidelines to not leave excess breast tissue, to reduce the risk of the cancer returning.

The article quotes Lisa Dunn, one of the directors of Solihull Hospital, who attempted to gloss over the reality of the situation: 'We understand that Mr Paterson was carrying out this procedure in good faith, believing it to be appropriate for his patients, to achieve removal of the cancer, but with a better cosmetic result than a traditional mastectomy.' She accurately describes how Paterson had now been told to stop, but failed to mention the lack of oversight leading up to the investigation.

The co-chair of Breast Friends, Lynn Bullock, wrote to the committee:

Some of you may have seen or heard about articles in today's Birmingham Post & Mail *and the* Evening Mail *with regards to Mr Paterson. These stories are likely to elicit contact from ladies who are concerned or frightened about the stories they have read and how they might be affected. Bethan [Lloyd Owen] is obviously very keen to ensure that our members are not unnecessarily frightened or worried by these articles and I wonder if you would mind forwarding the below round to the database as a global email please?*

Dear Members,
You may be aware that several articles have appeared today in regional newspapers with regards to an inquiry that took place back in 2007 regarding Mr Paterson's surgical technique for mastectomies. The inquiry in 2007 concluded that the procedure in question was safe, however, Bethan Lloyd Owen, Consultant Breast Care Nurse, has asked us to convey to you all that she understands how ladies (on reading the articles) may feel very concerned and frightened about their specific treatment and to this end has asked us to pass on her mobile telephone number so that anyone wishing to speak to her confidentially may do so. You can contact Bethan, who will do her very best to put your mind at rest.

Alternatively, Bethan will attend next week's Breast Friends meeting and will address the Group about this.

Lloyd Owen did attend the next meeting. She reiterated that the cleavage-sparing mastectomy procedure was safe, but she did not stick around to answer questions.

20

In August 2010, Mark Goldman stepped down from his position as chief executive of Heart of England NHS Foundation Trust. Goldman is the person responsible for treating the investigation into Paterson's cleavage-sparing mastectomies as an HR issue, which he would later claim was to avoid a potential lawsuit.

One clinician said, 'I also remember having a conversation with Mark Goldman on the phone … I was saying, you know, "Why don't you see the argument for suspending him?" What he said to me was they'd met with the Trust's lawyers and they felt that to suspend him without evidence – this was the problem – this lack of evidence of actual harm might blow up in the Trust's face and he might turn around and sue them if they didn't find this evidence at a later date. And I kept saying, "No, no, you can suspend him." Clearly, I thought you could suspend him without prejudice because issues of patient safety have been raised and your paramount duty is to protect patients, not him. I remember him saying particularly he was worried if he was suspended from the NHS the private sector would also suspend his practising rights. He was making huge amounts of money in the private sector. He could then turn around and sue them for loss of earnings if he was subsequently found to be innocent or without blame.'

Senior management also consistently failed to communicate about the issues, later described by an investigation as 'weak and indecisive' leadership. Goldman reassured the Board (of which he was a member) that all was well multiple times, the last being on 4 May 2010, shortly before his strategy imploded.

In February 2020, a *Daily Mail* journalist approached Goldman, who said, 'I am profoundly apologetic about the things I did at the time, that I did in good faith, believing them to be in the interests of patient safety. Clearly this did not contain Paterson's criminal behaviour, we know that now. I was not aware of the extent of his misdemeanours at the time.'

Mark Goldman retired from the NHS in 2012 with a £2.7 million pension pot.

Goldman was not the only one to step down during the recall in 2010. Ian Cunliffe, the medical director of HEFT, also resigned his position.

Along with the press coverage, Goldman and Cunliffe's resignations were a turning point for the patient recall. Cunliffe's replacement, acting medical director Dr Steve Smith, launched a new investigation into Paterson in early 2011. He immediately understood the patient perspective, later telling an inquiry, 'There was another element which, I have to say, was one of the things that really surprised me right from the start, is that the previous investigation through 2007 onwards had not considered the issue of consent … at all [Mr Hennessy had, as I have mentioned]. That was the most striking thing from my point of view, apart from the recall and everything else, that consent for this procedure was non-existent.'

This is the attitude that should have been present from the beginning, instead of panic about lawsuits. The investigation by senior management into Paterson's wrongdoing hadn't considered that the patients thought they were consenting to a proper mastectomy.

In an interview for an independent review into Paterson's activities at Spire, consultant surgeon Charles Hendrickse (who also worked for the NHS) said, 'I have looked at some of the breast reviews at the NHS where people have been consented for a mastectomy and there is no consenting for that. If you were consenting for a partial mastectomy, which is what this is, I assume, because I am not a breast surgeon, you would say "we are leaving some breast tissue on the chest wall, you need some radiotherapy afterwards".'

You don't actually need to be a breast surgeon to know this. Paterson's patients consented to a mastectomy, but received a partial mastectomy, also known as a cleavage-sparing mastectomy, or as Paterson sometimes referred to it, a 'simple' mastectomy. If breast tissue is left on the chest wall, then the patient needs to have radiotherapy. But if the patient believes they had a full mastectomy, and they are not given radiotherapy, then the cancer is more likely to return. Why would anyone consent to that?

BREAST SURGEON FACES PROBE AFTER 'CLEAVAGE-SAVING OPERATION LEFT CANCER BEHIND'
A top NHS surgeon carried out dozens of 'cleavage-sparing' mastectomies which led to at least one patient contracting breast cancer again and others fearing a similar fate.
Ian Paterson left small amounts of breast tissue around the cleavage in some NHS patients with the intention of giving them a 'better cosmetic result'.

The *Daily Mail*, Britain's highest-selling newspaper, was the first national publication to cover the unfolding Paterson story, on 18 February 2011. The piece contains details of Mrs Stone, a Paterson patient who had been 'substantially' compensated by the NHS for the return of her cancer following a CSM. The settlement was made out of court, meaning there is no publicly available evidence or paper trail for her case. This is not particularly unusual. Medical negligence claims against the NHS cost the taxpayer a staggering £2.6 billion a year – and rising. Of the 13,500 cases brought in 2022/23, half settled out of court, although not all of those settlements were financial. NHS

Resolution, the body which manages medical negligence claims, says settlements out of court are a good thing because they're quicker and keep costs down. This is true, but doing so also contributes to a lack of transparency.

By the time the Paterson recall story had made national news in early 2011, Lloyd Owen was in full damage-control mode. In November 2010, she emailed Breast Friends to say that cleavage-sparing mastectomies were safe. That was simply not true. The NHS runs an organisation called Pan Birmingham Cancer Network, whose job it is to issue clinical guidelines. I had heard through someone on the Pan Birmingham committee that they had been made aware of Lloyd Owen's email to Breast Friends, and they responded in a letter to our co-chair warning that there was insufficient data on cleavage-sparing mastectomies to claim they had been declared safe. A copy was also sent to Lloyd Owen.

That particular letter was not forwarded to us for several months. As soon as I received a copy, at the end of March 2011, I called for an 'extraordinary meeting', which in charity parlance is an emergency gathering of the committee to discuss an urgent matter. I had spent my career in a safety-critical industry, solving problems, reforming processes and demanding answers even when people were reluctant to give them. I knew I would have to switch into work mode if I had any chance of getting to the bottom of what was happening to us.

The first thing I did was ask Spire to send a medical representative to explain properly what the risk of cleavage-sparing mastectomies actually *was*. I wrote to the committee, 'My only aim is to get to the facts of this investigation so that we can make an informed decision about how and what we communicate to our members.'

I added part of an article from the *Solihull News*, which quoted a woman who had not been recalled and was due to have another operation:

'I had no contact from Spire Parkway. They reassured me that everything was okay. But my niece who works for the NHS told

me to contact Solihull Hospital in December 2010 after my
friend had seen an article about Paterson. I went and was told
that there was a 30 per cent chance of a recurrence. Spire would
not have called me if I had not called them. It makes me feel
more angry.'

I went on to say that I still had unanswered questions, and
listed them:

- Who is affected? A figure of sixty women has been
  quoted in some articles as the number of women being
  recalled.
- Has everyone now been contacted?
- Why did the lady in the press slip through the net?
- How do we know that everyone who should be informed
  has been informed?
- The communication from our co-chair and Bethan [Lloyd
  Owen] on the 04/11/2010 to allay fears stated the
  procedure was safe. But the Pan Birmingham letter points
  out that the investigation is still ongoing.

I couldn't know then that these five simple questions would be
the first of hundreds, and that my personal investigation would
turn into a national campaign that would change my life. I could
not have predicted that my face, voice and name would be on
televisions and radios throughout the world, or that I would
spend over a decade trying to get answers and justice not just
for me but thousands of other patients, living and deceased.

On Monday 11 April 2011, we held the extraordinary meeting of the Breast Friends committee. Lloyd Owen attended,
along with Joy Masters, matron of Spire Parkway (a modern-
day hospital matron is a nurse support and role model,
particularly in standards of patient care and accountability).

I immediately asked for a discussion of the Pan Birmingham
letter, and Lloyd Owen tried to deflect, reiterating a line about
the cleavage-sparing mastectomy procedure being declared safe

by an independent NHS inquiry in 2007 by West Midlands Cancer Intelligence Unit, with which Spire Parkway had fully cooperated. Sixty NHS breast cancer patients were recalled, and of those only one had had a recurrence of cancer, which, she reassured us, was well within normal parameters of 3 to 5 per cent. She also claimed that every patient who had been treated by Paterson for breast cancer over the past ten years would have been discussed at an MDT with other healthcare specialists.

Because of the press reports, the NHS was offering a second opinion and imaging for any breast cancer patient who was concerned, and Lloyd Owen reassured us that Paterson would be happy to see any Spire patient if they also had worries. All we needed to do was get in touch with her and she would set up an appointment with him.

She tried hard to place the blame for the concerns about CSMs on the press, and suggested that her email was merely reiterating what the newspapers had reported. She was adamant that when the medical director of HEFT contacted her because he had heard about her email, she showed him the contents and he was apparently happy with everything she had written. But it was clear she did not like us talking directly to Pan Birmingham, and told us that as we were not a political or medical group we did not need to get involved.

I told the group that women who knew of my involvement with Breast Friends had been contacting me because they were scared by the reports, and I didn't know what to tell them. I asked if Spire Parkway could issue a statement.

Joy Masters took this opportunity to clarify Spire Parkway's involvement in the events surrounding Paterson. When the West Midlands Cancer Intelligence Unit began its NHS investigation in 2007, it asked Spire Parkway to provide files of patients. At the end of 2007 the hospital was contacted by Mark Goldman to say that the investigation had been concluded, Paterson had been asked to stop carrying out cleavage-sparing mastectomies, and Spire Parkway must follow the same guidelines as the NHS.

Paterson confirmed that he would stop performing the procedure.

The press had been alleging that the NHS was recalling patients but Spire was not. The NHS recall was news to Spire Parkway, mainly because it wasn't true. At the time there was no proper NHS recall, just a handful of select patients. Spire had received many phone calls from worried women. But, Masters reassured us, Spire had agreed that they would do a full recall of all patients treated by Paterson between 2000 and 2007, and she believed they had now identified them all. That early number (later to prove a woeful underestimate) was 153 (122 at Parkway hospital and 31 at Little Aston).

I wasn't reassured by this, because there were clearly wider issues at play.

'Did those women know they were having a cleavage-sparing mastectomy before they had their operations?' I asked.

Lloyd Owen said she couldn't discuss it due to the ongoing investigation (despite earlier reassurances that there was nothing to worry about). Masters said that patients 'have a right to know, and if there is nothing for them to worry about then it is nice to put their minds at rest'. She reiterated that Paterson's recurrence rate was well within national guidelines and while there was no evidence to say they needed to do a full recall, Parkway felt that morally it was the right way to proceed.

I asked if we should share this information with our database, but the co-chair (a friend of Lloyd Owen) insisted we should refer our members to their medical professionals as we weren't medically trained. That may have been true, but I felt like only some of us were asking the hard questions, and this was all starting to look a bit like a cover-up. I held my tongue about that and instead returned to the Pan Birmingham letter. I wanted to know who to trust, so I asked if Pan Birmingham knew as much as the West Midlands Cancer Intelligence Unit. Masters replied that Pan Birmingham had taken a view without knowing all the facts.

I asked what we should say to our members who had asked about the newspaper articles, and Lloyd Owen replied that we should direct them to their breast care nurse. But of course, in the case of private patients, *that meant her*, and it looked very much like she was standing by Paterson. But at that time, in that meeting, I merely wanted answers to my questions and guidance on how to deal with the worried Breast Friends members who had no idea what to do. Spire may have been doing a limited recall, but what about NHS patients? I wanted Pan Birmingham to write a letter to distribute to the Breast Friends database to encourage them to get in touch with their hospital, but Lloyd Owen was adamant that the newspaper articles (even though she had earlier claimed they were full of 'blatant lies') were sufficient to prompt patients to contact their hospital.

The meeting truly was an extraordinary one. I did not get satisfactory answers to my questions, instead being told that the committee could not provide them because they were of a medical nature. I shot back that of course I didn't expect the *committee* to answer, but that Lloyd Owen as a medical professional would be able to. She insisted that newspaper reports about unauthorised cleavage-sparing mastectomies were wrong.

This was when I first started to feel isolated. The committee was annoyed that I'd called the meeting in the first place. I knew that something wasn't right, but at that time had no evidence to back up my suspicions. The meeting concluded with a vote about whether to email our database about the Pan Birmingham letter stating there was insufficient evidence to know if cleavage-sparing mastectomies were safe. That is, whether the procedure that deliberately left breast tissue behind to preserve a cleavage could result in the cancer coming back. The Pan Birmingham letter said that it was 'by no means clear' that cleavage-sparing mastectomies were safe, and that the procedure 'certainly was not recognised as best practice by peers'. But Lloyd Owen persuaded the committee that such an email would only upset and confuse patients.

Convinced by her reassurance that Paterson's recurrence rates were no higher than any other consultant, the committee voted not to contact the database. Instead, we agreed to write to Pan Birmingham asking them to send a communication themselves, warning patients of the potential issues around cleavage-sparing mastectomies, if that is what they thought. They did not send any such communication.

21

There was major fallout from the Breast Friends 'extraordinary meeting'. One member had cried, another had resigned. A group of women who had been through, or were still going through, the hell of breast cancer were being told the press coverage about incomplete mastectomies was just scaremongering. Tensions were high, but to me the stakes of not asking questions were even higher. If Paterson had done something wrong, then many of us were at risk of recurrence. The chair of Breast Friends sent an email describing the meeting as a 'hassle that we didn't need in our lives', which I felt was aimed at me for not simply accepting Bethan Lloyd Owen and Joy Masters' reassurances. My experience and instincts told me something was wrong. I distanced myself from a few of the committee as I knew my views were not popular, and because I knew their friendship with Lloyd Owen would muddy the waters. By now I simply didn't trust anyone employed by Spire to be honest about what was going on.

One of the consequences of the fallout was that the Breast Friends constitution was being amended to remove any right to question medical matters on the grounds that we were not medically qualified. Lloyd Owen played a big part in that change, emailing:

'Thank you for chairing a very difficult meeting so well. I confirm that I will remain as one of Breast Friends' principal

*officers with the understanding that our constitution is going to
be reviewed with my input. I trust this is acceptable and like you
hope we can all move forward providing support to the women
that need us.'*

In other words, shut up, Deb, and don't bring up the subject
of cleavage-sparing mastectomies again. Very convenient.

I was determined that I was not going to step down, even
though I felt isolated from the committee. There were a couple
of new members at the time who told me privately that they
agreed with me, and that helped to keep me going. I was, of
course, bringing this home to Bob, telling him I knew that something was going on. He knew that if I got the bit between my
teeth I wouldn't let go, but he was also worried for me. I didn't
trust Lloyd Owen and what I was being told, but at this point I
had no way to back up my suspicions with facts, and that can
send a person mad.

In February 2011, Mark Newbold entered the picture.
Previously a consultant specialising in gastrointestinal disease
and histopathology in Warwick, Newbold moved into management and became HEFT's chief executive. He inherited a mess.
Not only were the waiting lists still dangerously long, but the
limited recall process of Paterson's patients was clearly untena-
ble. HEFT now had to address the two major questions affecting
the breast unit: should Paterson's practising privileges be
revoked, and should there be a full recall of all Paterson's
Solihull Hospital mastectomy patients to assess if they had had
a cleavage-sparing mastectomy?

Efforts to identify which patients should be reviewed had
been hampered by Paterson himself, who was adamant the
whole thing was unnecessary and that his procedure was safe.
He was still re-operating on his own mastectomy patients,
despite the objections of his colleagues and the obvious patient
safety and consent issues. Bruce Tanchel, a pathologist at HEFT,
had raised concerns in 2003 that Paterson had left a tumour in
a patient. He was one of the signatories of the original whistle-

blowing letter to Goldman and later told an investigation: 'It was difficult because Ian [Paterson] was very defensive and would contest everything and anything and never conceded he'd ever done anything wrong and there were a lot of tensions.' The atmosphere of the MDT was described as 'difficult and unpleasant' by breast care nurse Clare Bates, who stated: 'Mr Paterson has expressed the opinion that "we" are raising anxiety unnecessarily and should be more reassuring with these ladies ... we are not able to have a valuable, unbiased and open discussion about these ladies in Mr Paterson's presence, partly because he cannot be unbiased in his opinions and partly because his being there inhibits discussion.'

Something had to give, and it all gave at once. In April 2011, finally, a full NHS recall was announced. It had been almost two years since the limited recall, but now all of Paterson's patients who had been given what he had written as a 'simple mastectomy' would be written to and invited for a review.

And then, on 13 May 2011, Paterson was suspended from the NHS for an initial two weeks, but he continued to perform surgery at Spire hospitals until 8 June 2011. In July, his registration with the General Medical Council (GMC) was made 'subject to conditions' for eighteen months. The conditions were that he could no longer do breast operations in the NHS, but he was free to carry on with his general practice. His patients in that period were not informed that the consultant carrying out their treatment was the subject of investigation, although some would presumably have read about him in the press.

Meanwhile, the private sector was scrambling to keep up. In June 2011, managers at Spire Parkway and Little Aston restricted Paterson's practising privileges while they started their own investigation. He carried out his last operations in the private sector that month, and a few weeks later Spire began a review of his mastectomy patients from 2007 onwards. They found that his patients had given consent for a full mastectomy, not any sort of 'cleavage-sparing' version, which might leave a bit of flesh for a bikini but would, of course, also leave potentially cancerous breast tissue. By August 2011, it was clear that Spire had to temporarily suspend Paterson's practising privileges while they tried to work out what was going on.

By October 2011, a whole list of terrifying allegations emerged. It looked very much like Ingle's claim that Paterson was doing unnecessary surgery was just the tip of the iceberg. Several Spire consultants who made allegations were claiming:

- Patients had had unnecessary surgery when there was no evidence of malignancy from the pathology and radiology results.
- Paterson had caused unnecessary worry to patients who believed they had precancerous cells and an increased risk of cancer when they in fact did not.
- He had used cancer codes on invoices for non-cancer treatments to generate more income.
- He followed up patients with more frequent imaging than was accepted as normal practice.
- There was no radiologist or histopathologist present at Spire breast MDT meetings and only Paterson and Bethan Lloyd Owen had access to pathology reports.
- Bethan Lloyd Owen was complicit in the above allegations.

The 2014 independent report that lists these allegations, undertaken by a company called Verita, also says that by 2011 there was evidence that Paterson had carried out procedures for which patients had not given consent, and given misleading information about pathology reports to his patients and their GPs. The cat was well and truly out of the bag.

Of course, I knew nothing of this at the time. I only found out Paterson had been suspended when I attended Spire Parkway for one of my regular check-ups. One of the breast care nurses told me the news, but explained that his clinic was to continue to be run for a short time by Bethan Lloyd Owen.

I sat in what I still thought of as 'Mr Paterson's office' while Lloyd Owen reviewed my notes. She seemed edgy and I found it odd that she had my huge stack of notes in front of her, something Paterson never had.

'Where's Mr Paterson?' I asked. 'He's out for a few weeks but will be back soon, I'm taking his clinic while he's away,' she replied. She wanted to get straight down to business. I watched as she slowly turned the pages of my medical papers, then she said, 'Let's start from the beginning. It says here you had grade one cancer with spread to one lymph node.'

'Erm, no … you never told me that before.' She looked at me, so I repeated, 'I was never told it had spread to my lymph nodes.'

I didn't understand why her tone was so forceful. 'Look, Debbie, it's here, it's written in your notes, and it is in your pathology report.' But I had never been told that the cancer had spread to my lymph nodes. I remember clearly being told on the results day, 'it was the best news they could have hoped for, there was no spread, no lymph nodes affected'. I'd written it in my journal. How could I have got it so wrong? Lloyd Owen wouldn't listen to my protests and was unable to offer an explanation. She just asked if I had any new symptoms to report and said she'd see me again in a few months. I didn't have my journal with me so couldn't push back on the lymph node issue, but I was horrified that my cancer might have spread after all.

When I got home I checked with my journal and Bob, and he confirmed, 'we were never told about the cancer spreading to your lymph nodes'. I was beginning to feel very scared that whatever was going on with Paterson was directly related to my own treatment. Had I had one of his cleavage-sparing mastectomies? Why did my medical notes say one thing when I'd been told another?

Nothing made sense, and it would be a long time until I had answers.

22

By January 2012, there were enough NHS Solihull Hospital patients presenting with cleavage-sparing mastectomies that it became clear the recall needed to be extended to patients who had received a mastectomy with an immediate reconstruction. These were more difficult to assess, because it wasn't always clear how much breast tissue had been left in place. Immediate reconstructions or skin-sparing mastectomies meant the surgeon removed the breast tissue through an incision, usually removing the nipple, then filled the skin with fat and tissue taken from the back or stomach still attached to the blood supply. This is the operation I had had, and the result is that visual or physical examination can't determine whether all the tissue has been removed.

Several women who had heard about the Solihull Hospital recall but had been treated by Paterson at NHS Good Hope Hospital in Sutton Coldfield or privately now presented with concerns about their surgery. They wanted to know if they had had one of the cleavage-sparing mastectomies they had heard about in the media. Many of them had.

It was now undeniable: the recall would also need to include patients from Good Hope Hospital. That meant a full recall of every single Paterson patient in the NHS.

You would expect or at least hope that was a straightforward enough admin process. Surely these major hospitals had a complete database of breast cancer patients? They did not. Identifying patients proved to be much harder than it should have been. Records were incomplete, missing, out of date. But the team tasked with managing the recall was doing its best and was now free from the constraints of HR and secrecy, and patients were beginning to identify themselves because of media coverage and word of mouth.

Once the NHS had started to look at patients who had had a mastectomy with immediate reconstruction, Spire would have to do the same. I, of course, was one such patient.

In February 2012, I had a phone call from Lynn Bullock, secretary to Ian Paterson and former co-chair of Breast Friends, saying they were recalling Paterson's Spire patients and that a number of independent consultants would be brought in to review our cases. She said she'd heard a consultant named Simon Harries was very good and she could arrange my appointment with him, which she duly did for a few days later.

On the day, I was thinking less about whether I'd had a cleavage-sparing mastectomy and more about Lloyd Owen's claim that my cancer had spread to a lymph node. I entered the hospital nervously and was shown to a downstairs office next to Paterson's old room. I met Harries, a consultant breast surgeon working out of Warwick Hospital. As promised, he was indeed lovely, shaking my hand and putting me at ease straight away.

I immediately asked if he could look through my notes and tell me what my pathology report said. He pulled out the relevant sheet and started reading it out loud. It *did* say that my cancer had spread to one lymph node. But I was certain I'd been told otherwise. Either I was going mad or something was wrong with the paperwork. I'd seen enough reporting errors in my career to know that the latter was more likely.

'Could you do me a favour, Mr Harries? Could you please check back through my notes to see if there is another pathology report in there, because I was clearly told at the time I had no spread to my lymph nodes.'

He looked through the file in more detail. Towards the back was another pathology report. My heart was racing as he confirmed that this was my original pathology report, and it said that there was no spread to my lymph nodes. He looked puzzled and surprised.

My hands were shaking as I took out my pen to write down the report reference numbers. To my surprise, it was the same reference number on both. So which report was correct? Harries wasn't able to tell me, but I asked him to investigate. He assured me he would, then sent me for an ultrasound scan to confirm I was definitely cancer-free, to determine whether there was any breast tissue present and to find out if I had had a cleavage-sparing mastectomy or not.

I asked the radiologist if I had breast tissue left. Given he was supposed to be checking for cleavage-sparing mastectomies, I had expected him to be more engaged, but he was rather dismissive, telling me, 'It's like having two boxes of cornflakes and mixing them together. You can't tell which ones are from the original box.' I thought, what the hell are you on about, comparing me to a bowl of cornflakes? He said couldn't tell which was breast tissue and which was reconstructed tissue. I felt angry. This was my health and my life. I told him I wasn't accepting that and wanted a second opinion.

I was then booked in to see a consultant breast surgeon named Philip Brookes on 8 May 2012 at Spire Little Aston. He was also part of the team employed to review Paterson patients and was based at Walsall Manor Hospital. When I got there, he didn't have any of my notes. That didn't help my anger. I was beginning to feel incredibly frustrated at the lack of care and reliable information. I wasn't someone who accepted being given the runaround. Brookes reassured me that my remaining tissue was 'fatty tissue' (where cancer couldn't grow) rather than breast tissue, but without my records I didn't feel like he'd done a thorough review. When I got home I rang Spire Parkway and explained the situation. I was very abrupt and by now I was beginning to be known on reception when I called, but I had to advocate for myself. I said my notes were missing so I needed another review.

On 27 June 2012, I received another letter from Spire signed by a woman named Emily Masters, who happened to be the daughter of Spire Parkway's matron, Joy Masters. She had been brought in to help with the admin side of patients requesting their records. The letter stated that in conjunction with the General Medical Council and HEFT, Spire Healthcare was investigating the practice of Ian Paterson. 'We do not believe there is any immediate risk to your health, however, we would like to ensure you are given the opportunity of a face-to-face appointment with an independent consultant breast surgeon at Spire Parkway hospital.' My appointment was for 15 July 2012.

This was progress, but the sort where I might be walking into bad news, despite the reassurances. I was one of hundreds of patients caught up in the recall, none of us knowing what to do or think. My trust in Spire, and perhaps medicine itself, was by now pretty low, but I was determined to get answers, however difficult they might be to hear.

23

Spire's recall was not going well, because the patients they had identified as potentially having had a cleavage-sparing mastectomy were only a fraction of the patients who needed to be seen. In July 2011, they sent recall letters to just eighty-three patients, those who had had a mastectomy between 2000 and 2007. By August 2011, fifty-eight had been seen and of those, half had residual breast tissue.

By March 2012, a further 143 patients received letters from Spire, which included those who had had a mastectomy with reconstruction (including me), and a further dozen contacted Spire themselves following press coverage. Of these, thirty were found to have residual breast tissue. The lower number may have been because of the difficulty in identifying breast tissue in patients who had had reconstruction. Brookes, one of the breast surgeons who had been brought in to do the initial reviews alongside his regular clinical practice, later told an inquiry:

'As the enquiries went on and we started recording patients that had had reconstruction, that became much more difficult to assess. If they had had immediate reconstruction it was almost impossible to assess whether there was any residual tissue ... MRI scans could help to a certain degree, but it was not obvious. If patients had had a delayed reconstruction, [it was] much easier because very often the plastic surgeon would have taken pre-operative pictures, so you have got pictures to see.'

Managing patients was difficult, because there wasn't much (if any) precedent for a situation like this, but also because many patients simply didn't want to believe what they were hearing. Brookes said:

'It was a very strange atmosphere for me to go as a complete stranger to Solihull to see patients that were extremely angry, and it was very difficult to start with. The first few months were pretty unpleasant seeing patients that were extremely angry, understandably so. Angry at me occasionally, and many people were very loyal to Mr Paterson and said, you know, "Who are you? Who are you to question this?" And I said, "I am not questioning it. I am just here to look at your notes," but it was very difficult. It got easier because, obviously, as things came out as to what was going on, people suddenly said, "Actually ..." you know, "... you are not the bad guy here".'

Eventually Brookes wrote to Steven Thrush and Dayalan Clarke, clinicians from other hospitals, to come and help.

'... I think it was just me seeing those patients, and following that I was made aware that there were concerns about patients that had had benign breast treatment under the care of Mr Paterson. At that stage I said to Spire, "Look, I cannot do this on my own. This is becoming too much of a workload."'

By July 2012, Spire had extended the recall to include women who had had wide local excision – a type of surgery that removes the lump and some surrounding tissue but not the breast itself

– sometimes referred to as a lumpectomy. By now the criteria included unnecessary surgery, the 'benign breast treatment' Brookes referred to. It had become clear that Paterson had been operating for no reason.

His modus operandi was simple, if evil. A patient with a breast lump but no other symptoms would first have a needle biopsy, where tissue is removed via a large needle and sent off to the pathology lab. The results, which only Paterson saw, indicated either malignant (cancerous) cells, benign (non-cancerous cells), or no viable cells detected, which meant that Paterson had missed the lump with the needle and merely collected regular breast tissue. The patient would also have a mammogram and ultrasound to see if there were any further clues about the lump, from which a decision about surgery could be made. If the needle biopsy results were uncertain (usually because he had missed), in theory the patient should then have a second needle biopsy, but this time guided by a scan.

Paterson had always been keen to recruit new customers to the private sector, even asking patients if they had female relatives who might benefit from being checked by him (on the grounds that breast cancer can be genetic). He saw a great money-making opportunity at Spire. He would write to the patient's GP to say that the ultrasound had shown a suspicious lesion, and that the patient had rejected a needle or core biopsy in favour of surgery. Neither claim was true, but it meant he could charge the patient not only for surgery to remove the 'suspicious' lump but could also then lie to them about the nature of the lump and sign them up for years of scans and mammograms. These patients had benign lumps but were told otherwise. In other words, they thought they had had cancer or were at risk of cancer when they absolutely were not.

In total, 597 patients attended a review. From an independent review of Spire's recall, '414 who had breast surgery were found to have had inappropriate treatment (unnecessary surgery, unnecessary follow-up), misleading diagnosis and/or misrecorded care (poor patient consent and/or miscoding). Twelve of the 597 patients were also found to have had inappropriate surgery for non-breast procedures.'

Brookes spelled out how lucrative their treatment plans were for Spire and Paterson: 'some of these women are coming, having an appointment, an operation, a follow-up operation and surveillance which could go on for four or five years for a condition which is entirely benign ... I had many patients coming back absolutely terrified, many of them saying, "I am sitting on a time bomb here", and you say, "You are not, no more than anybody else."'

Jade Edgington was one of Paterson's youngest victims. She was just sixteen in 2005 when she found a lump in her breast, and she consequently met with Paterson through Spire. 'He told me we needed to get it out. He said it wasn't anything scary, but that it was big enough to get it out.' Jade and her family trusted Paterson's opinion, and when she found three more lumps and Paterson said they should also be removed, they agreed. By the time she was nineteen she'd undergone four invasive operations.

'[We thought] he's the expert, he knows what he's doing. We went ahead with his advice.' Two years after her final procedure she met with another doctor who was investigating Paterson's work. She learned three out of her four operations were unnecessary as the lumps weren't at risk of becoming cancerous. The appropriate course of action would have been to monitor the first lump for twelve months, as removal was not necessarily required, and the other three operations should not have been performed given her age.

The cruelty of Paterson's actions can't be overstated, not just because of the fear of cancer, but because general anesthetic is not without risk. While it's generally considered safe to 'go under', absolutely no one should have it for no reason. While rare, complications can include nerve damage, allergic reaction, chest infections and even cardiac arrest. The mortality rate is less than 1 in 100,000, and practically zero in patients without other risk factors, but it is absolutely not something to take lightly. Of all the things I was most terrified of, dying during an operation was top of the list.

But I did have cancer. My operation and the months of chemotherapy, while terrifying and brutal, were lifesaving and necessary. My only query was whether Paterson had left breast tissue, not whether I should have had a mastectomy and reconstruction in the first place, right?

Wrong.

24

Throughout 2012 I'd been trying to move on from my breast cancer treatment and the trauma I'd experienced, but it was very difficult with the ongoing Paterson situation. Once I had received the first recall letter, I began to feel isolated. I didn't know exactly what was unfolding, or who I could safely talk to. The Breast Friends meetings were a very lonely place at that time, because there were still a lot of people within the group who didn't believe he'd done anything wrong. Those of us who knew we had been harmed by Paterson formed a tight bond. At times it felt like us against the world. One of the women I had trust in was another Paterson patient named Michelle Flavelle.

Michelle was a young mother who was diagnosed with breast cancer in 2005, aged thirty-nine, and had joined Breast Friends in the early days of her treatment. She was also someone who had frequently argued with Bethan Lloyd Owen, although I was unclear why. Lloyd Owen had done her best to poison the well, telling us privately, 'Michelle is loud, a troublemaker. She's not a very nice person.' Michelle told me that she had asked Lloyd Owen whether it was safe to have reconstructive surgery after her mastectomy operation from Paterson, as he had left a significant amount of breast tissue. Lloyd Owen had confidently told her that it was safe to go ahead. Michelle had also questioned the official Paterson story even before I did, because she was party to information via a Sutton member, a breast cancer patient who was also a nurse on Paterson's team at Good Hope Hospital. Michelle told me that any post or comment online supporting Paterson in any way badly affected her.

I had always got on well with Michelle and sadly at this time I learned that her cancer had returned, so I called her to talk about that and the impact of the Paterson news.

'I didn't truly understand until it was happening to me,' I told her.

I was still reeling at the idea that I might have had a cleavage-sparing mastectomy without my knowledge. By October 2012, it had been several months since I'd received the recall letter from Spire, and I did my best to put it to the back of my mind. It was still early days; I needed a sense of normalcy, and I had to live my life. Our house was always a busy one. On Friday 12 October, I was having a cup of tea with Jen and Bob when the doorbell rang. It was the postman with a letter for me, recorded delivery. Those are always ominous, particularly as I wasn't expecting anything. I opened the envelope, and my day was no longer ordinary. The letter was from the Head of Clinical Services at Spire.

Dear Mrs Douglas,

You may have read in the press that Spire Healthcare, in conjunction with the General Medical Council (GMC) and the Heart of England NHS Foundation Trust (HEFT) is investigating the practice of Mr Ian Paterson.

Supported by a team of independent breast surgeons, we are reviewing the medical records of Mr Paterson's patients who underwent specific procedures for benign

(non-cancerous) breast pathology. Our investigations have
revealed some irregularities in his practice that may go
against recognised treatment standards.

I read that paragraph several times as I tried to take in what it
was saying. Benign? Non-cancerous? 'I didn't have cancer?' I
said out loud. Then again, 'I didn't have cancer!'

My head was spinning. My first emotion was relief, even joy.
If I didn't have cancer in the first place then that meant I was
not at a high risk of recurrence or death. But this was immediately overtaken by fury as I thought of the implications. The
pain, the fear, the scars, the months of chemotherapy that had
wrecked my health – had these all been for *nothing*? It was
messed up. I had to process my anger at what Paterson had done
even as my brain was saying: *but you didn't have cancer*. Or did
I? It didn't seem possible that I could have had all the symptoms
if there was no malignancy at all. I didn't know what to think
or how to feel. Bob was shocked. Jen looked horrified. I said, 'If
he's taken my breast off and I didn't have cancer I'm going to
swing for him.'

There was no good outcome here. Cancer or no cancer, I was
still in the middle of something horrific and I needed answers
immediately. I tried to suppress my emotions as I called the
phone number on the letter, but as the phone was ringing I felt
a fury rise in my chest and thought to myself, *you're not going*
to get away with this.

I got through to Spire's direct reception line.

'My name's Deborah Douglas, I'm a Paterson patient and
have just received a recall letter from you, I need to speak to
someone about it.'

'I'm sorry, we are very busy as we've had a lot of letters go
out.'

Eventually I was given an appointment the following Saturday,
this time with a consultant named Steven Thrush. I was
exhausted at the thought of going through the whole story

again, especially as my notes seemed to be unreliable, but I was going to take whatever I was offered.

I was the last person to be seen that day, and the breast clinic was empty at Parkway. I sat on the waiting-room chair clutching my blue A4 journal, which was full of my deepest feelings, the poetry I wrote to get me through it all and, crucially, notes on my illness and the ongoing issues. It felt like a safety blanket, something solid to cling to, but also a useful backup in case of more admin incompetence.

'I'm sorry, Debbie, but Mr Thrush won't be able to see you.' Jane Walker, the nurse on duty came out to me as I was leafing through the pages. 'I'm afraid we haven't got any of your medical notes.'

I wish I'd been surprised. 'I want you to find them. I'm not moving,' I told her, trying to keep my composure.

'I'm very sorry, they may have gone to a central database.'

That wasn't good enough. 'I want to see Mr Thrush,' I told her firmly. I waved the blue book. 'I have notes in my journal.' She could tell my upset and frustration was turning to anger and went away to see what she could do. Eventually, Thrush agreed to see me, so I went through into his consulting room, accompanied by Walker. As soon as I sat down, he turned to me and said, 'Do you know what this is about?'

'No, not really.' I read him some of the notes from my diary and explained I'd recently had a letter which said my lump was actually benign.

'I'm afraid Mr Paterson has been telling people they have cancer when they do not,' he said. This was the first time I'd heard that he'd carried out breast surgery on people who didn't have cancer.

He also told me that Paterson had been falsifying booking codes to get more money. I could see he was upset and angry about it. It must have been a long day breaking the news to women that the surgeon they trusted had harmed them. As I read more notes from my journal, the nurse looked visibly upset. She said, 'We will sort this out for you, Debbie, don't worry.'

And then Thrush dropped a huge bombshell. The situation was so serious, the police were now involved. I couldn't believe what I was hearing. He didn't have any details, and I wondered where I could get more information. I had to leave without any answers about whether I had had cancer or not, because my notes were missing, but later that day Jane Walker phoned me and said, 'I'm really sorry about this, Debbie, we'll get to the bottom of this. I will find your notes and keep them safe even if I have to sleep with them under my pillow.' It felt good to have someone on my side, but I also thought, *what the hell is going on?*

I had expected that Thrush would be able to help once my file had been found. How wrong I was. My notes were there when I had the follow-on meeting with him a few weeks later at Walsall Manor Hospital, but his attitude was more guarded this time. I wondered if perhaps he thought he had told me too much. It was a frustrating meeting. He couldn't tell me whether or not I'd had a cleavage-sparing mastectomy or even whether I'd had cancer. He said the notes indicated Paterson had removed 585 grams of breast tissue. I asked how much a breast of my size weighed, and worked out there was probably around 40 per cent breast tissue left. That certainly didn't sound like a mastectomy. I would need an ultrasound to confirm. I told him I was going to speak to the police and asked if he'd put his findings in writing, but he said no, as he wouldn't want to testify against Paterson if it went to court.

I saw Thrush for the last time towards the end of November 2012. I had asked Spire to confirm which of my two conflicting pathology reports was correct, and whether or not I had had cancer. I didn't know which would be worse, to have had a mastectomy and chemotherapy without ever having had cancer, or having had cancer but an insufficient mastectomy, which meant it might return.

Thrush showed me a letter from the pathology service that confirmed that I did have cancer. Grade one, with no spread. The letter stated that the second pathology claiming spread to a lymph node was an error. So, I did have cancer. I felt numb and was back to the status quo, although still totally distrusting what I'd been told. Why had I received a letter from Spire saying my lump was benign? Another 'error', perhaps? How much more incompetence would I have to face? I now had to find out if I'd had a cleavage-sparing mastectomy and what that might mean for my health.

Thrush had written on a piece of paper a list of questions he thought I should pursue with Spire:

- Why a mastectomy?
- Why not a core biopsy?
- Why an axillary node clearance?
- Reconstruction – issues.
- Mastectomy – anything left behind weighs 585 grams?
- Why chemotherapy?
- Multidisciplinary teams?

I emailed the questions and details of my case to the then-chief executive of Spire, Rob Roger, but did not receive a reply for over a year.

In December 2012, I called the chair of Breast Friends Sutton Coldfield, the sister charity originally founded by Bethan Lloyd Owen. Some of their members had had cleavage-sparing mastectomies. The chair had arranged a meeting with Mark Newbold of HEFT, for early January 2013. The chair seemed to be party to a few more facts, and she told me that those patients who had immediate reconstructive surgery were at higher risk. She was happy for Solihull Breast Friends to join the meeting.

The meeting took place on 7 January at the Partnership Learning Centre in Sutton Coldfield. Mark Newbold and Aresh Anwar, HEFT's medical director, were there to give us information, and around twenty women turned up to hear what they had to say.

Newbold introduced himself and Anwar. He then apologised for the harm Paterson had caused to us and said it was his decision to suspend Paterson without pay, although he knew this could backfire on him if Paterson's solicitors sued the Trust. He came across as very sincere and genuine. It was quite powerful to hear our first apology from HEFT.

In my industry I was used to dealing with data and analysing the standard operating times of any process. I asked him what was the standard operating time for a mastectomy and immediate reconstruction. He said he didn't know, which I found frustrating as surely by now that was basic information. I also asked if he had a timeline of Paterson's wrongdoings and how many patients were affected. He did not.

I got talking to a young woman who had already accessed her medical records and received an independent medical report. Our cases seemed very similar, and she told me to contact Detective Sergeant Dale Robertson of the homicide team of West Midlands Police. The investigation was originally being led by the Economic Crime Unit, Serious and Complex Fraud team at Bradford Street Police Station, as the police were initially looking at whether Paterson had committed financial fraud.

A few days later I called Robertson. He was friendly, empathic and very understanding. Someone close to him had gone through breast cancer. We had a long conversation after which we made an appointment for me to be visited at home by female police officers. This was a whole new layer of complexity, something I could never have predicted. Frankly, it was a living nightmare.

25

Thompsons is a firm of solicitors specialising in medical cases. I first heard of them in March 2013, when my daughter Jen forwarded me their details from a local press advert. They were looking for Paterson patients. I hadn't really considered compensation; I was still trying to figure out what, if anything, had been done to me that shouldn't have been, but it was surely worth a chat. The police were interested, and everything I'd seen so far indicated I was one of what I refused to think of as Paterson's 'victims', but that did seem to be where it was heading.

I called Thompsons, but as the cheery voice answered and asked how they could help, I found myself unable to speak. Something about the situation hit me in a way it hadn't before. I managed to explain I was a Paterson patient calling to speak to a solicitor, but they wanted more details before putting me through. I couldn't do it. I put the phone down. It took me several aborted calls before I was finally able to give enough detail to be put through to a solicitor named Sian Thompson.

The first thing she did was engage the services of a professor of surgical oncology, to carry out an independent medical review of my case. I was desperate for this, as I didn't trust Spire and hadn't had anything like a satisfactory response from their consultants so far. She also asked more than once if I'd consider speaking to the press, but I pushed back, saying I couldn't talk with any authority to the press when I didn't know the facts of my own case.

My medical records were sent to the specialist for review.

In May 2013, I requested another recall appointment at Spire because the questions I had sent months ago still hadn't been answered, and the independent report hadn't yet come through. This time I met with a consultant named Dayalan Clarke. Just before my appointment was due to start, I saw Ruth Walker, Spire's head of clinical services, pop into his office, and I wondered if she was tipping him off about me. When she came out she apologised for delaying the appointment. I suspected I was being viewed as a troublemaker, which I absolutely was in this particular case. When I sat down with Clarke, my list of questions were sticking out of the back of my medical file along with a handwritten note saying someone had helped me with them. The tone of the appointment was much less friendly than I expected.

'So, did I need a mastectomy?' I asked. Clarke told me that yes, I did, that it was the correct treatment. I heard him say it, and I daresay he believed it, but the words didn't fit the picture.

I had an unanswered query on the weight of pathology from both Harries and Thrush. My pathology said I had 585 grams of breast tissue removed, but Thrush had told me that on a woman of my breast size it typically weighs one kilogram. Just over half the volume of my breast tissue had been removed, rather than all of it. I also had an MRI scan that Thrush said suggested that there was residual breast tissue present.

'Should I have had chemo?' I asked Clarke. This time he replied, 'I can't answer that.' There was a breast nurse in the room, one I had known from the start, who had always seemed loyal to Paterson. She seemed angry with me when I said, 'Look, I know there is something wrong.' I saw their faces and realised it was futile. Spire had too much to lose, I wasn't going to get to the bottom of anything this way.

'Forget it,' I said, trying to keep my upset and anger inside but failing. I felt like they didn't believe me. 'This is all bull. It's pointless. I'm leaving.'

I left with tears welling in my eyes.

I wasn't done with Spire yet, though. Not by a long shot. For a start, they weren't giving Paterson's patients any emotional support and were starting to be criticised for it. Now solicitors were involved, perhaps that would change.

I was supporting several other women through Breast Friends. One woman was phoning or messaging me most nights, as she was afraid to go out and told me how Paterson had described cancer to her as 'an army of ants on the move that needed to be stopped'. Her husband's job covered her for private healthcare, and Paterson gave her what she later learned was a cleavage-sparing mastectomy. She developed severe trauma to the point where when she saw actual ants in her kitchen, she put her house on the market.

I told Ruth Walker at Spire that they needed to provide counselling to recall patients who wanted it, and to my surprise she agreed. My own mental health was a struggle. I wasn't sleeping, and I was the daily point of contact for a lot of women who wanted answers or just someone to talk to. But I didn't have any answers. I was travelling with work and away from home but was also fearful that if I'd been left with an incomplete mastectomy, my cancer could come back. Spire referred me for six sessions with a therapist of their choosing.

The therapist had a room at one of Spire's clinics in Solihull town centre. I'd never had therapy before, but the waiting room was relaxing, with tea, coffee, biscuits and the obligatory fish tank. She wasn't a psychotherapist with a doctorate but a counsellor, and I wondered if she was in over her head with the extreme trauma she was hearing from all the Paterson patients; while I was explaining about my parents' deaths from cancer, she seemed to zone out. After the session I got into the car with Bob and said, 'Well, that was weird, I must be boring. She couldn't keep her eyes open.' We like to find a way to laugh about things but deep down it bothered me.

The following week I had another session, and exactly the same thing happened again. Always one to speak up, I said, 'Sorry, are you tired?' She sat bolt upright and panicked, 'Sorry! Did you notice?' 'Yes, and last week, too.' She seemed mortified and emailed me later to apologise for what she called her 'feet of clay'. The next time we met she apologised again and said she had taken on too much and hadn't put sufficient breaks in her diary to do herself or the other patients justice.

I think she was simply underqualified for the enormity of the job. We spent the final three sessions practising mindfulness, which consisted of deep breathing while listening to birdsong. I actually found that very relaxing and it helped me to stay 'in the moment', but I can't say we made a dent in the underlying trauma.

Throughout this time I continued to meet with an NHS breast cancer support group that had been set up in response to the Paterson situation, and I heard everyone's stories. They were terrifying and moving. I had developed a friendship with Gina, the young woman whose operation and treatment had been so similar to mine. She reminded me so much of my daughter Jen. We would meet outside of the group, and she also came to Solihull Breast Friends, even though it was a drive across the city for her. We would talk about Paterson and how there was no doubt in our minds that we would do whatever we could to get to the truth and see him brought to justice.

I met her parents on numerous occasions. Her mum told me how worried she was about Gina, and I briefly thought about how I'd cope if Jen had cancer, but quickly shook that off. Gina had had unnecessary chemotherapy that affected her very badly, to the point where her brother had found her collapsed on the bathroom floor. My heart hurt so much for her.

All the women in the group were traumatised and had been left mentally and physically scarred by what Paterson had done to them. The utter betrayal of trust inflicted on all of us was so damaging.

It was important that there was a place where we could tell our own personal stories and know that those who listened understood. But after a while the Trust ran out of funding for the room. Gina's father generously paid for a meeting room for us, but eventually we realised there was nothing new to say or share. Instead, action was needed. I continued focusing on Breast Friends and asking questions of HEFT and Spire about the recall process and care plans.

I had also been thinking a lot about the Paterson patients who had died. I wanted the data so I could see for myself, but it would be a long time until I got it.

Two female police officers visited me in June 2013. They had already interviewed a number of Paterson's patients, and although I hadn't yet had my independent medical report, my case was suspicious enough that it warranted their attention. I talked them through the timeline and details of my illness and treatment. I offered to read from my journal, which they readily accepted. When I got to the part where I'd written that I thought I was going to die and wanted my mum, my voice started to crack. I looked up and saw that they were both crying. I swallowed hard. 'Shall we have a cup of tea?' I said.

They asked if they could take my journal with them as evidence. How could I allow that? I didn't want to let it out of my sight, it was my most personal possession. Throughout the book were little sketches and poems and ramblings from the very darkest times, usually in the early hours of the morning when I couldn't sleep. But anything that helped the police in their case against Paterson had to be worth doing. I grabbed a stapler and sealed up some of the pages I wasn't willing to share, then reluctantly handed it over. They promised they'd take very good care of it and make a copy for their files. The two women spent nearly two hours with me and said they'd return soon.

After a few weeks I had another visit from them to return my journal and take a formal statement. It was surreal, but I kept a clear and focused head even through my anger. They confirmed that I might be called as a witness if the case proceeded to trial. I started to imagine facing Paterson in court. I thought of him as a bully and a narcissist, and it would be an important responsibility to give evidence in person. I wasn't afraid of him.

I signed my statement to confirm it was a true and accurate account of my dealings with Paterson. If my independent medical report proved that I had had unnecessary treatment, my operation would be considered a crime.

The police also interviewed my brother and his wife as they had attended a few of the appointments with me, and then I had to wait to see how the Crown Prosecution Service wanted to approach the trial.

Sometime later I got another call from one of the police officers. She told me that I wouldn't be asked to give evidence after all. The prosecution was building a case around ten of the strongest examples of Paterson's wrongdoing, patients who had had unnecessary operations but who had never had cancer at all. My case was more complicated because I did have cancer, just not the sort that would normally be treated with a mastectomy and chemotherapy. It was thought that the testimony from patients with cases like mine might confuse the jury. I was disappointed I wouldn't get my day in court, but the logic made sense. All that mattered was building the very best case in the hopes of a guilty verdict. It was hard to believe they would finally get him to face trial, and I was worried it would all fall apart.

Around the same time, Spire published a statement on their website saying they had engaged the services of independent company Verita to undertake a review of the governance arrangements at Spire Parkway and Little Aston hospitals in light of concerns raised about the surgical practice of Ian Paterson. This review would become known as the Verita Report.

Spire wrote to over 700 of Paterson's patients who had attended a recall appointment, inviting them to contact the Verita inquiry team. They received 157 calls in response. We all received a questionnaire to complete so that Verita could determine whether we were able to contribute to the terms of reference of their review. After reading the questionnaires, they conducted nine patient interviews face to face and four via telephone. On the afternoon of Tuesday 30 July, I headed to the Balmoral Room of the Macdonald Burlington Hotel in Birmingham to meet Lesley Sargeant and Jess Martin of Verita.

I had been the day before to accompany Anne Ramsay, a Breast Friends member, to her interview, and she returned the favour and came to mine.

I had told the story and its impact on me and my family so often, but I still hadn't found the strength to talk about it without emotion. The investigators introduced themselves and explained that Verita was an independent organisation investigating Paterson. The room in the hotel was dimly lit. I sat at a large table next to Anne and the investigators sat on the opposite side, almost like an interrogation, although they were sympathetic and friendly. They asked me to tell them when I had first met Paterson and what he said to me. It was hard to start at the beginning and go through the sequence of events while they made notes, feeling the weight of what was no longer just a medical case but multiple formal investigations. I explained what had happened to me as they made notes, and I got the impression they were taking it all very seriously. I left feeling drained but that progress was being made, and perhaps as well as a criminal case against Paterson, Spire might finally be held to account.

26

In August 2013, I received my independent medical report. It had felt like an eternity, but finally I had the definitive answer about what had happened to me and whether I'd been through hell for no reason.

I read the report with hands shaking, and I saw the words I had dreaded the most. My mastectomy and chemotherapy at the hands of Ian Paterson and his colleagues had not been necessary, and I had had a cleavage-sparing mastectomy.

The report was thirty pages long, but here's the pertinent detail:

'*Mrs Douglas presented with an 18mm lesion which was deep to the left areola margin in the 9 o'clock position. It had a benign nature on mammography and therefore the cytology, although malignant, was discordant with the mammograms and the clinical impression of a potentially benign lesion.*

'*It is the requirement of the NHS breast screening programme QA guidelines for surgeons that if a surgeon is performing a mastectomy, they confirm the lesion is malignant, in the face of discordant triple assessment, by a core biopsy. Additionally, before an axillary dissection is carried out, it is mandatory that a core biopsy is carried out to confirm the lesion is an invasive malignancy and not pure ductal carcinoma in situ (DCIS). Although less than 5 per cent of mass lesions are pure DCIS, the presentation of a mass lesion needs to be clarified with a preoperative diagnosis using core biopsy.*

'*Therefore, it was not acceptable practice to carry out axillary node dissection or mastectomy without having done a core biopsy to clarify there was an invasive component to this lesion. This was a breach of duty by Mr Paterson.*'

The report said that the 585 grams of tissue removed was unlikely to be the full amount of breast tissue. This was confirmation that I had likely had a cleavage-sparing mastectomy.

'*In any case, Mr Paterson described a subcutaneous mastectomy, which usually involved leaving substantial tissue on the skin flaps to improve the cosmetic result and I think it's unlikely that Mrs Douglas had anything other than a cleavage-sparing mastectomy (CSM). She has certainly not had a complete mastectomy.*

'*The difference in size from the weight to what would be expected of a 38G breast is one reason, the description of subcutaneous mastectomy is another. I do not believe that this was explained to Mrs Douglas at the time. The consent form from Mr Paterson was in fact consented by Dr F. Bannourah on the 4th Dec. and stated 'left skin sparing mastectomy and axillary node clearance and left immediate breast reconstruction using TRAM flap'.*

'The doctor concerned (not one of the consultants involved) did not describe the intended benefits of the procedure or serious frequently occurring risks and did not state the risk of any blood transfusion.

'I remain unconvinced that Mrs Douglas understood the issues or had been adequately consented, despite the consenting process involving a clinical breast care nurse.

'The consent form itself should have been signed and consented by the Consultant carrying out the operation and the risks and benefits of the operation should have been listed. I consider the consent to have been below the standard required by the GMA in carrying out consent for a major surgical procedure.

'The absence of any comment about breast-conserving surgery suggests that this patient was persuaded into having a mastectomy as the first choice.

'This is a breach of duty by Mr Paterson [and] Bethan Lloyd Owen … This is difficult to defend but will depend on a statement from Mrs Douglas about what was said to her at the time surgery was discussed.'

I can confirm that the ONLY treatment that was offered to me was a mastectomy. The report states that the recommended treatment for cancer of my type is a wide local excision, an operation to remove the lump rather than the breast. If I'd been offered that I'd have taken it in a heartbeat.

'There appears to have been an MDT meeting where it was decided that Mrs Douglas would have chemotherapy but no radiotherapy, Dr Latief stated that he informed Mrs Douglas that she had a 3–6 per cent benefit from chemotherapy.'

That wasn't true. Latief told me there would be a 6 per cent benefit. But even so …

'This in fact was a gross overestimate and misrepresentation of the benefit by Mr Latief. By contemporary standards of 2003,

the prognostic indices widely used was Adjuvant! Online. This showed a 94.6 per cent chance of being alive 10 years later and a 0.9% benefit in reduction of breast cancer death using CMF chemotherapy. Mrs Douglas also had a 2.4 per cent chance of dying of causes other than cancer.

'The benefit from adjuvant tamoxifen over 10 years would be a 1 per cent reduction in mortality and a 0.9 per cent benefit in reduction of mortality from breast cancer with the addition of chemotherapy. Any discussion about the benefit of chemotherapy is usually about mortality benefits and therefore the statement by Dr Latief of a 3–6 per cent benefit is misleading and inappropriate.

'The reason relapse is not used to discuss chemotherapy in the situation of a grade 1 tumour is the risk of relapse is likely to be due to contralateral breast cancer and the risk of epirubicin is that approximately 0.5 per cent develop venous thromboembolism or neutropenic sepsis during the course of their chemotherapy, which can lead to their death during chemotherapy and in addition even in 2003 it was apparent that 10 years later, there was a 1 per cent risk of leukaemia with epirubicin.'

The report was saying that the chemotherapy presented a risk of causing leukaemia that outweighed any potential benefit. The standard in the UK is to not offer chemotherapy to patients with a less than 3 per cent benefit in mortality. The benefit to me was just 0.9 per cent, nowhere near the 6 per cent that Latief said. It made me feel very sad and scared about future implications to my health. The correct treatment, had I had a wide local excision, should have been radiotherapy. That's no walk in the park either, but it often has far less severe side effects because it targets just the affected area rather than the whole body and every organ. It's also a treatment done over the course of several weeks rather than several months.

'There has clearly been a significant risk that has been accrued, both at the present time and ongoing, in terms of risk of leukaemia in the future, from the use of chemotherapy in Mrs Douglas.

'*Axillary node clearance was not justified in the fact that it was a small, less than 2cm, Grade 1 cancer which had more than a 50 per cent probability of being node negative and there was no evidence this was an invasive cancer.*'

The report also offered an opinion on the scans I'd received.

'*In my opinion, the fact that bilateral ultrasound was requested, including ultrasound of the reconstructed breast, indicates that Mr Paterson knew there was breast tissue left in the reconstructed breast and that this was an unnecessary investigation which could have been avoided had he carried out a complete mastectomy.*'

What a bizarre situation. I didn't need the mastectomy, but if I'd had a proper one I wouldn't have needed additional scans. Instead, I'd been given numerous CT scans, X-rays, MRI scans and, most damaging, five PET scans.

'*I wish to put on record that PET scanning, which has been used by Mr Paterson in many of these cases, has no role in the regular surveillance of breast cancer patients post-operatively.*'

I thought back to every scan I'd had, every visit to Spire Parkway and how each had brought back the stress and worry that my cancer had returned. The further I read into the report, the harder it became to understand why they had done this. The report provided a possible motive.

'*Further, all the radiologists involved should have been aware that only mammography was indicated and there was no reason to carry out ultrasound apart from the financial gain they would incur by carrying this out.*'

The report also criticised the matter of my two contradictory pathology reports, one of which said the cancer had spread to a lymph node and the other (which I understand to be the correct one) that said it had not.

'*This is clearly unacceptable and Spire Pathology Department, as a hospital, should have provided the correct report and had it clearly annotated. The fact that Mr Thrush and Mr Harries were asking the matron at Spire to clarify the exact pathology cannot be defended and it is a breach of duty by Spire hospital in their performance of providing pathology for patients.'*

The report concluded with some harsh words on the clinical nurse specialist who had treated me, Bethan Lloyd Owen, saying she had influenced decisions about chemotherapy and the surgical operations I should undergo for breast surgery.

'Whilst [the breast care nurse's] *duty is to provide the role of advocate for the patient,* [she has] *advised the patient in a paternalistic way, the correct treatment to pursue.*

'The treatment has to a large degree been detrimental to the patient's care and I do not believe Ms Lloyd Owen's actions have been satisfactory, safe nor considered the other treatments that could have been undertaken with much less morbidity.

'I believe that [Lloyd Owen] *has breached their duty as Clinical Nurse Specialist to provide the evidence of current practice within the UK to the patient at the time she was making the decision and ... unduly influenced her treatment decisions.'*

It was so much worse than I had been expecting. I had been badly advised, given an unnecessary mastectomy that left breast tissue behind, unnecessary chemotherapy that could cause more harm than it reduced, and I'd been hugely over-scanned. For what? Profit? I'd been put through the most horrendous regime, lost my hair and almost my sanity, and the only people to benefit were those who charged my insurer.

Finally, I had the truth, which although hard to hear was a relief. At last, I could read in black and white exactly what had happened and how I was failed. Everything I suspected had happened was borne out in the report. I knew I could now speak with confidence about Paterson and the harm he had caused because finally I had my own truth. I read the report out to my family. Their reaction was one of disbelief and collective anger, that Paterson could butcher me for money. I thought of the ten patients who never had cancer but whose treatment was so severe, they were now the legal victims in a criminal case. And then I thought of the women who did have cancer but whose cleavage-sparing mastectomies meant their cancer returned, and who later died. Women I had known, who I had supported and who had supported me.

27

It was time for action. Now I finally had some answers about my health, I could start focusing on the bigger picture. Who knew what, and why had Paterson patients been so misled? Bethan Lloyd Owen had told the Breast Friends 'extraordinary meeting' that our mastectomies had been safe, that Paterson had done nothing wrong, and that I was overreacting.

I emailed the Breast Friends committee with what I had discovered from the independent review of my medical records. I explained that I had felt isolated from the committee because I kept asking questions, but that I hoped they were now under no illusions about what was going on. I ended by saying, 'I really do just want to get across that there are going to be many more recalls and that our support group will be needed more than ever to help ladies in this situation, so let's see what's said tomorrow at the Trust's meeting, which will be all about how this was allowed to happen.'

I got a response from one of the newer ladies on our committee who had been operated on by Paterson.

'As a group we were advised not to respond to certain emails which were classed as scaremongering, and we were advised by Bethan, who spoke at one of the meetings, that we should not be concerned about the rumours going around, Mr Paterson's record of secondary operations was no higher than the average. No mention was made of the many unnecessary operations performed in the private sector for what can only be seen as financial reward.'

The Trust meeting I referred to had been arranged by Gillian Waterhouse, a project advisor for HEFT, to be attended by HEFT and patients or volunteer representatives from Breast Friends Solihull. It wasn't possible to separate the NHS side of Paterson's actions from the private sector side, in part because there was so much patient and staff crossover between the two but also because the NHS had been leading the investigation. In my line of work, the obvious next question after 'how and why did this happen?' was 'how can we stop this happening again?'. This was as true for medicine as it was aerospace.

One of the women who attended was Shena Mason. She joined Breast Friends in 2005 after being diagnosed with cancer, and Paterson had given her a right-breast, cleavage-sparing mastectomy in the NHS in July 2005. After waking up and still having a mound, a breast care nurse told her, 'That's how Paterson likes to do it, so you're left with a cleavage.' Her cancer returned in 2007 after she found a lump on the original mastectomy scar, which had metastasised to her spine. In the meeting she suggested that HEFT allocate more time from a breast nurse specialist for those with secondary cancer, which they said they would. She emailed me shortly after saying she thought the meeting was very constructive and hoped that with a bit of added pressure from Breast Friends things could really start to improve.

She was incredibly dignified in how she met the return of her cancer. When she gave evidence to a later NHS investigation, she said:

'Some of us will always have rotten bad luck and carry on and the disease will develop, that is going to happen, but rotten bad luck is easier to live with than the thought that your surgeon may have damaged you ... You have this gnawing suspicion that maybe if you had woken up with a nice flat chest wall the day after the operation, maybe you would be feeling well now, but I'm never going to know.'

I'd known Shena slightly from the Breast Friends meetups but didn't properly get to know her until we both started attending the NHS breast cancer patient support group for Paterson patients. She was older than me, and I liked her a lot. I found her caring and intelligent, with a mischievous twinkle in her eye. She told me about her career as an editor for a major jewellery trade magazine, and her love of the outdoors and natural history. She had been a key figure in helping to research and document Birmingham's heritage, working on projects including the award-winning Museum of the Jewellery Quarter and the restoration of Soho House, the one-time residence of the great industrialist Matthew Boulton. She had published several books on the topic.

Shena and I were both devastated when, just a few days after the HEFT meeting, we learned that our friend and fellow Breast Friends member Michelle, who had been one of my trusted allies in questioning Paterson's practices, had died. Michelle's secondary cancer had been aggressive and spread to her liver and stomach, taking her life in August 2013, aged just forty-seven.

I was used to losing friends – it's part of the deal when you work with a cancer support charity – but August 2013 was one of the worst months of my life. Not long after Michelle died, another Breast Friends member and Paterson patient, Jackie Goodman, passed away a month short of her eightieth birthday. Jackie was a true lady, very articulate and extremely kind. At a funeral for Cathy Coyne, another of our Breast Friends ladies, Jackie had stood next to me outside the church and said sadly, 'I don't know why I'm still here and that young woman is not.' It really hit me. Cathy was the same age as me, with a young family, and one of the first people I spoke to when I joined Breast Friends. I thought, that could be me.

Always wanting to see the best in everyone, Jackie couldn't see why anyone would want to tarnish Paterson's name, believing him to be an honourable man that deserved our support. I understand why she felt that way, as the alternative was, for some, too devastating to bear. She had printed posters and suggested that Breast Friends hold a rally to demand Paterson's reinstatement, believing Lloyd Owen's claim that it was all a witch hunt by jealous colleagues. She was disappointed when the committee said no to her idea. My heart breaks when I think of how she was misled.

After her death, I called Shena Mason and said, 'We will get Paterson, justice will prevail.' I vowed that I would do everything I could to fight for the truth and stop this happening ever again.

On Friday 30 August, Shena and I went to the funeral of my young friend Michelle Flavelle. The sky was bright blue and the sun shone brightly. The church was packed to its beautiful wooden rafters. A large screen showed photographs of Michelle's life and how she had lived it to the full, her beautiful smile beaming out and lighting up the church as her family and friends remembered her life. I thought of those who were no longer with us, and those who would not always be.

The last time I saw Shena Mason was at one of the support group meetings. We later spoke on the phone and she told me that the tumour was in the same breast. She died aged seventy-five on 31 January 2014.

I remembered my vow to her, to carry on the fight for justice for all of us, and how she had told me how mine and Bob's Route 66 trip across the US on a Harley-Davidson had filled her with tears, enthusiasm and hope. She raised a fist in the air when she was telling me, saying, 'Good for you girl! Good for you!'

28

Sir Ian Kennedy is an academic lawyer and vice-president of the College of Medicine who specialises in the law and ethics of health. He was invited by the board of HEFT to investigate the Paterson case from an NHS perspective. I met him in October 2010 at a meeting organised by Gillian Waterhouse, to give him my story and ask questions.

On 19 December 2013, his review was published. Over a period of twelve months Kennedy's team had collected sixty-six witness testimonies from members and former members of staff of HEFT, Solihull, Heartlands and Good Hope Hospitals, their patients and their relatives and friends. Kennedy had no powers to compel anyone to testify, so he relied on goodwill, offering anonymity to those who wanted it.

We had waited a long time for this review and I was excited to get more pieces of the puzzle into place. Kennedy gave a press conference at Solihull Hospital, which was well attended by press and NHS management. I had been invited with a few other women from Breast Friends, and we were handed hard copies of the report. I liked Kennedy; he had come to address the Paterson support group a few times and I was hoping his report had fully understood the patient impact side of the story. Almost daily another Paterson victim had come forward to tell their story, and by now I was supporting multiple women and advising them on how to navigate the recall and legal process. I watched as Kennedy stood outside the hospital in front of assembled journalists and officially launched the report.

'How many times have we heard stories about patients being let down?' he said. 'It's a depressingly familiar theme. In an NHS which by and large works very well we keep having scandal after scandal, and it does have to do with the culture of the organisation.'

I felt heartened that he was using such strong words. This wasn't going to be a whitewash.

The same day, the CEO of HEFT, Mark Newbold, released a statement to the media apologising to Paterson patients.

'Firstly, patients were harmed by Paterson himself, carrying out an unauthorised operation, and secondly by the delay in acting by the previous Trust management team, which meant that more operations were carried out than would have been if they'd acted earlier. I'm profoundly apologetic to all those affected.'

When I got home I sat down and eagerly read the report. It opens with a personal statement from Kennedy saying that while he personally had not had previous involvement with the Trust, his brother Stuart had been a surgeon at two of the involved hospitals. 'He ceased to operate after contracting hepatitis from a patient around 1990 and died of liver disease in 1999. It was partly in honour of his memory that I agreed to take on this Review,' he wrote. I appreciated the personal touch.

The report is 166 pages long. The first part of the executive summary reads:

'This is a tragic story. It is not a story about the whole of the NHS. It is about something that happened in one corner of one hospital trust in one part of the NHS. But, it has lessons for the whole of the NHS.

'It is a story of women faced with a life-threatening disease who have been harmed. It is a story of clinicians at their wits' ends trying for years to get the Trust to address what was going on. It is a story of clinicians going along with what they knew to be poor performance. It is a story of weak and indecisive leadership from senior managers. It is a story of secrecy and containment. It is a story of a Board which did not carry out its responsibilities. It is a story of a surgeon who chose on occasions to operate on women in a way unrecognised by his peers and thereby exposed them to harm.'

It was such a relief to finally see that in writing. It was a powerful opening statement, and he wasn't mincing his words. As I read on, the NHS side of the story began to emerge. Most of it was new to me, and I felt anger rising as I read about Goldman and Cunliffe and how they were able to hide behind 'HR confidentiality' to keep everyone in the dark. I would describe the Kennedy report as damning.

I read about the Board not being informed:

'They were not told of Mr Wake's Report, nor the less-favourable views expressed by the initial and follow-up QA visits in

2004, *and the recommendations which followed. Good news was preferred to true news.'*

Of course, I don't know if the Board would have taken different action if they had known, particularly as Goldman was a member and Paterson had been threatening legal action even while sheltering behind his prolific surgery rates and old boys' network. One section about Wake (who declined to be interviewed by Kennedy) jumped out:

'I asked for and, very belatedly, was given documents (only a very few) relating to the annual appraisal of Mr Paterson. Annual appraisal of Clinical Leads in Cancer was introduced by Mr Wake, as Lead Cancer Clinician, in 2003. I have seen Mr Wake's Note of his appraisal of Mr Paterson in 2003 and in 2006. They are both bland. They give no suggestion of the difficulties which I shall describe shortly. The appraisal of 2006 is noticeable principally for its congratulatory tone regarding Mr Paterson's workload and output.'

The report explained what had happened with the MDTs and the wider culture that was endemic. It's hard to believe Kennedy was describing a hospital, where everyone was supposed to work together with the shared goal of patient safety.

'The culture of the organisation at the relevant time was hierarchical and seen by some as oppressive. Inappropriate behaviour by consultants went unchecked. Speaking out about concerns was not easy, particularly for younger members of staff. The Board was passive, responding to what it was told by the Executive rather than actively exercising effective governance.'

He called the initial recall procedure 'hopelessly flawed', criticising the involvement of Paterson himself in selecting which patients were reviewed (it should have been all of them).

He also gave short shrift to the Trust's attitude to data collection, which he suggested was actually a wider NHS problem:

'One of the lessons of history from the many occasions when things have gone wrong in the NHS, it is that senior managers

and doctors who are reluctant to confront what is actually happening, take refuge in the call for ever more data. The view was that data was needed to establish whether Mr Paterson's surgical practice exposed patients to an increased risk of harm. (The issue of consent, which did not require data, was simply overlooked and not pursued formally till mid-2011.)'

I've detailed much of what was revealed in the Kennedy Report in earlier chapters, and a post-mortem of it could be a whole book in itself. The recommendations alone are a dozen pages, and are largely concerned with matters of governance, but there are some key takeaways. Kennedy refers to the Board as a 'passive recipient', suggesting it becomes proactive about data and patient welfare. Most patients, I suspect, would believe this was already happening, as it's obviously crucial for safety and accountability. He also wants senior management to create better lines of communication for staff when they have safety concerns. This is an ongoing problem in healthcare, and part of the anti-whistleblowing culture that remains despite interventions (a 2015 initiative entitled 'Freedom to Speak Up' was supposed to create change, but I hear mixed reports of its success, and some NHS staff don't even know it exists). Kennedy also recommends staff should be more informed about their duty to report issues to the GMC or other regulators if management aren't listening.

None of that is possible if Kennedy's next recommendation is ignored: stop hiring bullies. Kennedy phrases it thus: 'A person appointed may be technically sound but have personal qualities or characteristics which mean that s/he will not best serve the interests of patients and the Trust. This may be because of her/his attitudes to colleagues or to patients, or both', and suggests personality and 'team player' skills should be a deciding factor'. Nice idea, but in practice there aren't enough clinicians to go around and the hiring process is often criticised as biased from the top down. Paterson had a track record of malpractice and lying with the Gill Dallow controversy in 1996, but he was hired anyway. 'The notion of "working around" difficult consultants has no place in the NHS. They should be confronted and required to change their behaviour. Their performance should then be monitored and action taken if there is no improvement in behaviour,' wrote Kennedy. But in practice, bullying is baked into the system and if an aggressive consultant is also getting the waiting lists down, who do you think management will prioritise?

Kennedy has a lot to say about patients, which can be summarised by his line 'patients are entitled to be told the truth' about their medical treatment and when things go wrong. He also talks about consent, one of the major aspects of the Paterson story. Informed consent is sacrosanct; without it the entire patient/doctor relationship is destroyed. Kennedy has strong words:

'A growing practice has emerged of talking in terms of "consenting" patients. This is wrong. It trivialises what is a central feature of the relationship between patients and healthcare professionals. It completely undermines the respect that patients are due. It reflects a complete failure of understanding on the part of professionals about the nature of the transaction between them and their patients. It seeks to reduce a matter of great ethical significance to the level of an administrative chore.'

He also made lengthy recommendations about QA visits, NHS regulators, disciplinary procedures and clinical governance which can best be summarised as 'talk to each other more'.

'It is not the role of this Review to hold people to account,' wrote Kennedy. Perhaps not. But it was *someone's* role. His report was important, and the recommendations essential, but would anyone pay attention? The more I read, the more determined I became to make them.

29

Thompsons solicitors had asked me to have an assessment of my scarring by an independent plastic surgeon, Nicholas Parkhouse. Bob offered to come with me, but I joked, 'I'll be fine. I've got my boobs out plenty of times now, I'm used to it.' I had my usual rush to get across town to the appointment and parked outside a beautiful white Georgian house in Edgbaston, the most affluent area of Birmingham and very popular with private medical consultants. I knew Paterson used to live round there and wondered which was his house.

While I'd digested the medical facts of the independent medical report, I hadn't really come to terms with the psychological impact of being told that all the extensive scarring and disfigurement I had was unnecessary. Perhaps my reassurance to Bob wasn't so true after all. I started to feel anxious as Parkhouse asked me to get undressed. I stood there topless while he took out a fabric tape measure and started to document my scars. There was no chaperone nurse in attendance, and I hadn't been offered one, but I just wanted the whole thing over with so I did what I was told.

Then he asked me to stand against a white wall with my hands on my hips, facing forward while he photographed me. As I did so my trousers slipped down to my ankles. He ignored that, and asked me to put my hands behind my back and turn slightly to the side, and then face side on. I felt horribly exposed and ridiculous with my trousers around my feet while he took pictures of my body. He described my scarring as 'extensive'.

'I hate the contours of my body,' I told him. 'My abdomen is distended on the left side and this bulging below the scar line causes me anxiety.' I never wore anything fitted in that area because I was so self-conscious about it. At Breast Friends we were able to laugh about it because we all had scars of one sort or another. At the Sydney Harbour Bridge climb I got into a tight jumpsuit that made me look like I was wearing a codpiece. My friend Chris had howled with laughter when I pointed it out. It was different here, though. I was practically naked in front of a stranger having to point out all the defects, imperfections and harm that Paterson had caused.

I pulled my trousers up, went behind a screen to get fully dressed, then sat down at the desk in front of Parkhouse. He started talking about how he might be able to do something about my 'dog ears'.

I hated that phrase. So dehumanising. He was referring to the overhangs of flesh and skin from where material had been taken from my stomach area and then stitched back together. Somehow it didn't quite fit as the hips and stomach widened further down my torso, so I was left with a flap of excess tissue. I later learned that 'dog ears' is the common medical term for them. It shouldn't be. We are not dogs. Medical literature also says they are generally preventable, and yet are somehow still common.

I started crying. I could barely breathe. 'They've done all this to me and for nothing but money,' I gasped. He looked uncomfortable and, perhaps wanting to reassure me, he told me that he could surgically remove the 'dog ears' and improve the depressed area of scarring in the supra-pubic area at a cost to me of £5,000, but he wouldn't be able to fix the bulging in my groin and upper abdomen. No chance. I wasn't going to have more surgery and I didn't have five grand.

I left Parkhouse's office and sat crying in my car. There was no way on earth anyone was touching me again. I wasn't going near another consultant. I rang Bob and he said he should have insisted on coming with me. 'I thought it would be easy,' I said. 'But it wasn't. It was one of the worst things I have ever gone through in my life.' I knew work wouldn't mind if I didn't go back in, so I composed myself and drove home to a big hug from Bob.

*   *   *

The support group for Paterson patients had been set up by Gillian Waterhouse. I'd already swapped dozens of emails with her up until that point, and she had been a helpful and very sympathetic liaison. She was facilitating an important meeting at the Ramada Hotel in Solihull in April 2014 with Mark Newbold alongside Lisa Thompson, HEFT's Director of Corporate Affairs, and she had asked me to take the minutes. This was the second time we had met with Newbold, but the first since the Kennedy Report.

The meeting was crowded; most attendees were patients and their partners. I sat with my notebook and pen to take the minutes as Newbold stood up at the front to address the room.

First, he apologised for the harm Ian Paterson had caused and said he could understand the anger directed at the Trust. He said that the patients affected and the Trust were both on the same side and he hoped that the group would inform and have input into the way breast cancer services were developed in the future.

He opened the floor to questions.

'What have you done to improve the breast care services at Solihull Hospital?' someone asked.

He assured us that services were being reviewed, although he didn't give details. He said that when he initially joined HEFT in 2010, he had been told that the most significant problems with Paterson had been addressed. Over the next two years it became increasingly clear that was not the case, particularly when the police got involved.

There were some small wins. The patient support group had said that attending Solihull Hospital for recall appointments was re-traumatising, so the Trust agreed to allocate facilities at another hospital. Newbold clearly recognised the anger and confidence issues that patients had, but I wasn't going to take anything on face value.

'Why was the first recall not done properly?' I asked.

Newbold replied that the Trust had employed a programme director, Richard Brown, to handle the ongoing recall full-time.

He had almost completed his database of affected patients. I already knew this and had been told several months ago that Brown still had around sixty patient records left to review. 'Why has that recall data not been completed yet?' I pressed. I was thinking of patients who had had cleavage-sparing mastectomies but had not yet been recalled. If they were at higher risk of recurrence then surely time was of the essence. Newbold said that there were difficulties because of the state of Paterson's record-keeping, and that a full set of data had not been available from the cancer registry until December 2013.

Newbold then confirmed what I had been pushing to know. The data *did* show that there was an increased risk of local recurrence in Paterson patients.

Newbold clarified that the data from the cancer registry was still being formatted, but at this stage it indicated that a single cancer had an increased risk in Paterson patients of 8–9 per cent at ten years. Terrifying.

Newbold talked about staffing issues. There was a shortage of breast radiologists, which was holding things up, and the Trust planned to make a clinical psychologist available for the breast care nurses who had been deeply affected by it all.

The issue of staff was a thorny one. I had no doubt that many of Paterson's colleagues had no idea what he was doing, but the Kennedy Report had been clear that there were also those who were arguably complicit or who did not prioritise patient safety.

'After apologies and admissions of culpability, why has no action been taken by the Trust to discipline senior members of staff who have put our lives on the line?' someone asked.

Newbold replied that the senior members of staff named in the Kennedy Report, Mark Goldman and Ian Cunliffe, had left HEFT. He said there was nothing specific in the Kennedy Report that could be used to discipline them, but that the report had been sent to the General Medical Council, who had not yet responded about Goldman and Cunliffe.

He also said that it was difficult to take action against junior staff when senior staff were the ones who knew what was going on. But he assured us that patient reports about staff behaviour were being listened to and action taken, including the recent exclusion of a member of staff on the basis of complaints. 'Days when doctors are beyond criticism are over,' he said. On Paterson himself, while he was suspended and under police investigation, there had unfortunately been delays to his GMC tribunal after a psychologist deemed him incapable of providing instructions. Therefore he was unable to participate in any forthcoming hearings. This was the first I had heard of Paterson claiming to be unwell, something that would become a major pattern over the next few years.

Other questions were about HR and the 'cloak of secrecy', workstreams and other procedural issues. Newbold assured us that reforms were underway.

The meeting concluded and I left feeling satisfied that Mark Newbold had been as open and honest as he could be. He had apologised up front and that felt quite emotional to hear. There was no doubt the harm done to us had been fully acknowledged. But would the promises of reform and cultural change come to anything? None of this work was worth a damn if the system didn't change to stop it from happening again.

30

A TV version of this story would want a dramatic arrest scene. Perhaps at the hospital, the actor playing Paterson would be escorted out in handcuffs, flanked by officers. 'Ian Stuart Paterson, you are under arrest!' In fact, he was never arrested, a strange quirk of the legal system that many people are surprised to learn of. A suspect does not have to be arrested to be charged with a crime. The reality of Paterson's charges was far more banal, a matter of paperwork rather than handcuffs.

After investigation under Operation Kempton, Paterson voluntarily attended for a police interview on 8 January 2013, and again on 24 September 2014. He was interrogated in a room that looked like an office. There is footage online, released by police to the media. In it, Paterson is seated on a brown leather sofa, in a dark suit, white shirt and red spotted tie. He is wearing an expensive-looking gold watch. A woman's voice is heard asking him questions about cleavage-sparing mastectomies. To every question, he replies, 'No comment.'

It's very unusual for someone of his demographic to find themselves in an interrogation room. He was adamant he had done nothing wrong. One of my sources told me that upon searching his house the police found confidential patient medical records that should not have left the hospital.

A year later, in September 2015, the Crown Prosecution Service gave authority to charge Ian Paterson with twenty-one counts of Wounding with Intent under Section 18 of the Offences against the Person Act 1861. This charge is more commonly known as GBH, or grievous bodily harm. As I understand it, it was the first time a surgeon had been charged with that crime for actions undertaken during the course of his duties.

Paterson was in the US at the time, and flew back into the UK on 20 December 2015, where, rather than be arrested, he was served what is called a charge requisition notice. It's basically a summons that says you're being charged with a crime and you have to appear in court.

The twenty-one counts of wounding with intent were for harm caused to a final total of ten patients. These were patients that the prosecution felt were the strongest cases, with the most easily understood evidence.

Paterson did everything he could to resist prosecution. His legal team argued that he was unfit to stand trial on mental health grounds. A psychiatrist had diagnosed him with adjustment disorder. This is a term that was coined in the late 1970s and is sometimes used as a defence plea in criminal trials. The idea is that someone's mental health is so affected by a 'stressor', for example, the prospect of going to trial, that they cannot cope. It's usually treatable, and one expert told me that it usually goes away in about six months, but there have been cases where it is persistent. But if it's used as a reason to plead unfitness for trial, then justice cannot be done. Anyone who went from a career as a rich surgeon to being charged with serious violent crimes is going to struggle to adjust. How long could he keep playing the same card?

I understand adjustment disorder because, just like Paterson, I was diagnosed with it. In November 2013, I had a psychological assessment arranged by Thompsons solicitors. The report was nineteen pages long. Under the section headed 'causation', the doctor wrote:

'While the diagnosis of cancer is in itself traumatic, and in this case complicated by her previous experience of bereavement and being at her mother's bedside when she died, in my opinion and on balance of probabilities, this Claimant's ongoing emotional problems are, in the main, attributable to her treatment with Mr Paterson, and the incorrect procedures used, and the discovery of unnecessary treatments.'

No surprises there, of course. While Paterson was presumably terrified of spending his future in prison, what he had done to me sometimes robbed me of the idea of a future at all. At the time, I was often in a dark place. The report says,

'The Claimant says, "I do feel like my future is cut short ... I don't think I'm going to live until I'm old." She feels she has to fit things in because she's not going to be here. She tends to live for today.'

But unlike Paterson, I coped. I had my career, my amazing family and the great Douglas toughness that I'd always drawn on to get me through just about anything.

Besides, there was work to do. Every time I thought one

aspect of the Paterson story was resolved, something new would crop up.

Paterson was, of course, incredibly wealthy, and presumably he could afford excellent lawyers. He sold his eight-bedroom Grade-II-listed Georgian mansion in Edgbaston in July 2013 for £1.2 million and moved to a converted barn in Cheshire. He also owned properties in Cardiff, Manchester and Florida, and had a valuable collection of fine wine.

And yet, despite his obvious wealth, he was granted legal aid of £216,542. Legal aid is a taxpayer-funded scheme to provide funds for the legal defence of those who cannot afford it, or, in some circumstances, if the accused's human rights are at risk. It is remarkable that Paterson was able to access these funds when clearly neither situation applied. How was he able to claim he had no money when he so obviously did?

He had divorced his wife Louise just before his trial in April 2017 and she appeared to be the recipient of his assets. His Florida property is in the name of his wife and children. It isn't clear how Paterson was able to successfully claim legal aid, as recipients must usually have a current household income of £37,500 or less. Paterson would have had to demonstrate financial hardship. There was potential to recoup the money, though. Savings and other capital aren't considered upfront, but are assessed at the end of the case, and those with more than £30,000 in disposable capital may be ordered to repay the legal aid. I wasn't about to let the whole thing go with 'no comment'.

31

Paterson's mental health claims also affected the ongoing fight for compensation. In November 2014, his legal team argued, via a psychiatric report, that he could not participate in a lawsuit brought by five Solihull women who had unnecessary operations because he 'lacked capacity' to give instructions to his lawyers. The high court judge agreed to an eight-week postponement, saying that Paterson had 'become increasingly unwell due to the pressure he was under'.

In December 2014, he lost the financial support of the Medical Defence Union (MDU), whose insurers had previously been paying for his solicitors to defend the claims for compensation. Paterson was claiming he was medically unfit to instruct his solicitors, and his solicitors were saying they couldn't act on his behalf anyway because no one was funding them. An application was made to the High Court to see if his solicitors could be forced to act for him regardless (despite him being unable to instruct them, an almost comical catch-22), which he lost.

The issue of insurance and its role in private medicine is a major part of the Paterson story. This doesn't just affect private patients, but the NHS too, which is increasingly outsourcing to the private sector. Patients reasonably assume that when they are treated, the clinician is insured in the event that something goes wrong, including negligence or malpractice. This insurance is called 'indemnity'.

When I tell people the following fact, their response is often disbelief:

If the malpractice by a clinician turns out to be criminal, the indemnity insurance is void.

This is quite obviously a huge and appalling loophole. What patient would agree to be operated on by a surgeon if they knew they weren't properly covered by insurance?

Linda Millband, the solicitor from Thompsons who led the class action lawsuit on behalf of Paterson patients, said:

'This was the first time this had ever come on my radar, that there may be people in this country operating without insurance. And that's horrific. Apart from Paterson, I think that is the one thing about it that the public are aghast about. They've said, "What? We can go into a private hospital and we're not insured?" It became this massive nightmare.'

I first heard about this in December 2014, when I received a letter from Thompsons solicitors.

'We have also started to receive confirmation from the MDU that they have identified cases where they will not be indemnifying/insuring Mr Paterson for claims brought against him. On those cases, Mr Paterson's solicitors are no longer instructed. This is as a result of a decision taken by the MDU and their insurers only, but please bear in mind that Mr Paterson is still being investigated by the police and the GMC. I am sure you are aware there is little point in pursuing an uninsured Defendant because they will not have the capacity to pay you any compensation if you are successful. However, please rest assured we are continuing to press Spire, who is insured, and we are in receipt of positive advice from our QC in these claims despite these issues.'

This might have been reassuring, had Spire not also been trying to get out of paying. They wanted to proceed to court with test cases to ascertain the extent of their liability. Their argument was, in a nutshell, that despite operating in their hospitals under their brand, Paterson was merely 'renting a room', operating independently, and therefore they couldn't be held responsible for his actions. They also argued that because the NHS had known about Paterson's wrongdoing for some time, the whole thing was an NHS problem. Even if they did agree to settle out of court, they wanted Paterson's insurers to contribute, and his insurers had said 'actually, we aren't covering that'.

All of this was massively complicated by Paterson's alleged inability to instruct his solicitors, meaning ongoing compensation claims like mine ground to a halt.

Over the next few years, the NHS settled all Paterson-related claims against them out of court, to the tune of £17 million. Those of us who had been operated on in the private sector were left in limbo.

But I'm not one to sit in limbo. I kept up the pressure, protesting outside Spire and via multiple TV, radio and press interviews. Without the patient voice at the forefront, there was a risk that we would simply be forgotten.

After more than three years of legal wrangling, finally a court date for the compensation claims was set for October 2017. There had been a pre-trial review in July 2017, in which the judge refused to postpone the hearing against Paterson, although she did request further information about his financial status and mental health.

Thompsons wrote with news:

'I can tell you that some positive and serious negotiations are ongoing, and it is very highly likely that a compensation package can be agreed which will include payment of damages (compensation) as well as legal costs, which will include all the costs of medical reports, insurance premiums and other costs that have been incurred. The offer from the Defendants started at £27 million, however after negotiations, the sum has now increased to £37 million.'

This sum was for 750 litigants, but also included legal costs – around forty solicitors were working on the case.

'The MDU have now effectively withdrawn cover having repudiated his insurance and are unlikely to make any payments in respect of damages. We are in negotiations with Spire, who have agreed to make payment in full by way of the £37-million lump sum. It is a mystery why Spire allowed their reputation to be tarnished for so long and did not do this beforehand, especially when at an early stage, the Medical Defence Union (MDU)

might have been persuaded to contribute as well. We can only speculate but they may have been trying to obtain a contribution from HEFT.'

Any award we received would be a one-off, regardless of whether our health deteriorated any further, but it seemed like the best option. The stress of a lawsuit cannot be underestimated. There isn't really an amount of money that can compensate for the hell we'd all been through, but that amount certainly isn't 'zero', and I wanted the whole thing over and done with. It was utterly exhausting.

'The legal position is very complex,' wrote Thompsons. 'This leaves the Claimants to prove that (in addition to Ian Paterson) either Spire or HEFT are also liable for their injuries when they were treated by Ian Paterson in the private hospital. Although [the QC] has previously stated and remains cautiously optimistic about succeeding in the claims against Spire in the cases which occurred after 2007, the issues for the court to decide at trial in October (contained in an agreed list of 63 generic issues) are complex and some raise novel points of law. For example, proving liability against a private hospital for injuries caused by a self-employed surgeon would be a significant extension of the current legal position where responsibilities are generally only established against an in-house surgeon.'

This is another key point that often causes disbelief. Not only can a surgeon not be insured for harm they cause, the hospital they operate in can try to claim it's not their problem. When I had my treatment, I considered myself a customer of Spire, not of Paterson. My insurer, BUPA, paid what was later Spire but at the time was a BUPA hospital. BUPA and Spire provided the building, admin services, nurses, food, medicines and every other aspect of my care. When Paterson wasn't available, they provided another clinician. In what world was I not their patient?

Likewise, HEFT was able to argue that in law they did not owe a duty of care to patients treated in the private sector, despite many patients being 'shared care'. This included private patient cases being discussed in NHS MDTs, and NHS GPs referring patients to Paterson under the promise that it would be faster to be treated privately. Paterson's practising privileges and training were the NHS's responsibility, and they had undertaken internal investigations into his wrongdoing long before Spire was aware that anything was amiss. Despite that, HEFT was successful in claiming that Paterson's private patients were not their responsibility.

Lesley Cuthbert was a patient who had started off seeing Paterson in the NHS. In 2006, her GP referred her to him after she discovered bleeding from her right nipple. Paterson said that she had cancer in her right breast and precancerous cells in her left breast and needed an urgent operation. His NHS waiting list was months long, he told her, but if she paid for it through the private sector, it would be a matter of weeks. She and her husband had a small BUPA policy that would cover it. Paterson removed the milk ducts from both of her breasts. 'When he told me I was clear of cancer the next day, he was my angel doctor, my saviour.' Her recovery was long and painful, and Paterson brought her back to Spire for regular check-ups.

Eight years later she found herself back at Spire once again, this time having the news broken to her that she never had cancer. Her left breast had been totally clear, and her right breast had had some precancerous cells that did not require an operation. She was represented by the solicitor Kashmir Uppal, of Shoosmiths, who said:

'The claims for the women who had surgery on the NHS have all been settled because the NHS accept that he was their employee, he was acting negligently, he was carrying out operations. Those women have had compensation which provides them with some comfort and ability to get on with their lives, they can pay their bills. Women have lost their jobs, they couldn't pay their mortgages, they didn't have any income, so they've got something to move forward with.

'*However, the women who had surgery in the private sector, and a lot of the time when they were deceived into having surgery in the private sector, such as Leslie, by being told that there was too long a wait on the NHS. Those claims are still outstanding because Spire healthcare, where the operations were performed, are saying that he was not their employee and therefore they're not liable for his acts or omissions.*'

But someone had to pay. That harm was done wasn't debatable, despite legal best efforts. Spire's problem, and therefore our problem, was that Paterson's indemnity insurers, the MDU, had originally insisted they didn't have to pay it. It was only after pressure and legal threats that they agreed to cover the first £10 million. The rest of the £27 million on offer would have to come from Spire's assets. At the time Spire's revenue was £856 million.

My solicitor was saying that we, the patients, were probably better off accepting the pot of £37 million rather than going to court and fighting for more.

'*There could be appeals to the Court of Appeal and possibly the Supreme Court, particularly if we are asking the judge to deal with novel issues never before tested in law during this trial. [The KC] fears that it may be at least 2–3 years and possibly longer before the lead litigation may be finally determined, and within that time, the commercial reputation of Spire may become so tarnished that the current offer from them may not be available at the end of this protracted litigation.*'

'*In light of all of this, Lizanne Gumble,* [the KC who acted on behalf of 750 Thompsons clients] *and her team have advised that attempts should be made to accept the offer of settlement in order to complete your individual case before the trial date for the lead cases and finally bring your long and arduous claim to a conclusion.*'

'*We will then write to you separately to discuss the value of your claim.*'

The victims were uncertain about how much compensation we should expect. We'd had no guidelines from the solicitors, who wanted to settle. I was contacted by a number of patients who wanted to know how much money they should expect to receive. I could feel the desperation in the emails and calls I received at the time, but I was at a loss to help. I was in the public eye, so it was assumed by many that I had already been given an offer. This was far from the truth. I'd concentrated on the fight for compensation, and I hadn't pushed my own solicitor for an offer, so I was one of the later claims to be settled.

On 27 September 2017, the £37-million settlement fund was agreed. The October court case against Spire was cancelled. I had a call from a very upset claimant saying that her solicitor had given her a compensation figure, but BUPA insurance wanted its money back, which was a third of the amount. Her solicitors' fees were another third. I called the solicitor Tony Mikhael first thing and said I was appalled that a BUPA insurer in a then-BUPA hospital could ask for money back. I threatened to go straight to the press and let them know.

The amount of compensation for a victim of Paterson ranged between £1,000 and £250,000, although very few were at the upper end of the scale. One patient who had been given a lumpectomy by Paterson under general anesthetic, after which he told her it had been a rare type of fibroadenoma that would have become cancer quickly, received £6,000 compensation. The lump he had removed had actually been a harmless swollen lymph node. Patients who had had cleavage-sparing mastectomies received between £30,000 and £40,000. There were more than forty firms of solicitors representing almost a thousand patients. The initial £37 million has now been increased to £50 million. To my knowledge it's the biggest medical class action lawsuit in British history – and is still ongoing.

32

My daughter Jen and her husband Scott called round. It was December 2015, and they had amazing news. 'We're going to have a baby!' I could not have been happier. This would be our first grandchild and we were elated.

Around the same time, Jen found a lump in her neck, but she dismissed it as pregnancy hormones. She told a colleague who said, 'If you don't go to the doctor, I'm telling your mum', a jokey threat which nonetheless did the trick. After a period of watchful waiting, Jen's GP referred her to the hospital for further tests. She phoned me, crying with worry for herself and the baby. I was at work but told my boss I had to leave, jumped in the car and drove across town. 'They're probably just taking precautions,' I reassured her, not wanting her to be stressed in her pregnancy. Surely the odds of the lump being anything bad were low, though? She told me that the GP, a woman, had said it was probably nothing, but if Jen was her sister, she'd want to make sure. Over a cup of tea and a laugh we both relaxed a little, but it was a tense wait for her appointment.

She had been referred to the Queen Elizabeth (QE) in Birmingham, one of the largest medical buildings in the country and a well-respected teaching hospital. I knew cancer wards because of my experience with my parents at Heartlands, but I never expected one of my children to need one. Jen was given tests and then the devastating news. At eight weeks pregnant, she was diagnosed with Hodgkin's lymphoma, a type of blood cancer. It was unbelievable.

She was young and fit, and was in excellent medical hands, but there was a long road ahead and I would have done anything to take away the pain she had coming. At fourteen weeks pregnant, Jen was started on chemotherapy. The delay was to reduce the risk, as the baby would by that time have its own blood supply. The QE had only fifteen recorded incidences of chemotherapy in women who were more than twelve weeks pregnant not passing drugs to the placenta, but there was no way of avoiding the treatment without Jen's life being at risk. Bob and I put on a brave face for Jen and Scott, but we were terrified.

'Are you sure you've told me everything?' I gently insisted. 'You're not refusing treatment because you're pregnant?' I couldn't think about the baby until I knew Jen – *my* baby – was going to be all right.

She reassured me she was following the clinicians' recommendations. At 16 weeks pregnant, Jen and Scott were able to listen to the baby's heartbeat for the first time.

The baby was closely monitored with regular ultrasound scans throughout Jen's treatment and seemed to be developing normally. On Jen's part, she tolerated the chemotherapy well, and to the outside world she looked healthy. She finished her treatment six weeks before giving birth. We all prayed she and the baby would be all right, so when she called on the night of 22 July to say, 'Hello Mum and Dad, you're grandparents. Meet Sophia Rose,' I burst into tears.

'Thank God, she's a little miracle,' I cried. We couldn't wait to get to the hospital to meet her. Baby Sophia was healthy, and seemingly unaffected by the chemotherapy. She was so beautiful, and so like her mum. It was one of the happiest days of my life, but there was still the dark cloud of Jen's illness over us all. The only diagnostic tool to say for certain whether the cancer had gone was a PET scan. This involved injecting a radioactive liquid into Jen's veins, which would show up any remaining cancer in her body under the scan. She kept putting off the scan as it meant leaving Sophia for at least eight hours, the duration that the radiation would stay in her body. Eight weeks after giving birth, Jen finally had the scan. There was no sign of cancer. She was in complete remission. I thanked God and the doctors for two miracles.

Jen and Scott moved house to be closer to us, and I went part-time at work to support them and help with Sophia. I was relieved, as I'd just about been holding it together through all the stress, and I wanted to spend as much time as I could with them. Jen went back to her job as an engineer at an aerospace firm, and we fell into a new normal.

In May 2018, Jen was asked to tell her story to the local newspaper to raise awareness of Hodgkin's lymphoma and was honoured to be asked to start the Birmingham leg of Race for Life. I stood proudly and listened as she took to the stage to tell the story of what the newspaper called her 'miracle baby' and her treatments at the QE. She thanked the crowd for their support, saying, 'If it wasn't for events like this funding research to advance cancer treatment, we wouldn't be here today so give yourself a round of applause.' She also challenged herself to do a 100-mile bike ride for Bloodwise, cycling into London down The Mall in the pouring rain watched by her family. Little Sophia cheered her on, shouting 'Mummy, Mummy!' at the top of her voice. It was a joyful moment, and a thankfully healthy year.

And then, more joy. When Sophia was almost three, during a visit she said out of nowhere, 'Mummy's got a baby in her tummy.' It was fantastic news, particularly as Jen's chemotherapy could have left her infertile. But here was another little miracle. The pregnancy was closely monitored, with some alarm when the baby was discovered to be breach and could not be turned, but a C-section was performed and Sophia gained a beautiful baby sister, Bella. The joy I felt at having two incredible granddaughters helped to undo so much of the pain and harm we had all experienced over the past years. The Paterson saga was ongoing, but I could do the work knowing how much strength and love there was in my growing family.

In July 2019, four weeks after Bella was born, the men went to 'wet the baby's head' down the pub while we ladies had a night in, with my husband Bob texting me progress photos of their antics. The mood was one of elation and peace. Once Bella and Sophia were asleep, Jen opened a bottle of wine. We were enjoying a glass when she ran her hand over the side of her neck, and her face suddenly changed.

'What's the matter?'

'I think I can feel a lump,' she said. My heart stopped. I asked to feel the lump, and played it down, saying, 'It's probably your glands, just a virus, but let's get it checked.' The unspoken potential hung in the air between us. Neither of us would say it, because it was unthinkable. What if the cancer had come back?

A nurse at the QE examined the lump before calling in Ram Malladi, a consultant in stem cell transplantation and cellular therapy for lymphoma. He immediately sent Jen for a chest X-ray and told her, 'If you don't get a call this afternoon then everything is fine.'

We went home to Jen's house and sat chatting about anything other than the results of her X-ray. It was unthinkable that the cancer might have returned, so we acted like it hadn't. Just after 2pm, Jen's phone rang. I felt sick to the pit of my stomach. I knew it was bad news. Jen ended the call and said, 'They've found something on the scan.' I put my arms around her and hugged her tight while we both cried.

The following week, Malladi confirmed that Jen's cancer had returned. She once again had Hodgkin's lymphoma, but this time in both sides of her neck and in her chest, too. He tried to reassure her, saying that there were options, but in reality, those options turned out to be much more aggressive chemotherapy and a process called apheresis, wherein her own stem cells would be harvested, then transplanted back into her body. It would be brutal. The treatment would wipe out her immune system and she would spend a month in hospital.

She began the chemotherapy straight away. The first time, she had lost very little hair, but this time it all fell out after just a few treatments. Her veins began to collapse, so the clinicians fitted a peripherally inserted central catheter (PICC) port into her arm. It was an aggressive schedule to prepare her stem cells for harvest, and then transplant, and she became quite ill. By August 2019, she had progressed to a portable chemotherapy unit and was fitted with a black backpack and stand that she would be attached to at home overnight. Because Bella and Sophia were so young, there was a risk of spillage from the dangerous chemo drugs, so she decided that while it was being administered, she would stay with us.

I was very nervous. What if the pump stopped? What if the battery failed on the pump? I couldn't help but think of my own chemotherapy, and I wished I could take the treatment and risk in Jen's place. But all went as well as it could. Jen was able to sleep a little, even with a drip hanging out of her arm. I felt happier that at least I could spoil her and do my bit for her. And so we settled into a routine, albeit one that revolved around sickness. Jen couldn't change Bella's nappy for risk of infection, so I would stay every day and help with the kids until Scott came home from work. I took Bella for her first vaccine injection, as Jen couldn't risk the clinical setting. All the while, Jen's body was being prepared for the stem cell harvest, and on 1 September 2019, she was admitted to the apheresis ward to begin the process. Her blood count was excellent. She texted me, 'they look for 15 and above to start collecting stem cells with 50/60 seen as good and mine were 180!' It was impossible not to be hopeful and even excited about this. Surely a good sign. The next day, after a small setback during which the clinicians couldn't get a line into her arm so they moved her to the main hospital to make an incision in her groin, her stem cells were harvested without issue. She went home sore but happy.

There were a few weeks before the other end of the process, where her own stem cells would be reintroduced into her body, during which Jen had to lie low because of her compromised immune system. At the end of October 2019, she was admitted to the apheresis ward to begin the process. Scott had started a new job a few weeks before, but thankfully his new employers were understanding. I would have the children during the day while Scott stayed with Jen at the hospital. In the evening Bob and I would bring her whatever she felt like eating. Initially it was comforting to know that we could help in a small way, but later when the daily regime of treatment kicked in her mouth was too sore to eat, and we felt as helpless as any parents ever have. We kept her company but didn't hug her for fear of passing anything on, as her immune system was all but dead. She'd lost weight, was pale and so weak, and she missed her babies dreadfully. We would just sit with her while she slept, the morphine she'd been given for the pain knocking her out. She was incredibly brave and never complained. She just got on with whatever treatment she was given, always trying to reassure us.

On 18 November 2019, her line was removed and she was told she could go home. I sent her a card telling her what an inspiration she was. I could have told her to her face, but I would have blubbed like a baby trying to say everything I really wanted to say. Jen still had severe bone ache but she managed as best as she could, with the amazing Scott by her side, and we all started planning for Christmas.

33

Three years before, in among the worry about Jen's health after her first diagnosis and recovery, the efforts to bring Paterson to trial were continuing. On 26 May 2016, the police brought Paterson to the Old Bailey to assess his fitness to stand trial. It had been three years since he had been charged, and his solicitors had so far successfully argued that his mental health was too poor for him to stand trial. The argument in such cases is that if a defendant is unable to represent their side of the story, give evidence or discuss the case with their legal team, then the trial would not be fair. It's an important part of the justice system, but the delay had been horrific for the victims, particularly those whose cases formed the basis of the prosecutions.

Thompsons asked me to prepare a statement for the press in the event that the judge ruled in Paterson's favour. By now I was used to being in the media, but I was hoping that this time it wouldn't be necessary. I did not want any more delays or injustices, and I did not believe Paterson was unfit to stand trial. I had first-hand experience of his ability to present himself one way while the reality was quite another.

I once again did not sleep all night, then spent the day restlessly pacing up and down until finally my phone rang. It was the Thompsons' solicitor Tony Mikhael, who was overjoyed to tell me that the judge finally rejected Paterson's excuses and the trial would be going ahead.

This was incredible news, overwhelming and terrifying, but also hugely uplifting. Paterson would have to stand up in court and account for his actions. We had been through daily torture for years. He had been suspended in 2011, charged in 2013, and now in 2016 there would finally be a chance for the victims to see justice done. It was going to be a rough ride for everyone, but it had to be done.

Over those intervening years I'd met with many victims of Paterson; those that contacted me through Breast Friends, those who were part of the NHS support group, and those who had seen me in the media. I was helping to push for changes in the breast clinic at NHS Solihull Hospital and was heavily involved in supporting breast cancer patients as well as Paterson victims.

In 2016, I was approached to be part of a national support charity, Breast Cancer Haven, which had been awarded a £2.65-million government grant and had secured a property near Solihull to provide free support to breast cancer patients and their families. The location was chosen due the high incidence of breast cancer in the area and to recognise the particular needs of Paterson patients.

Gillian Waterhouse of HEFT asked if she could come to my house with Pamela Healy, CEO of the charity. They were both really keen to get me on the committee. However, this was when Jen had just been diagnosed with Hodgkin's lymphoma, and so I explained this to them and that she was going through treatment while pregnant with her first child, but that I did want to do what I could. I was by now Chair of Breast Friends, but I agreed to also join the Breast Cancer Haven committee. It was important work and it also helped to distract me from the impending trial.

It took almost a year for the trial to begin. I had vowed to be there as often as I could, and by the time it started I was free to attend the trial, as I'd reduced my job to three days a week to support Jen when she was going through treatment and she was now in remission.

I sent an email out to the NHS Paterson support group to say I was going to attend court on the day Paterson took the stand and asked if anyone else wanted to come with me. I was contacted by one other patient who asked if I could pick her up as she too wanted to attend. We drove into the centre of Nottingham, circling the court a couple of times until I saw a sign for a car park and eventually parked up. My stress levels were at maximum and now I was running late.

Nottingham Crown Court is a 1980s angular construction of stone and glass, an unassuming municipal building that from the outside doesn't look like the place where murders and other violent crimes are tried. I was dressed in my usual work attire – a smart blouse, black trousers and a grey over-coat – looking like I meant business. I could have been there for any reason.

We headed through the entrance into the court building to be greeted by a security officer who escorted us to a metal detector and searched our handbags. I asked what court Paterson was in then walked down a short corridor and pushed open the heavy door into the courtroom. It was smaller than I had imagined, with rows of chairs on either side of the door. As I walked in to find a seat, I saw Ian Paterson. It had been a few years since I had seen him in person. He had lost weight and his hair looked greyer. I did a double take, at first not sure it was really him, then my stomach turned over and my body filled with adrenaline like I was facing a threat. He was dressed in an expensive-looking tailored suit, shirt and tie, just like he had been when he was my doctor. I stared hard at him. For a moment he made eye contact with me, and the corners of his mouth turned up in a thin-lipped smile of recognition. I suspect that for a second he thought that I was there to support him, as some members of Breast Friends still did. After all, he had been the charity's patron. I didn't blink, I just stared coldly at him. His smile dropped and he looked away.

I headed across the courtroom and took my seat next to my solicitor, Tony Mikhael, who leaned towards me and whispered, 'Have you seen who is sitting behind you?' I looked over my right shoulder. Bethan Lloyd Owen was just a few rows behind me. She looked unkempt, nothing like her former confident and very smart self. I stared at her and she blushed and looked away. I thought of her as complicit in Paterson's treatment of me and was furious to see her. She began to chat to the woman next to her, who I later found out was the daughter of a Paterson patient who had died.

Paterson was seated in front of me just a few feet away, facing the judge, and looking down at an iPad. His daughter was sitting next to him for emotional support. All the way through the trial he had a family member by his side. He was charged with seventeen counts of Wounding with Intent, contrary to section 18 of the Offences Against the Person Act 1861, together with three counts of Unlawful Wounding, against ten victims (nine women and one man). Their names are Rosemary Platt, Marion Moran, Judith Conduit, Patricia Welch, Carole Johnson, John Ingram, Leanne Joseph, Frances Perks, Joanne Lowson and Rachael Butler.

I thought Paterson would be taking the stand first, but the judge – Mr Justice Jeremy Baker – called Caroline Williams of HEFT, who I would be in contact with on numerous occasions after the trial.

Caroline confirmed she worked at Heartlands Hospital and explained how she had been asked by the police to search for all the medical records of the ten patients. She said that as well as personally checking for medical records that also included the records of MDT meetings, two of her colleagues had individually searched for electronic and paper copies.

Nick Barraclough, for the prosecution, asked whether private patients were also discussed in the NHS MDTs. Williams replied that they can be, depending on the arrangements made with the consultants and the private sector, but that such patients are flagged to the MDT coordinator as private, and relevant records sent over to the NHS. There were no records for any of the ten patients to show that their cases had been discussed at an MDT.

On cross-examination by Nicholas Johnson KC, Williams was asked about record retention and what the procedures were that had been in place in 1997 (the earliest case of wrongdoing by Paterson). She found it difficult to answer, not having a reference for that period, but added that procedures are reviewed every three years or so, depending on the record. For example, blood transfusion records were kept for thirty years. I was getting frustrated at this point. In the aerospace line of work, records and procedures were everything. I was used to strict controls, protocols and a thorough history of any changes. Human lives can depend on such record-keeping, as do investigations if anything should go wrong. How else can mistakes avoid being repeated?

Ruth Walker of Spire was called next to answer similar questions. She said that the MDT notes for Spire and Little Aston were kept and stored in five or six lever arch files which she had discovered during an office move. They were kept in Bethan Lloyd Owen's office. Walker said that Paterson did not have his own office, which I found odd as during my appointments the large corner room in Spire was always referred to as Mr Paterson's office. Walker explained that these MDT notes were not kept in individual patient records because they referred to multiple patients, so they were kept separately. When the police requested records for the ten trial witnesses, Ruth Walker searched these files but found only scant notes for just three of the patients, whose names she couldn't recall. Barraclough reminded her it was Frances Perks, John Ingram and Marian Moran.

Walker confirmed that when she left her role in August 2015, the MDT files were still on the shelf in the office. She was aware they were put into storage and were retrieved for legal proceedings much later. She could not, however, explain why some MDT records only recently surfaced or why some may not have reached the police earlier, but she said that all available records at the time were provided as requested.

I was getting more and more angry as I listened. Why was record-keeping so lax in a healthcare company that was worth billions?

Finally, it was Paterson's turn to give evidence.

Butterflies rose in my stomach as he was called to the stand. He put down his iPad, picked up a blue folder, and strode confidently to the witness box, no sign of mental frailty or even nerves. He was as cool as a cucumber, ready to defend himself.

After he was sworn in he placed his folder down and smiled at the jurors. The judge said, 'Mr Paterson, you may be there for a little while, so if you at any stage would like to sit down, please feel free to do so.'

Paterson's defence lawyer, Johnson, went through the formalities of asking Paterson his name and date of birth. Johnson said, 'That makes you nearly 60.' There was less than 12 months between our ages, and I was struck that while we were in the same courtroom, our lives were now even more different than they had been before.

His barrister began by asking about his career. Paterson described his training in Manchester and his medical specialisms, his two-year placement at Harvard University and his move to Birmingham in 1991. He boasted of his progress up the ranks of medicine, describing his years as a registrar as 'the next step up the ladder. It's a very high rank in the structure training. You're a lot more autonomous but you still have senior supervision available and immediate. You've reached the stage where your peers and the people on the appointing committees think that you probably have what it takes to become a consultant.' I felt sick. He then began to describe his achievements in sports, boasting of his rugby prowess. 'I played for Sale and was capped for Ireland,' he beamed. I thought, why the hell is he talking about rugby? Surely it was a tactic of some sort, to make the jury think he was a fine, upstanding member of the community. I looked at their faces, a mix of men and women of all ages. All seemed to be listening intently and taking in everything he said.

Paterson began to talk about his children, and how happily married he was (he later divorced, but at the time of the trial he was living with his wife in a barn conversion in Cheshire), painting a picture of an eminent surgeon and all-round devoted family man. He described his move from Good Hope Hospital to Solihull hospital in 1998, conveniently leaving out the fact that he had been suspended for almost killing Gill Dallow and trying to cover it up. Why isn't the prosecution questioning him about why he moved, I thought? Why were his claims about how great he was going unchallenged?

And then he started to explain how he dealt with cancer patients. He said that he would use a 'shades of grey' scale when explaining their results, where white was benign and black was cancer. 'Between these two extremes there are shades of grey and everyone can get that. It's a very straightforward thing that's not patronising but easy to understand,' he said.

In the statement read by prosecutor Nick Barraclough, he said: 'He has never pressured any patient to undergo surgery.

He gave patients time to make their decision. All surgical procedures taken by him were appropriate and necessary and he denied any allegations of unnecessary surgery or bad faith.'

He never pressured anybody into surgery? I was fuming. He put the fear of God into me, called me back two days later to tell me my results were back from the lab and that I had cancer, but he could cure me if I had the operation. That wasn't pressure? Or how about the single mum that he told would orphan her son? Or the many, many women I had spoken to who all had similar stories, including those who never had cancer while he looked them in the eye and told them they did. I was terrified the jury would just believe what he was saying, this confident, charming man who had fooled so many of us when we were under his care.

During a break I went outside and called Bob in a panic. 'He's going to get away with it,' I cried. Bob reassured me that the trial was only just beginning, and I gathered myself to go back inside. As I took my seat, a woman in the row in front of me turned to me and said, 'Are you one of Paterson's victims?'

'Yes,' I said. She handed me a business card.

'Anne Delaney, BBC.' She asked about my story and I told her everything. She would become a great ally.

During the afternoon break, I introduced myself to two women who were sitting nearby and asked them if they too were Paterson patients.

'I'm not,' said one, 'but Jane is.' She indicated her friend and we said hello. Jane is ten years younger than me, with blonde hair and a vaguely familiar face.

'I think I know you,' I said. 'Where are you from?'

She told me the name of the council estate where she grew up and the name of her parents. I knew them, and laughed delightedly. It was such a lovely moment of nostalgia and coincidence, the last place I had expected to find a connection that was nothing to do with Paterson. I told her my maiden name. 'Patty and John Maher's daughter!' she said. 'I remember your mum, you're so much like her.' The courtroom melted away as I thought of our mums and dads as young parents, us kids playing out on the streets of Birmingham. In that moment, Jane Smith and I became friends. She told me her story.

After finding a breast lump, Jane wanted to go private and had been referred to Paterson at Spire. She never saw her pathology results, but he told her the lump was cancerous and he needed to remove it. A week later, she woke up from the operation and saw with horror that instead of a small incision for a lumpectomy, Paterson had removed half her breast. A large incision ran into her armpit. She went from a 36FF cup to a 34B.

Paterson wrote to her GP saying she had cancer. At a follow-up appointment he said she was very lucky. She had had a grade two oestrogen-positive cancer, but he'd removed it and she was curable; she just needed to go on tamoxifen. She never had cancer. In September 2012, she was recalled by Spire and told her notes had been falsified. Paterson had claimed he had performed a fine needle aspiration, when he had not.

Jane and I travelled to Nottingham together the next morning, chatting about how our parents had been friends. Our dads even grew up together in the same part of Dublin. Then we talked about Paterson. We both admitted to some dark feelings at times. I'd heard from other victims and family members about their rage and sadness, how they wanted Paterson to suffer like they had. The thought of him being found not guilty, becoming free to go back to his privileged life and perhaps even his surgical practice, filled us with horror.

I saw Bethan Lloyd Owen again as we entered the courtroom. This time she looked more like her old self, in a smart suit, heels and make-up. I ignored her as we took our seats. In front of us was Anne Delaney, who became a regular fixture of the proceedings.

I had a direct eyeline to Paterson who was just a few feet away, directly opposite the jury. At one point during the trial he turned up with a vicar, who sat next to him. I was very surprised that Paterson was able to just wander around among the victims and witnesses. After a lunch break, he was just ahead of us as we left the canteen. He opened the door and held it open for me. I recoiled. There was no way I was going to let him do me even this smallest of favours. I stood there unmoving and stared at him. He stared back, and I thought I saw contempt and arrogance in his eyes. Did he not realise he was the baddie in this scenario? I thought, fuck you, Paterson, I'm not going to look away first. He let go of the door and made his way back to court. I didn't show any fear, but inside my stomach was in turmoil.

Anne Delaney was very friendly straight away and said she felt like she'd known me for years. She would always phone me in the evening to ask how I was feeling and get my thoughts on the trial. We would talk through the court proceedings daily. If I wasn't in court, she'd update me, but I was beginning to be frustrated at how little press coverage there was. It was seen as a Birmingham story rather than a national one with cultural and structural issues that affected every single NHS and private patient. As far as I knew, there had never been a prosecution like this one. I wanted it to be front-page news. But of course, Paterson hadn't been found guilty of anything yet, nor had he been struck off the medical register. It was still possible that it would all come to nothing.

Paterson hadn't shown any signs of mental health unfitness during the trial, presenting himself with confidence and even charm. But on one occasion, he let his mask slip and showed his arrogance. One of his victims, Rosemary Platt, took the stand. As she told the court of 'the butchery she suffered at his hands', he could not control himself.

'Lying bitch,' he muttered.

34

*BREAST SURGEON IAN PATERSON DENIES COURT
VERBAL ABUSE*
*A breast surgeon accused of carrying out unnecessary
operations has denied verbally abusing a witness while she
was giving evidence against him.*

*The prosecution asked Mr Paterson whether he had
called Dr Platt a 'lying bitch' as she took the stand at
Nottingham Crown Court.*

*He replied: 'No. Why would I use language like that
about a patient?*

'I said that I thought she wasn't telling the truth.'

*He also told the court he was not saying the ten alleged
victims were 'liars', rather he believes their memories had
become confused over time.*

The BBC headline was one of several to report his slip of the
tongue, including coverage by *Birmingham Live*, the *Daily Mail*,
Bristol Live and the *Irish Independent*. I was horrified for
Rosemary Platt and all the patients, who were holding up
incredibly well as they faced their abuser. I don't think anyone
expected him to verbally abuse one of them in open court, and
yet at the same time, I wasn't entirely surprised. He couldn't
hold back his true nature for ever. Here was the Paterson who
had contempt for everyone, the aggressive bully who cowed his
colleagues and attacked whistleblowers like Hemant Ingle.

I knew one of the ten victims in the trial personally. Carole
Johnson was a publican who ran a pub around the corner from
where I had lived in Birmingham. I worked for her as a barmaid
when my children were young. I couldn't believe it when I saw
her photo in the papers a couple of years before the trial took
place. It was such a shock to see that she, too, was a victim of

Ian Paterson. I had called her at the time to say how sorry I was to read what had happened to her. She told me how she never doubted anything he said and totally trusted him. To her, he was 'God'.

She first had problems with her breasts in 1998 and was referred to Paterson privately, as she had health insurance provided by her employer. By 2002, she had undergone a series of radiological tests, none of which had revealed any suspicious masses. However, despite this, Paterson wrote to her GP suggesting that there was a solid lump which looked like a fibroadenoma in her right breast. Although a fibroadenoma is a benign condition, he falsely described this to her GP as being a 'dangerous and difficult diagnosis in a lady of this age', advising her to have the lump removed.

Paterson carried out an excision biopsy in 2002, and two further operations in 2004 and 2005 with Spire. Her health insurers queried the need for so much treatment, and Paterson wrote to them claiming the latest histology showed premalignant potential in her breast. The insurers declined to fund any further treatment.

Carole trusted Paterson completely, and she decided to pay for her treatment herself. In 2006, she found a lump on her left breast, but an ultrasound scan showed nothing suspicious. Paterson wrote to her GP claiming the scan showed 'a rather worrying ridge of differing echo texture', advising the removal of the lump. Carole believed him, and paid for the operation the same year. In 2007, he carried out a sixth excision biopsy that also wasn't justified by the scan. All six operations were carried out under general anaesthetic.

Carole told me that she had received a letter from Spire Parkway recalling her for a consultation to discuss her treatment after Paterson was suspended. She was seen by Hemant Ingle, and a police officer was in the room with him. Ingle asked if she understood why Paterson had operated on her so many times. 'Because I had cancerous lumps in my breasts,' she replied.

Ingle gently explained that she never had cancer and she was one of Paterson's patients who had been operated on unnecessarily. She told me she just kept saying, 'No, I did have cancer, he told me.' She was so stunned she couldn't take the truth in. She had lived for years full of fear and anguish, and now she was hearing it was all for nothing. I knew Carole to be a strong and fiercely independent woman, able to handle the pressures of running a pub, standing up to unruly customers and everything that entails. But Paterson had a devastating effect on her. She didn't think she'd be able to give evidence, but with the support of her husband Barry and her family she eventually decided to take the stand and testify against him.

The prosecution alleged that over a fourteen-year period, Paterson deliberately misrepresented medical results, exaggerated cancer risks, kept patients' names absent from multidisciplinary team meetings and lied to victims, their GPs and to his own colleagues about diagnoses. As the ten brave victims and their families gave testimony alongside three experts, I began to feel more confident about the case.

Paterson's defence tried to claim that the erroneous information could have been an unknowing error, or communication problem. Paterson tried to challenge witnesses' recollections of what they had been told, tried to suggest that they were lying or had been coached into what to say. He did not call any experts to his defence.

But his misrepresentation of test results was surely too consistent to be simple error or coincidence. There were major disparities between the risk of cancer that Paterson claimed and the indication of radiological and histological reports. The same pattern came up over and over. I prayed that the jury had understood all the evidence and could see what was, to me, as plain as day.

May Bank Holiday was coming up, and the trial was coming to an end. I was about to break up from work and had booked off a few extra days. My colleagues tried to persuade me to go away for a short break to get my mind off things, but I couldn't do it. The stress was tremendous, and I had no respite from it, but now was not the time to look away. I was terrified the jury hadn't understood the case. At one point late in the trial, on a day I couldn't attend, Anne Delaney had called to tell me the jurors had asked the court to explain again what a cleavage-sparing mastectomy is. I was glad they were being thorough, but I couldn't help imagine the worst-case scenario, that Paterson would successfully hide behind complex medical details.

Jane and I decided to stay overnight in Nottingham on Thursday 25 May. The trial would have to finish on Friday 26 May or be postponed until the following Tuesday, due to the Bank Holiday. The prospect of more delays was agonising. One of the jurors had booked a weekend away for her boyfriend's thirtieth birthday, but the judge refused her request for leave, saying the victims had waited long enough for a verdict.

We had booked a local hotel within walking distance of the court. We were both on edge not knowing if the verdict would be announced and if it was, would they find him guilty? Our conversation was consumed by the fact that he *had* to be found guilty. We discussed the jurors, did they look like they understood all the medical jargon and would they be taken in by Paterson's version of events and his shades of grey analogy to describe a scale of cancer? We didn't stop talking all night, firstly about Paterson and then about our families. How we'd both lost parents to cancer, how my dad was at her parents' wedding and what they would think of us now fighting together against the harm that Paterson had inflicted on us and hundreds of his patients. We were made of the same stern stuff, growing up on the same tough estate, both taught to fight for what was right.

I spoke about how I limped about in the morning when I was on tamoxifen for my oestrogen-receptive cancer and how it affected my joints. Jane told me Paterson had prescribed tamoxifen when she didn't have cancer at all, which caused her permanent bone damage. She had to wear a mouthguard as she would grind her teeth during the night. We got a fit of the giggles and then hysterics when she put it in. If we didn't laugh we'd have had to cry instead.

The following day we were both running on adrenaline. We went to court early as we decided we'd eat breakfast in the court canteen. We were deciding on what to order when Paterson and his daughter walked in and sat down a few feet away from us behind a Perspex divider that was on their table. We were both fuming. It felt like he had been afforded every luxury in court, going in and out through a side entrance so journalists couldn't get to him. I joked to Jane, shall I accidentally walk over and spill my hot coffee in his lap? I kept looking over to see him hunched forward to speak to his daughter. We walked down to the courtroom to take our seats and wait for the jury to be called in.

I sat in my usual position, which was on the left-hand side of the court facing the jury, with Paterson sitting at a desk with his daughter near the middle of the courtroom.

After the morning's proceedings, the judge told the jury he would take a majority verdict. He sent the jury away and the court broke for lunch. Jane and I walked to the local pub to get some air. It was very busy, but we managed to find a table. I went to the bar to order a couple of sandwiches and soft drinks. I had to wait for my order to be taken, and when I got back to the table I pulled my phone out of my bag. I had several missed calls. I checked my messages. Anne Delaney had texted me: 'The jury's back.' In a panic I shouted, 'The jury's back! Oh my God, we can't miss the verdict now after all this.' We grabbed our coats and bags and ran out of the pub as fast as two middle-aged women with health issues could. We got to the court puffing and sweating. Jane shouted, 'Let us through! We've got to get into the courtroom!'

'I'm sorry, ladies, you have to go through security,' said the guard. We threw our bags onto the conveyor belt and walked as fast as we could through the metal detector. Thankfully it didn't beep.

As soon as we'd cleared security, we ran down the corridors to the courtroom. The doors were shut, but we burst through them with a bang, like a dramatic scene from a TV show. The courtroom was packed and we frantically looked around for a seat. I heard Anne whisper my name, and gratefully sat down beside her, Jane behind us.

We had made it just in time. My heart was beating incredibly fast as the judge was passing the verdicts on a piece of paper to the clerk of the court

The rest of the room disappeared. I could barely breathe from the mad dash and the extreme stress of the moment. Paterson was right in front of me, level with my eyeline. I fixed my eyes on him as the clerk asked the foreman of the jury to give the verdicts. The clerk said in a loud voice:

'On count one, wounding with intent, guilty.'

On count two, guilty.

On count three, guilty.

Guilty, guilty, guilty. On all twenty counts.

35

'Debbie.'

I heard someone say my name, but I was rooted to the spot.

'Debbie!' It was Anne. The court was clearing. 'We have to leave.'

I turned to her and she said, 'I thought you were going to jump over the seats and go for him.' I had been staring so intently. I looked over to where the police officers were sitting. One of them was crying. They were comforting each other. I could see how much it meant to them to get a guilty verdict. They had heard the personal testimonies of over 200 people throughout the investigation. It wasn't a moment of celebration but of relief.

I composed myself and gathered my belongings. We left the court and I looked around for Jane. We hugged with palpable relief. 'We've got to get out of here,' I said. We headed for an empty corner of the building and I phoned Bob.

'Guilty!' I shouted.

Bob started cheering, then said, 'Yes! The bastard got what he deserves.' I couldn't talk for long because I had to address the press, who were waiting outside. Jane and I walked down the stairs and saw Lesley Cuthbert, another Paterson patient who had been in court to hear the verdict. She was shaking and in tears. I put my arms around her and said, 'It'll be alright.'

As we got outside, my solicitor, Linda Millband, walked over and asked if I was ready to speak to the press. I felt faint. I hadn't eaten or drunk anything, my abandoned lunch long in the past. Linda ran to get me a bottle of water, and I readied myself for the assembled journalists and cameras, who had been organised into a group by Anne. I took my place in front of them on the courthouse steps.

The first person to give a statement was Detective Chief Inspector Caroline Marsh, who thanked the victims on behalf of West Midlands Police and the Crown Prosecution Service.

'We really hope that today's verdict will help victims move on with their lives and start to recover from what happened to them. We can see that Mr Paterson hasn't shown any remorse for the terrible things he's done, and he's really damaged the trust that the public have in the health service and in our health professionals. We really hope we will never see a case like this again. The man has shown no remorse.'

She talked about not being able to adequately describe someone who has done such awful things and mentioned the 240 patients who had given statements.

'There has been lots of speculation into why he has done what he's done. That includes financial gain. Some of the victims said he wanted to play God with their lives or he got some satisfaction out of giving them bad news then making them better. We really don't know. It's a fact that when you go to your doctor you go there with the belief that they will treat you as best they can and you absolutely trust what they are doing and who they recommend to you. This has caused huge damage to the trust that the public have with the health service and their health professionals and it's going to take a long time to repair.'

She ended by saying that over the four years of investigation, Paterson was the only person they felt was appropriate to bring to trial and they would not be pursuing anybody else. The last bit of the statement didn't sink in until I watched the news coverage later. I was disappointed, as I was certain from all the evidence so far that others were complicit.

And then it was my turn. I had never faced such a large group of press before. By now I was used to being in the papers or on the news, but this was a responsibility on a whole other scale. I was thinking about the patients who continued to suffer because of Paterson, and of those who had died. My friend Michelle Frances, another Paterson patient, had called me a few days before the trial, as she wanted my help to get a hospital bed delivered to her house. She was nearing the end of her life and probably knew she wouldn't be around for the verdict I vowed we would get justice and she told me to fight on, he's got to be found guilty. Michelle sadly died on the 27 March 2017, a few weeks before the guilty verdict. One of the last messages she sent to me was about Jen being diagnosed and me going part-time at work in the new year. She said, 'Do it and enjoy life, don't waste a minute.'

I stepped forward to face the press, full of emotion. A journalist asked, 'How do you feel?'

I hadn't prepared a speech, but I'd been thinking about this guilty verdict for five years. I heard myself speak. 'Just so relieved that justice had finally been served. It's been a really traumatic, hard journey not just for the victims but for our families.'

'Did you have faith in him?'

'Utter faith in him.' My voice started to crack and tears filled my eyes. Somehow I got through it.

'I told everyone I was lucky to have the best consultant. I told everyone that I was lucky to be in Spire and BUPA and have private medicine so that I could get in straight away and get treated, and then all those years down the line I find all of that's been betrayed and I've been left physically damaged. I feel like I've been mutilated. All the scars I thought were there because they were a badge of honour, for nothing.

'I am angry that we've waited so long. This has not only physically damaged patients, it's mentally damaged patients. I know ladies that phone me every night and say they can't sleep, they just pray that justice is served because they can't go outside their own house. They've had years of mental anguish, so thank God justice has been done. We had to fight for this. I've had to fight for information in my own case. Lots of things were hidden. So thank God for these brave people who spoke up in court and got the right verdict.

'He's never admitted it. I still hold him in contempt; he has never given anyone any peace.

'I did have cancer, but I didn't have the operation that I needed. I should have just had a wide local excision, but I had a full mastectomy and I had chemotherapy that I didn't need.

'To me it was a money-making machine, but he did have some kind of almost God complex where he tells you he's cured you, you're cured now. I know consultants don't say "you're cured", it's not a term they use in general, but he used to use that term and I used to walk out thinking, he's brilliant, he's actually cured me. Other patients I know got secondaries because he left breast tissue.'

I spoke about those who had died, quoting the late Shena Mason as I addressed the cameras. 'As a friend of ours once said, "some of us will always have rotten bad luck and carry on and the disease will develop, that is going to happen, but rotten bad luck is easier to live with than the thought that your surgeon may have damaged you … You have this gnawing suspicion that maybe if you had woken up with a nice flat chest wall the day after the operation, maybe you would be feeling well now, but I'm never going to know". I remember all those ladies because I knew a lot of them personally. It's been a really really traumatic, hard journey for our families and not just the victims. And for the ladies that are no longer with us, I'd like to say thank you to the jury, they got the right verdict.'

I spoke for several minutes, adding my thoughts about the cover-up and missed opportunities, then stepped back, my eyes full of tears and my voice cracking.

Linda Millband followed, saying Thompsons had acted for approximately 350 women who were victims of Paterson in the private sector,

'There are an enormous number of people who have suffered through having an incorrect diagnosis and have had totally erroneous treatment and others that have been overtreated.

'Our case is not only against Mr Paterson, it is against Spire hospitals and the Heart of England Foundation Trust, and our allegations are that neither of the hospital authorities took the necessary steps to protect our clients.

'We've never had a case where the recall has gone into hundreds, and there may still be victims out there who have not come forward.'

As the journalists dispersed I went over to Jane to hug her, and the tears I'd been trying to hold back came flooding out.

The same afternoon we were called back in by the judge to hear the bail hearing. I was exhausted as I took my seat. The judge noted Paterson's mental health had improved and didn't feel he was at risk of harming himself or that there was a flight risk but said that his passport would be withheld. And that was that. It was over, for now. He was out on bail, and we didn't yet have a sentencing date. Paterson was once again let out of the building through a side entrance to avoid the press. Anne had asked if I'd stick around for a live BBC piece outside the court for the *Six O'Clock News,* so Jane and I popped to a local cafe for a sandwich and cup of tea.

Back outside the court I was feeling cold. It had been a long day. I was fitted with an earpiece and talked through what was going to happen, and then suddenly I was live on BBC News. I was asked again, 'How do you feel about the guilty verdict?' I reiterated that 'I wanted to speak up for those that couldn't because they were no longer with us.' Finally, Jane and I headed to the train station and collapsed into our seats as the train left Nottingham. We were exhausted but elated. My phone kept pinging with messages of congratulations from people who had seen me on TV. I just wanted to get home.

On Saturday my phone didn't stop ringing. Journalists, supporters, Paterson patients. I had work to do, but as soon as I woke up I realised I was ill. I was aching all over, shivering and fluey.

The majority of the national newspapers led with headlines about Paterson. '**Butcher surgeon mutilated "at least 1,000 victims" as he ruined lives with needless ops including mastectomies**', said the *Daily Mirror.* The *Times* headline read, '**Liar betrayed patients who adored him**'. The *Daily Mail Online* read, '**Breast surgeon with a "God complex" is found GUILTY of wounding patients with "completely unnecessary" operations – as it's revealed there could be a THOUSAND other victims**', while the front page of the printed *Daily Mail* newspaper exclaimed, '**Why did NHS fail to stop butcher surgeon?**'. The *Daily Express* went with '**EVIL cancer doctor played God, "could've wounded thousands" with UNNECESSARY operations**', while *The Telegraph* led with '**"Cover-up" let rogue surgeon play God**', and '**The NHS must cut the risk of another Ian Paterson**'.

I was following the coverage online while juggling media appearances and interviews. It was incredible to me that finally this was national front-page news, even though that only lasted a few days. I was invited onto the *Victoria Derbyshire* show the following Tuesday at the Birmingham BBC studios. I took a couple of paracetamol and somehow got through the radio interview, then went home and straight to bed and stayed there for days. I couldn't eat, could barely function. Eventually, I went back to work, but my mind wasn't on my job. Paterson was out on bail, living with his wife in Cheshire. He was approached by the ITV journalist Stacey Foster with a camera crew while he was walking his dog. She asked him, 'What happened, what went wrong? Have you got anything to say to your former patients?' A weird grin came across his face, but he ignored her as she questioned him, got into his car and drove off. But the next time he walked his dog, he was wearing a T-shirt that had emblazoned across it 'I'm a little ray of sunshine'. He knew he would be photographed wearing it, and he knew that it would wind up his victims. He couldn't care less about us, and he was arrogant in his defiance.

36

'Ian Stuart Paterson, you are fifty-nine years of age and are to be sentenced for seventeen counts of Wounding with Intent, contrary to section 18 of the Offences Against the Person Act 1861, together with three counts of Unlawful Wounding.'

It was 31 May 2017. My son Robert was working in Taiwan and Bob and I had booked a holiday to visit him for a few weeks. Paterson was out on bail following the trial, and we hadn't known how long it would take before he was recalled for sentencing. I had really wanted to be there, but the date wasn't announced until weeks after the trial. I'd have had to put my life and plans on hold, and frankly I'd done enough of that. Paterson had been found guilty, that was the main thing.

I wasn't the only one on holiday. While on bail, Paterson's passport had been confiscated to ensure he couldn't flee the country, but he took advantage of his last bit of freedom to visit Northern Ireland. I thought that was stretching his bail conditions too far.

I enjoyed Taiwan as much as I could, but as the day of sentencing approached I was on edge. I'd had problems sleeping for several years, and even the change of scenery couldn't fix that. We walked around the town where Rob lived with his fiancée, Mary, then headed back to his apartment. I apologised for taking up their time but I couldn't now miss the sentencing. We sat huddled around the TV as Rob found BBC Ceefax. As I waited for the news to refresh I was texting with Jane Smith, who said she was at the court but the situation there was difficult. Some patients and their families were left outside as the courtroom was too full.

Jane was faster than Ceefax. She messaged with the news. Ian Paterson had been sentenced to fifteen years in jail. She said she was 'gutted' that it was not longer. He'd be out in half that time. A second later the news was confirmed via Ceefax. I had mixed feelings. I agreed that fifteen years wasn't long enough, but I'd been expecting less. He would be locked away. The harm done to his victims was finally acknowledged by the justice system, and for that I felt a great sense of relief.

We arrived home a few days later. I caught up with the news properly and listened to John Ingram – the only male victim – give his victim impact statement. He had been told the lump in his breast was 'pre-cancerous', Paterson's usual words. 'He drew a diagram with one end which said "not cancer", then "cancer", and drew me part-way along the line. He said the line only went in one direction, towards cancer.'

John already had a phobia of surgery, but Paterson gave him no other choice. His mother had died of cancer, and he was terrified of the same fate, so he went ahead. The first attempt ended in a panic attack, so was rescheduled. Eventually he had the surgery, needing sedation to get him into the operating room, but a few months later Paterson told him he needed a double mastectomy. He trusted Paterson completely, so agreed.

John never had cancer, pre-cancer, or any sort of dangerous condition. His test results had actually shown he had gynaecomastia, a benign condition where the body creates excess breast tissue. Paterson knew this the whole time, and he had simply lied.

John still lives with the physical and psychological pain of the surgery, but he and the other victims demonstrated the most extraordinary courage in taking the stand at the trial. His speech after the sentencing was powerful: 'Today Ian Paterson has been convicted of what was called in court "dark and grotesque crimes". He used his position, his obvious charm and charisma to lure patients into a system where he was able to drug and operate and remove body parts from patients, whom he had convinced had cancer or were on their way to cancer.'

He described how Paterson had sat in the dock 'shaking his head in disbelief as if he was the victim'.

I was to meet John virtually during lockdown and in person after lockdown. John is a trained psychologist, and we bonded over trying to understand the psychology and personality traits of Paterson and people like him. We can't know for sure what motivated Paterson, but as John said in his victim statement: 'Throughout the trial he has made no attempt to show any remorse for his actions and may be revealing his true character rather than the charming professional man we all thought he was.'

I had been sent a copy of the judge's sentencing remarks. I read Mr Justice Jeremy Baker's summary of each of the ten patients one by one, in which he describes how Paterson had inflicted untold horrors and anxiety on all of them. It didn't matter whether they were sixteen or sixty, he would prey on their worst fears of having cancer and their desire to do whatever it took to save their own lives. So much of it was familiar to me, even though I had had cancer and they had not. It was there in black and white, proven in court and punished with fifteen years in prison. The judge said:

'*You deliberately exaggerated the risk that the patient would develop cancer and advised either the necessity of undergoing continued surveillance of their symptoms at further consultations, or, on some occasions, the undertaking of various surgical procedures. The reality was that, unbeknown to the patients, there was little, if any, need for continued surveillance, and none of the surgical procedures, which are the subject matter of these offences, was necessary to maintain their health.*

'*All of them have suffered the pain and discomfort associated with surgery, whilst some have suffered the debilitating longer-term effects of complications arising from the unnecessary procedures; especially those who have undergone mastectomies with immediate subcutaneous reconstruction.*

'*All of them have been left feeling violated and vulnerable, whilst some have suffered prolonged psychological conditions, including post-traumatic stress disorder, anxiety and depression, which has required professional intervention and treatment.*

'*All of them have been left with physical scarring to their bodies, and those who underwent mastectomies have had their breast tissue removed. The one man who was affected by this type of procedure has spoken eloquently of the effect that this procedure has had upon him, and it is probably difficult to overstate its psychological effect upon the women to whom it took place, which is best encapsulated by one of the victims, who puts it in these terms, "Now and probably for the rest of my life, when I look in the mirror I see a victim of Paterson, who took away part of being a woman".*'

He called Paterson charming and charismatic to those who support him, the very characteristics he 'deliberately misused in this case, both to manipulate your patients into believing what you were advising them, and in your evidence at trial, when you sought to persuade the jury about the righteousness of your position. Unfortunately, I am also satisfied that there is a less attractive side to your character, and that is one of arrogance, which not only may have misled you into believing that you were untouchable, and that no one would dare to question your authority, as somewhat belatedly has now occurred, but has contributed to the complete lack of remorse which you have shown for your offending throughout these proceedings.'

The sentencing remarks are available online. They are lengthy but incredibly powerful, and I encourage everyone to read them in full.

I was relieved, emotional. I could finally breathe again knowing the judge saw him as we did. I felt vindicated. But I was becoming concerned that his sentence was too light compared to other criminals convicted of multiple serious violent crimes. I wondered if his former position as a highly educated surgeon, a golf-playing member of the elite classes was a factor. Mr Justice Baker had considered the character evidence which showed that Paterson did 'a good deal of charity work', but much of that charity work was with Breast Friends, from where he recruited many of his patients for needless operations and benefitted from our fundraising for equipment for his department. It was self-serving.

On 7 July 2017, I got a text from one of the victims in the trial to say that the police had called her that morning. The Crown Prosecution Service was trying to get the sentence increased.

Solicitor General Robert Buckland had referred the case to the appeals court, arguing that the sentence was unduly lenient for offences that are so serious and exceptional that a jail term significantly higher than fifteen years was required. It should merit a sentence of at least twenty years. He said the surgeon's crimes had 'caused a very high degree of physical and psychological harm to vulnerable patients'.

I had been introduced by Anne Delaney to a freelance journalist, Richard Vernalls, who was following the events. I phoned to tell him that Paterson was going back to court. He wanted to cover the story. He suggested he come to my house to record me and Jane Smith watching the judges' ruling as it was announced live on TV. On 3 August, Paterson attended the Court of Appeal from prison, via video link. There were three judges, led by Lady Justice Hallett, the first woman to chair the Bar Council and the leader of the inquiry into the 7/7 London bombings. She told Paterson his crimes were 'brutal and sustained', that his victims had been 'left feeling violated and vulnerable' and that they had 'lost their trust in others, particularly some in the medical profession.'

Paterson's solicitor, Nicholas Johnson KC, said Paterson had to be kept in isolation in prison because he was a 'marked man'. I had heard from a source that he had been briefly sent to a Birmingham prison, clearly a dangerous decision given how many women in the area had been affected by him. He was quickly relocated back to HMP Nottingham, where he had started.

Jane and I sat on the sofa as a cameraman set up. I always get nervous before being filmed and said as a joke 'Debbie Douglas, News at Ten', which started me and Jane laughing. 'The ruling is coming up,' said Richard and I tensed up again, all jokes forgotten.

The judge was on the TV in front of us as we heard the words, 'Ian Paterson you had been sentenced to fifteen years in jail. That's now been increased to twenty years.' We gave a loud cheer and hugged each other. Yes! I was so relieved. I later watched the footage on BBC News. On camera I said that it sends the right message. The patients have all got life sentences, and twenty years means he wouldn't be out in just a few years. The fight wasn't over by any means – there was still the matter of compensation, of systemic change to ensure this never happened again, and a proper examination into who knew what and when. But Paterson would be behind bars for at least half of his sentence, and that was something to be grateful for.

37

Given Paterson would not allow for any suggestion of wrong-doing, despite obvious and overwhelming evidence of his lies and malpractice, it wasn't entirely surprising that he would attempt to appeal his conviction.

In August 2021, a few years after his conviction, West Midlands Police emailed to say Paterson was granted leave to appeal. I got a text message from one of the witnesses at the court trial. She was devastated. I spoke to her at length on the phone, she was petrified at the thought that she might have to face him again in court. I called DS Dale Robertson, who told me that Paterson would be appealing on the claim that the judge did not direct the jury properly and that the usual timescale of twenty-eight days post-sentencing should not apply to him. He asked for an extension to this date due to him changing his legal representation.

My legal contacts assured me this new attempt was a very long shot. In fact, there is even provision for a financial penalty if an appeal bid is considered frivolous. Whatever the outcome, it would be at least a year before his application was heard, due to a backlog in the courts. By now I was used to doing the rounds of press interviews whenever Paterson was in the news. I was quoted in the *Independent* and elsewhere as saying, 'I can't believe he has a hope in hell. It is him trying to get back control; he is playing games and it can't be a coincidence that this is coming in the middle of the recall and inquests being held by the coroner.'

I got another text from a Paterson victim saying, 'You're the only person I can really ask about this. I'm having awful night-mares again, I'm getting no sleep at all. I won't go into graphic detail but I'm dreaming he is in prison nearby and he could get out. I don't suppose you know where he is?' She had contacted

Victim Support and been told they weren't allowed to disclose his location. I knew he was in solitary confinement at HMP Nottingham for his own safety, as he believed his food was being spat in and he was at risk of attack following his experience in a Birmingham prison. I later learned he had been moved on from HMP Nottingham to HMP Long Lartin, in Worcestershire, the Category A prison that had been home to some of Britain's most notorious offenders, including Charlie Kray, Ian Watkins and Jeremy Bamber. It had been the scene of multiple inmate riots, too. A report found that many prisoners were living in 'squalid' conditions, with some cells infested with rats. The prison holds over 500 men, and some of them had to use buckets for toilets. Violence and drug use was very high, training and education was substandard, and prisoners were locked in their cells for too long. I couldn't help but imagine Paterson living in those conditions.

On 23 November 2021, my late mother's birthday, Paterson was given leave to appeal in the Court of Appeal in London. There had been no warning this time from the police, but I was on HM Courts and Tribunals' mailing list and happened to search the appeals. There it was, Ian Stuart Paterson, leave to appeal. I called DS Dale Robertson to ask if he knew about it; he said he hadn't been informed.

As Paterson was appearing via video link, I dialed in via the court phone system.

His grounds for leave to appeal against all his convictions were that 'the judge's directions to the jury were wrong in law. It is submitted that the common law has decided that a doctor does not commit assault wherein either the surgery is necessary or where there is consent, or both.'

I was called by ITV reporter Alison Mackenzie, who was covering the appeal via Zoom and who told me, 'He's appealing on the grounds that patients consented to those procedures.'

I was furious. 'I consented based on the lies he told me, as did everyone else he harmed. It was not proper informed consent,'

I said. He seemed to be arguing that it is the right of a surgeon and not a criminal offence to carry out any procedures, operations and treatment he wanted on a patient whether their condition warranted it or not. His lawyer talked of a man with an unblemished record, which of course was untrue, as there had been questions dating all the way back to the beginning of Paterson's career and the near-death of Gill Dallow. I saw a criminal. The victims in the trial saw a criminal. The jury and the trial judge saw a criminal, a man who had lied, deceived and manipulated patients at their most vulnerable. The sentence appeal judges saw the same. A man so arrogant, so evil, that he has never once admitted guilt for the harm he caused and the behaviour that led to 'the unnatural deaths' of hundreds of patients now being investigated by the Birmingham Coroner.

I'm pleased to say his appeal was thrown straight out. I was elated at the thought of it being over. I couldn't see any reason the appeal had been allowed in the first place, given there was absolutely no new evidence. He had employed a top lawyer, and that night he would know he was staying in prison. I called one of his victims straight away; she had been so terrified he would get out of prison. She said, 'Thank you so much for letting me know. I'm opening a bottle of champagne to celebrate.'

One of the questions I'm asked most often is why Paterson wasn't pursued for proceeds of crime. This is where assets are recovered if they have been deemed to be the result of criminal activity. Paterson got wealthy from selling operations and treatment in the private sector that were not necessary, so why couldn't that money be recovered?

In 2019, I had contacted DS Dale Robertson to ask why the police were not going after Paterson's assets. The simple answer was that it would not be cost-effective for the Crown Prosecution Service to pursue fraud charges alongside the Wounding with Intent. As only ten patient cases were being prosecuted, only the profits from those cases would be recoverable by police, and that wasn't worth doing. In any case, any money recovered would most likely be awarded to insurance companies to compensate them for their financial loss, rather than to victims.

The other issue was that there is in essence a 'statute of limitations' on proceeds of crime. Because Paterson's malpractice dates back to as far as 1997, it was simply too late to pursue.

However, it was possible for the solicitors representing the victims to pursue Paterson's assets under a civil restraint order. Both Thompsons and the firm Slater and Gordon had thousands of Paterson victims on their books, but it would have cost them too much money to do it with no benefit for them.

Six houses, a cellar full of vintage wine, cars and bank balances do not simply disappear. But there is no appetite by authorities to pursue it and, by now, no legal mandate.

38

There had so far been two formal investigations into the wrongdoing of Ian Paterson. The Kennedy Report in 2013, which looked at the NHS and HEFT specifically, and the Verita Report, which reviewed his activity in the private sector at Spire. After Kennedy, the then Conservative MP Caroline Spelman had called for an inquiry, but nothing happened. I didn't see any significant progress in changing the culture and systems that had allowed Paterson to thrive, which meant it could easily happen again. It needed intervention at the highest level.

Government inquiries are a mixed bag. Since 1997 there have been at any one time at least five on the go at once (at time of writing there are no fewer than twenty). They're governed by a standard set of rules, and initiated by a government minister who chooses a chairperson who then appoints a whole team of people. The chairperson is most often a judge or former judge, but it can also be someone of professional standing who has a high level of trust from the public (ironically, this includes doctors).

There have been many medical inquiries, some more famous than others, including the 2013 Francis Inquiry into failings at Mid Staffordshire NHS Trust, led by Sir Robert Francis KC, a senior barrister specialising in medical law. This inquiry is important to the history of British medicine because it led to significant reforms and the founding of Freedom to Speak Up, an initiative intended to help whistleblowers (although I have spoken to a great many medical workers over the years and I am unclear that anything has actually changed in regards to their protections or treatment when speaking up).

The most famous inquiry in healthcare is perhaps the Shipman Inquiry, which took place between 2000 and 2005, and produced five reports. Harold Shipman was a GP who was found guilty of murdering fifteen patients, and had likely killed hundreds more. The Shipman Inquiry was chaired by Dame Janet Smith, a former judge, with medical advice from Professor Aneez Esmail. Smith also chaired the review into Jimmy Savile's actions at the BBC, one of many inquiries into Savile's offending. Several more were led by the Department of Health, who looked into Savile's abuses at thirty-two hospitals, where he had been given unsupervised access to vulnerable patients.

After Paterson's sentencing in May 2017, I began to fight for a public inquiry in earnest. There are two types of inquiry: non-statutory (in other words, no one can be compelled to give evidence or talk to investigators), and a statutory one, where witnesses are legally compelled to talk. Obviously, I wanted the latter, not trusting that the truth would come out otherwise, and the recommendations from non-statutory inquiries didn't always have the required impact. I started an online petition addressed to the Health Secretary at the time, Jeremy Hunt, which attracted some press coverage.

I also began emailing Hunt to demand an inquiry, as did other affected patients, including my friend Jane Smith.

He couldn't keep ignoring us, especially as the press were involved.

Shortly after, I received a letter inviting me to a round table meeting with Philip Dunne, the then Minister of State for the Department of Health, to discuss Paterson and my request for an inquiry. At last, I felt things were moving forward. I called Jane to see if she had her invite – she had! I immediately alerted my press contacts to ensure there would be coverage on the day.

On 5 October 2017, Jane and I boarded a packed train from Birmingham to London together, both feeling nervous but excited. I was in no mood for messing, so when I saw a young man in the seat I'd booked I abruptly told him he needed to move. Jane joked that I gave him my best 'Pat Butcher look'. Damn right.

I had alerted Stacey Foster, who agreed to meet us at Whitehall, where she was waiting with a camera crew to film us going inside for a piece and an interview with me to be shown on that evening's *ITV Evening News*.

The meeting was held at Richmond House, which was at the time the headquarters of the Department of Health. The facade was impressive; the courtyard frontages with staircase towers like large columns were broken up by long leaded windows of glass. The entrance opened onto Whitehall. It was the most expensive public sector office building in the UK. We entered the heavy oak door to a cramped dark entrance hall with a security desk to the side of us. A security guard gave us all a personal pass to gain entry into the office areas and we were asked to walk through a metal detector as our bags were searched. We sat for a while on wooden chairs waiting to be collected by a young civil servant, who then led us through long corridors and into a lift that took us down a level to more long corridors, where I caught a glimpse of cramped offices stacked full of paper and the odd photocopier. By contrast, Jeremy Hunt's office was a grand, light-filled space. In total, seven patients had been invited. Alongside me and Jane Smith were Alison

Bromfield, Andrea Baker, Sarah Jane Downing, Lesley Watts and Sonya Cerruti, all of us affected by Paterson and all fighting for an inquiry. We made a formidable group. I was hoping Hunt himself would be there, but we were greeted by Philip Dunne and other representatives from the Department of Health: William Vineall, Jennifer Benjamin and Paul Stonebrook from the Quality Patient Safety and Investigations team.

We took our seats around a large oval table. I sat next to Dunne. There was a tea service directly in front of him, and he asked if I would like a cup of tea.

'Yes please,' I said. To my surprise he asked one of the female civil servants to pour. She had to get up and walk around the table to do it. I should have just done it myself, but I wasn't thinking that quickly. Still, it wasn't the best first impression and I remain surprised that he was unable to pour a cup of tea himself. Perhaps that's how things are done in government.

Dunne began by saying, 'you're in Jeremy Hunt's office', perhaps to impress us or to prove he was taking us seriously. But then he said something along the lines of 'Paterson's been brought to justice, you've got your compensation' and I realised he was quite bad at being charming. Paterson being locked up was hardly the end, and nor was the financial settlement. There were still too many unanswered questions and, as far as I could see, no pressure for change particularly in the private sector.

'How did he get away with it for so long? And what has changed to stop this happening again?' I asked.

I explained we were at higher risk of a cancer recurrence and that we needed proper monitoring and follow-up, and that a great many Paterson patients who had had cleavage-sparing mastectomies had died. We each related the harm Paterson had done and how we had all lost trust in the medical profession as a result.

I said we need a statutory public inquiry, to which Dunne replied that they are costly, very slow and not always effective. But he was not ruling out an investigation entirely. He suggested a non-statutory review could be possible. 'The one undertaken in Morecambe Bay was very effective.' This was a reference to a 2015 investigation into neonatal and maternity care failures in several NHS hospitals.

I said, 'But you can't compel people to speak to that sort of inquiry.' The room was very hot. I pressed my point on the need for legal backing, 'How was he allowed to move to Solihull Hospital in 1998 after he'd almost killed a patient at Good Hope? He was under a supervision order, yet he was employed by one of his cronies, the old boys' network.' I thought I saw Philip Dunne stifling a smile when I used that term.

The meeting lasted an hour. I felt quite frustrated and still annoyed at Dunne's comments about compensation and Paterson being in prison, as if he was saying 'job done'. It was far from done for me.

At the end of the meeting Jane stood up and said she felt faint because the heat had got to her. One of the civil servants got her some water and Philip Dunne asked her if she felt all right, and for the first time I saw a glimpse of his caring side.

Outside, Stacey Foster was waiting to interview me for the *ITV Evening News*. I'd got to know Stacey as she had followed the case from the beginning, so the interview went well. I reiterated the need for a public inquiry. The interview finished and some of the assembled press took photos, then Jane and I headed back to Euston Station for a large glass of wine and our train home.

Afterwards, I requested the government notes via email and was sent a summary by Paul Stonebrook, in which he noted those present wanted urgent action for private healthcare patients to have the same levels of safety and protection as NHS patients, and that the industry should be subject to the same regulatory requirements as NHS hospitals. We also wanted better safeguards around consent, particularly as there is a culture of overtreatment in the private sector. We were concerned that only Ian Paterson had been held fully accountable and called for a full public inquiry. Stonebrook's summary also acknowledged our concerns about the length of time it took for Paterson's NHS mastectomy patients to be followed up on, and the need for the follow-up of all breast cancer patients treated by Paterson, not just those who had undergone mastectomy.

I then wrote to Philip Dunne:

Dear Philip,

Thank you for the update to our meeting. I am not happy that you are still talking about a review/investigation and not a public inquiry. I mentioned that we had had two reviews within the NHS, neither of which have brought about any real change.

I received a letter last week from a lady in Surrey who had also been left with breast tissue after a mastectomy and got secondary cancer requiring further surgery. There is also the ongoing case in Stoke of the breast consultant carrying out inappropriate operations. How can the system allow this to happen?

This whole case exposes weaknesses in the system. The Care Quality Commission is not asking the right questions and whistleblowers are still penalised within the NHS.

I fear a cover-up and I will not stop fighting for the truth to come out. There are hundreds of Paterson patients that have died because he left breast tissue and exposed them to secondary cancer. The private sector has washed its hands of Paterson patients and are asking them to go back to the NHS for their ongoing reviews, certainly in my case they made it clear they will not be carrying out any future monitoring, even though within the NHS findings are that patients who were given a mastectomy by Paterson and had an immediate reconstruction are at higher risk of recurrence and should be monitored for fifteen years.

He wrote back immediately to update me and express gratitude that I was able to attend. He said the government 'remained committed to making sure that we have a thorough investigation that looks into the circumstances and practices that have affected so many patients, and that there is every opportunity for patients and their families to take part and contribute'.

It was a nice enough email, but it didn't really reassure me. From data I'd seen, more than half of Paterson's mastectomy patients were dead, and in particular I wanted someone to look into that. I was happy to be a thorn in Dunne's side until something was done.

39

'In October 2011 a group of consultants with practising privileges at Parkway and Little Aston told the hospital's management about new concerns that had come to light since Mr Paterson's exclusion. They alleged that Bethan Lloyd Owen was complicit in the above allegations.'
Verita Report 2014

'I do not believe Ms Lloyd Owen's actions have been satisfactory, safe nor considered the other treatments that could have been undertaken with much less morbidity.

'I believe that [Lloyd Owen] has breached their duty as Clinical Nurse Specialist to provide the evidence of current practice within the UK to the patient at the time she was making the decision and ... unduly influenced her treatment decisions'.
Independent Medical Report of Deborah Douglas 2013

Lloyd Owen's tenure at Spire had not ended well. In October 2011, Ruth Paulin requested she be suspended because of her work with Paterson, pending investigation. In an email she noted 'the distress caused to patients who Mr Paterson had led to believe they had cancer – or were at greater risk of cancer – when they were not. Apart from the unnecessary worry, many would have had increased insurance premiums'. She also noted that the consultants Paulin had met with believed that Lloyd Owen, as a breast care nurse 'should have known what was being done was wrong'.

The resulting tribunal was messy, with Lloyd Owen claiming it was a witch hunt because she had complained about colleagues (Paterson's supporters also made this claim about him). But she had been his closest associate, undertaking an audit for Spire that was 'generally reassuring' about his work. It should have been done by an independent consultant. The later Verita Report, which Lloyd Owen refused to give evidence to, found that her audit 'fails to compare Mr Paterson's practice to other consultants and only includes basic details of the breast care service'. She was the person communicating with the pathology lab, eventually accompanying Paterson to confront a pathology manager who had complained about them. Only she and Paterson had access to pathology reports, due to the breakdown of the MDTs. The pathology manager said she had misrepresented information and was pleased when Paterson moved pathology services to Walsall, because it would mean 'less hassle and abuse from the breast care team'. His allegations against Lloyd Owen included her asking for expensive unnecessary tests on samples. Another colleague described her as Paterson's 'rottweiler'.

Paterson also used her as leverage, telling Spire matron Joy Masters that the company 'could lose Bethan' because of the ongoing complaints by patients and colleagues. And, of course, she was the one falsely communicating with Breast Friends that cleavage-sparing mastectomies were safe and that the allegations against Paterson were untrue, giving her phone number to anyone worried to be reassured by her personally. She failed to pass on the letter to us from West Midlands Cancer Network that contradicted her claims. These latter events, and our extraordinary meeting, were documented as evidence in the Verita Report.

There was no doubt she was dedicated to her career, but she was also dedicated to Paterson, even taking his suggestion to name her dog Gordon 'after her favourite drink'. She started as a chef in Manchester but had always wanted to be a nurse like her parents. She trained at Good Hope Hospital from 1985 and had a commendable early career. She won an award for her work in breast cancer care and used the prize money to attend the Institute of Cancer Research at the Royal Marsden Hospital in London, then eventually earned a degree in cancer nursing in 2001. She founded multiple support groups, eloquently writing in a 2005 Breast Friends newsletter, 'I have always passionately believed that there is an aspect of support that we in the breast care team cannot always provide for our patients; this can only be given by someone who has had breast cancer.' Yet Breast Friends had been used to recruit patients to the private sector, to provide funds for equipment benefitting their department, and to massively advance the reputation of Ian Paterson. This is hard to reconcile.

The report also notes that a patient who had had five operations under Paterson 'told us that she phoned Bethan Lloyd Owen because she was confused about the conflicting information [another doctor] had given her. Ms Lloyd Owen reportedly reassured her about Mr Paterson. Patient B told us that at the time Spire was saying that Mr Paterson was taking a break, and that she asked Ms Lloyd Owen whether he was being investigated about carrying out operations that were not necessary. She said that he was not.'

'Bethan Lloyd Owen is complicit in the above allegations and supporting subtotal mastectomies and that it was not appropriate for her to see patients with concerns,' concludes the Verita Report about those events. In the summary, it says, 'No one we spoke to said they had noticed anything unusual about Mr Paterson's practice at the time. However, several people told us that they thought other people should have known what was happening. There was no consensus on who did know other than Bethan Lloyd Owen, Mr Paterson's closest associate at Parkway and Little Aston.' The Verita Report then states it was unable to find definitive evidence of what she knew.

Lloyd Owen sought an injunction against her suspension and disciplinary hearing on multiple grounds. These included that she had been told she was now the subject of a police investigation, which therefore made it unfair to continue, that further details of the reasons for the disciplinary action were being withheld from her, and that she had been refused the right to legal representation on the grounds that this was not a criminal investigation but an internal disciplinary. She said she had dyslexia, citing 'difficulties with speed of reading; ability to understand information quickly when reading; a difficulty when she was on the spot; a difficulty with spelling; a difficulty with working memory; problems with word-finding when she is under pressure of time, and feelings of lack of self-esteem.' She stated that her dyslexia affected her competency to defend herself. The injunction application was rejected on all counts, with expert evidence from an educational psychologist and the agreement to keep the disability aspect under review.

After her suspension from Spire, Lloyd Owen took a job as a consultant nurse at a private practice in Birmingham.

She must have been under a great deal of stress. On 31 May 2017, a journalist covering Paterson's sentencing live on TV news commented something to the effect that Lloyd Owen was next in line to face justice 'for her crimes'. As Lloyd Owen hadn't been accused of any crimes, she considered this libellous and began legal action. Rather than go to court, the news outlet decided to settle, and Lloyd Owen was paid a five-figure sum.

She had been getting a fair amount of pressure from the media. At one point, I received a message from a member of the Breast Friends committee asking me to stop sending journalists to 'doorstep' Bethan Lloyd Owen, saying she was 'completely exonerated'. Both things were untrue. In no way had she been exonerated – at the time she was still being investigated – and in no way had I sent anyone to her house. I was offended by the accusation. It's common for journalists to approach people outside their home, and some had done so with Ian Paterson and Mark Goldman. As Lloyd Owen was closest to Paterson professionally, it was inevitable the media would want to question her, but I also appreciate it's a deeply unpleasant and invasive experience.

Her entire world had fallen apart. She was potentially facing a criminal inquiry and a medical disciplinary tribunal. Whatever her involvement with Paterson's crimes, unwitting accomplice or conscious collaborator, she stood by him all the way through the investigations and trial, supporting him to the last.

In January 2018, Bethan Lloyd Owen suffered a major stroke and died. She was buried on 7 February 2018.

I heard about Lloyd Owen's death via a friend who was at the hospital at the time. I was babysitting my granddaughter at Jen's house, chatting on the phone with Jane Smith, when I got a text message on my work mobile. It simply said, 'Bethan's dead.' I stared at it for a moment in shock, then exclaimed to Jane, 'Bethan's dead! Bethan's dead! I'll call you back.'

The details were scant, but my friend at the hospital confirmed the news. I phoned some of the committee members and some of the patients I knew as part of the support groups, then tried to work out my thoughts. She was the key to a great many questions that would now never be answered. Her death ended the police investigation and the disciplinary proceedings into her actions which might have provided proof either way. She had known so much, and had had a front row seat to everything. She had had a huge amount of power and was Paterson's second-in-command at Spire, with practically no oversight. Paterson would break the news of cancer to patients, then Lloyd Owen would comfort them, explain the medical procedures and handle the paperwork. They were widely considered a team.

To this day it's difficult to know how to feel about Bethan Lloyd Owen. She should have been my advocate, but she failed me. I recently revisited the Breast Friends newsletter she had written, in which she describes her career and passion for helping breast cancer patients, and I wondered how it had all gone so wrong.

40

On Thursday 7 December 2017, I was on an early shift at work. At 8:30am my mobile rang. It was Paul Stonebrook, the civil servant I had met during the Whitehall visit. He said, 'I'm pleased to announce that the government is to open an inquiry into Ian Paterson. We are phoning the people that took part in the meeting in Whitehall back in October as it's shortly to be announced in Parliament.'

This was incredible news. I asked if it was a public inquiry, where witnesses would be legally compelled to give evidence. 'No, it would be a government-led one,' he told me. Not quite so good, but it had been hard enough to get this much and we'd have to take what was being offered. It would be quicker, but I wasn't sure if that was necessarily a good thing. I asked who would be chairing it, hoping for a senior medic or legal professional.

'The Right Reverend Graham James, Bishop of Norwich.'

Interesting choice. I had never heard of him. 'What qualifications does he have to lead this inquiry?'

Stonebrook said something to the effect that Reverend James was used to speaking to a lot of different people and would have a team to help him that would include medical professionals. I figured that the rationale was about trust, and the government's reasoning was that a bishop was a figure who could bring a high degree of empathy to the proceedings. Or something like that.

I thanked Stonebrook and said I'd be in touch. This was a huge milestone; I had an enormous amount of evidence to present to the inquiry, and I'd need to contact the press to ensure patient voices were represented in any coverage. But first I called Jane Smith, keeping my excitement down because I was in the middle of a busy office. 'We did it, we got the inquiry!' About an hour later Philip Dunne announced details of the inquiry to Parliament. I was still on the clock at work, but I rang round my press contacts with the news and was interviewed for TV, print and radio.

The government issued a press release saying:

> 'The Inquiry follows a pledge by the Health Secretary earlier in the year in which he committed to hold a "comprehensive and focused inquiry". Following this, and Health Minister Philip Dunne's meeting with the victims of Paterson and their families, the initial scope of the investigation has been widened in recognition of their feedback that broader issues about care in the independent sector needed attention. This includes whether any further action is needed to strengthen CQC's inspection regime in relation to the private sector.
>
> 'Philip Dunne, Health Minister, said: "Ian Paterson's malpractice sent shockwaves across the health system due to the seriousness and extent of his crimes, and I am determined to make sure lessons are learnt from this so that it never happens again in the independent sector or the NHS.
>
> '"I believe an independent, Non-Statutory Inquiry, overseen by Bishop Graham James, is the right way forward to ensure that all aspects of this case are brought to light

and lessons learned so we can better protect patients in the future."'

I wanted to believe he was serious about reforming the medical sector, particularly private hospitals, which were increasingly taking NHS funds. But it was equally possible the inquiry would be a whitewash, a way to draw a line under the whole thing. I would need to double down on getting data. My main concern was the apparent lack of investigation into those Paterson patients who had died. Frankly, I didn't trust anyone involved and I needed to do my own investigation and keep up the pressure. I wrote to Kevin Bolger, the chief executive of HEFT, to request the demographic of the patients involved in the recall and patients who had died. I also asked if wide local excision (lumpectomy) patients, and the families of deceased patients had been contacted.

He replied with the age breakdown of Paterson patients, and said that because it had taken so long to write to mastectomy patients, wide local excision patients had been pushed back to the beginning of the New Year. He confirmed my fear that no one was contacting the families of deceased Paterson patients.

I took the age data of deceased patients that Kevin had sent, opened my spreadsheet and dropped it alongside the data for breast cancer survival rates by age that I'd got from Cancer Research UK. I knew I hadn't got the cause of death for the 675 patients and that this was rough-cut data, but it scared the crap out of me. For my age bracket, 51–60 years old, Paterson patients had a 61 per cent chance of survival compared to a 90 per cent chance of survival for non-Paterson patients. The only difference between the data contained in a wider number of breast cancer patients is they were not operated on by Paterson and breast tissue was cleared during their mastectomy operations. The data sent me into a dark place for a few days. I couldn't discuss it with Bob and my family for fear of upsetting them. I would save it for the inquiry.

I had been invited to give evidence. Jane and I booked adjacent slots on 23 May 2018 so we could attend together. The meeting was in the Zellig building, part of Birmingham's famous Custard Factory built by Alfie Bird in 1906, in the Digbeth area, once home to many more factories and warehouses but now a thriving hub of arts venues, restaurants and event spaces.

I was nervous about giving evidence as I knew how important it was. I'd met Reverend James a couple of times already, when he was first introduced to an assembled group of NHS and private patients at a support group meeting at the Greswolde Hotel, in Knowle. I asked him then if he would speak directly at a Breast Friends meeting and he agreed. Of course, I had googled him already and learned that he was born in Devon, went to an all-boys grammar school, was married and had studied theology at Oxford. A member of the House of Lords at the time, he was also a regular contributor to BBC Radio 4's *Thought for the Day*. But there was nothing to suggest a qualification in medicine or law (I later learned his wife had been a nurse, but she was not part of the inquiry team).

He had a warm, calm, pastoral air about him, not aloof or superior in any way. He introduced me to Jane Pawson, the engagement lead, and Martin, a trained counsellor who was there to give emotional support. I also saw Rebecca Chaloner, secretary to the inquiry, who I had also met at the Greswolde Hotel meeting. She had an impressive history of involvement with high-profile inquiries, including the independent investigation into the Jimmy Savile sex abuse scandal, as well as leading governance and implementation projects for the Department of Health and the NHS. Jane went off with Chaloner to be interviewed while I sat down with Graham James. It was surreal sitting opposite a bishop. The last time I had spoken about my health to a man of the cloth was in the confession box before my operation. Over a cup of tea James put me at ease, telling me the idea of the interview was to focus on what had happened to me and any other information I wanted to pass along.

I started at the beginning, at my first meeting with Paterson and Lloyd Owen. I had got used to reeling off details of my story to the press, but this was much more difficult. I could see the look of concern on James's face and noticed Pawson clenching her jaw as I described the details of my operation and the aftermath. I spoke about my mum, and the harm Paterson had inflicted on my whole family.

I described the conflicting pathology reports with the same report number, the lack of corrective action or accountability, how it took almost a year before Spire was able to confirm which report was correct. How could I believe anything they told me? How could Spire brush it off as human error when there were no checks and balances in place to ensure it never happened again?

I described how Paterson had left 40 per cent of my breast tissue, something I never consented to, and my breast had been reconstructed over the top of an incomplete mastectomy. I talked about the unnecessary chemotherapy given by Latief, the physical and psychological damage, and the ongoing fight for justice.

We had had to fight for years to get acknowledgement of the harm and then fight again for compensation. Spire dragged its feet even while hundreds of women were being diagnosed with secondary cancers. 'It felt like they were waiting for us to die,' I told James.

When compensation was finally offered to victims, a lot of them felt they couldn't wait and many feared missing out on compensation completely, so they took the first offer. There was a single pot of money from which the solicitors and insurance companies took their cut. Those affected, mainly women, did not want to delay any longer or fight on. I talked about the impact this had on everyone, particularly when we discovered that Paterson's insurers were able to claim he wasn't covered and Spire tried to insist he was simply 'renting a room'.

Then I presented the data showing the numbers of deceased mastectomy patients under Paterson. This included stats from

Kevin Bolger comparing the age of death of Paterson patients overlaid with national breast cancer data and from Martin Lee's 2017 NHS report. It was a simple visual representation but showed clearly that if you were a mastectomy patient treated by Paterson for breast cancer you had a more significant chance of recurrence and death than if you had had a different surgeon. The bottom line was that of the 1,206 mastectomy patients operated on by Paterson, 675 – almost 60 per cent – were now dead.

I went over every detail I knew about Paterson and produced emails and evidence to back it up. It was exhausting, but I knew I didn't have many more chances to be heard. James finally closed the meeting and we gathered outside the room. Jane had finished her interview, too; the emotional strain took its toll on both of us. For weeks before and after the interview we were having to relive the events of what had happened. I was constantly going over the facts in my head, worrying I'd missed something, or if what James had was enough to go after others involved and to get justice for those who had died.

41

The year 2018 was my sixtieth birthday year and I was going to make the most of it. The inquiry was underway, Jen was recovering well, my granddaughter Sophia was thriving, and my health was improving. We spent a lot of time together as a family. I had decided to fulfill another challenge on my bucket list: to do a wing walk.

A wing walk is where you are strapped, standing up, to the wing of a biplane, which then takes off and flies around for a bit. I'd always wanted to do it, for the challenge and for the sensation of truly flying. It was also a great chance to raise much-needed funds for Breast Friends. When the day arrived,

Bob drove me to a small airfield in the Cotswolds, followed by the rest of the family. It was a perfect day: blue skies, no wind, bright sunshine. The director, Alison Millar, had asked me to film the wing walk for a documentary called *Bodies of Evidence* that she was making about the Ian Paterson story, so was there with her assistant Sian and a camera.

I was very nervous, but I was reassured by a professional wing-walker, who showed me a safety video of a few people going up. I was heartened by the fact that one of them was an elderly man of at least seventy. I thought, if he can do it I can. We walked out to the airfield towards the 1934 Breitling biplane. My greatest trepidation was whether I could climb onto the wing, but a small step at the bottom to help me up was all I needed. I shuffled forward onto the edge of the cockpit, hooked my arm around the strut and pulled myself up to a standing position. My instructor fastened me into the harness and explained what to do if there was a fire in the tail of the aircraft. My entire career in aerospace safety flashed before my eyes. I was sure it would be fine. She securely strapped me in, climbed down from the plane and signalled to the pilot, who started the aircraft. I had been given instructions by the pilot to face both thumbs down if I wanted the flight to stop. The propeller started spinning loudly as the plane moved across the grass. It was a bumpy ride and my back was banging against the metal pole. The plane turned then took a run up for take-off back towards where my family were cheering me on. As I started to lift off, I could hear them all chanting 'Nanny, Nanny, Nanny' at the top of their voices, and I started to laugh as I ascended into the sky.

My laughter quickly turned to nerves. Bloody hell, I thought, I'm not sure about this. But I held my arms out and waved to my family as I flew past. I could see for miles over fields and barns and the beautiful Cotswolds landscape. My stomach was doing somersaults, but I relaxed into it and felt the wind blowing hard against my face. It was exhilarating. I heard the sound of the engine change as the pilot put the plane into a dive. I thought he had looped the loop, as my view quickly flipped from sky to the ground (I later found out it was a manoeuvre called a rudder turn) and I screamed, 'JESUS, MARY and JOSEPH!' The plane righted itself and an incredible flow of adrenaline surged through me. 'Top of the world!' I shouted. The plane did a few more circuits and then we descended for a gentle landing.

Alison was waiting with her camera when I climbed down from the plane. In her quiet Irish voice she asked, 'How do you feel?' I was full of emotion and told her that this wasn't just about raising money for Breast Friends, it was about challenging myself, showing I'm not afraid of anything, least of all Paterson. He had mutilated me, lied to me and betrayed me, but he couldn't touch my spirit. I felt strong and empowered and ready to take on anything.

My second interview with the inquiry team was on 24 September 2018. This time I was there in my capacity as chair of Breast Friends Solihull. Graham James once again chaired the meeting alongside Jane Pawson from the inquiry team, and I was introduced to Karen Harrowing, the independent advisor on healthcare to the inquiry. James explained that they wanted to talk to me about issues related to Breast Friends 'and then we will go on to look at the organisations and regulators as well as Spire, then Karen will explore just what their responses were to you, so that when we see them we have got some evidence from your experience as to how the different regulators, let alone the hospitals themselves, responded to you, and how seriously they took the approaches that you made, issues to do with insurers, Medical Defence Union, and so on. And then Jane will look at the experience of the recall from your members in relation to the group, because that concerns us, too, and then we can cover any other issues you want to, you know, about the drilling down in relation to statistics and numbers, and all that sort of stuff about how that happened.'

This interview was just as painful as the first, as I recounted how Bethan Lloyd Owen first introduced me to Breast Friends and how she and Paterson were held in such high esteem by the group and the local community. Paterson convinced all of us that if we did as he suggested we would be all right. He could cure us, for a price.

'One of the things we're exploring is just how much Bethan and Paterson used Breast Friends, let alone others, as a means of grooming the whole community. I mean, you have just illustrated it in a way,' James said after I had finished speaking. That word really struck me – groomed. That's exactly what had been done to us. Vulnerable women were targeted for our health insurance and sold treatment we didn't need. Breast Friends had unwittingly been the perfect recruiting ground for that.

'Yeah, absolutely we were used,' I replied. 'One of our committee members only recently said to me, "I have been in denial for years. I couldn't face this. You seemed to catch on a bit quicker than everyone else, Debbie." And I said, "Well maybe I did, but I started listening to what people were saying, things were coming out in the local press about women who were being recalled because they had a cleavage-sparing mastectomy"'. I told the inquiry about Lloyd Owen writing to our database to reassure us that the procedure was safe, how close she was to the committee, constantly reinforcing how important a support group is to newly diagnosed breast cancer patients.

And it is. There is nothing more powerful than seeing someone who has already been through breast cancer and come out the other side. The support we provide to each other, emotional and practical, is essential. Not everyone has a family or friends who can help or understand the journey we go on, and Breast Friends fills that role. To exploit it for gain is beyond a crime, it's a sin. I told James about Lloyd Owen's invitations to meals out where she would press us to fundraise for equipment for Spire, and then I handed over the minutes from the extraordinary meeting.

The evidence showed that Bethan Lloyd Owen and Joy Masters at the time said that the cleavage-sparing procedure was safe and how they had quoted evidence from the West Midlands Intelligence Unit apparently showing that Paterson's recurrence rates were in keeping with everyone else's and in some cases lower than those of other consultants. Lloyd Owen used this data to convince us that there was nothing untoward going on and nothing to worry about.

I talked about the Pan Birmingham letter that contradicted Lloyd Owen's claims, how it wasn't initially shared with us and how she convinced the committee not to forward it to our members. How she then had our charity's constitution rewritten so we could no longer discuss medical issues. I described how many Breast Friends members were in denial about Paterson and believed everything Masters and Lloyd Owen told them, potentially to the detriment of their own health.

'What was really hurtful was that people were dying on our committee, friends were dying, because they had never acknowledged that Paterson could have left breast tissue, and because Bethan had told us that the procedure was safe so our members didn't come forward to be checked,' I said.

I told the inquiry how, because of a failure of the recall process and denials and complications by Spire, I was left to help women who didn't know where to turn. One Breast Friends member had a lumpectomy and then a mastectomy, because she had a recurrence shortly after her first operation. She had necrosis, and had to have further reconstructive surgery from her back. She had also had hernia operations and a lot of complications from her surgery, and for years I had been telling her and others to get their records and have them assessed before it was too late. Recently she had realised that she had been in denial, and had come to me to ask what to do. "I have tried to get hold of a solicitor; nobody wants to take me on, I'm out of time to claim and can't afford to pay someone to look into it," she said. I showed her how to apply for her medical records. When they arrived, it looked very much like Paterson had not cleared the margins when he operated. I forwarded everything to Thompsons. There was no money left in the Spire compensation pot for her records to be assessed by an independent consultant, but she was offered a measly £1,000. I intervened, writing a letter on her behalf showing how Paterson had not cleared her margins. The offer was increased to £5,000, with a take-it-or-leave-it attitude, as she was out of time and there was no money left.

'There are others now coming forward after the announcement of the inquiry who will not get any compensation,' I continued. 'I get people contacting me all the time. A nurse called to say she had lived with the fact that she thought she had cancer, and had been in denial about Paterson. She couldn't get all her records, critical information was missing, her personal circumstances were such that she couldn't handle going through the fight. She has been on antidepressants for fifteen years. I am being asked medical questions because no one else has been there to sort it out.

'One of my worst experiences was when I was given the records of a deceased woman to look at by her husband, who asked if I thought he had a case. I had to read about the last minutes of her life. This man wanted to know if Paterson wrongfully killed his wife. I had to tell him I simply didn't know. That's what's so upsetting for the families left behind, they may never really know.' Only inquests could give them answers, and in the meantime I was the only person they could turn to who would listen and help them work through their case.

Harrowing asked, 'And do you think that is in your capacity as chair of Breast Friends?' I felt like shouting, of course I bloody don't! But instead I calmly said, 'No. It shouldn't be, but that's what's happening to me, because there is nobody else answering. Nobody else has been there, literally, for our group and for all the victims. Nobody.'

James realised that I had two different roles: Deborah Douglas, Chair of Solihull Breast Friends who was now a campaigner and media figure, and Deb the Paterson patient and cancer survivor. 'You tried to keep them separate, really, in a certain way,' he said.

'I did. I was conscious that Breast Friends were a support group for all breast cancer patients, both NHS and private.' Perhaps in some way I was trying to be the anti-Paterson, to undo the harm he had done by grooming and disenfranchising us. I wanted women to be aware of the risk to their health if they had had a cleavage-sparing mastectomy, to be compensated, to know if they definitely had cancer and whether any of their treatment had been unnecessary. I was fighting so hard for that, even while knowing that compensation or acknowledgment could never truly undo the harm we'd suffered at Paterson's hands. And then there was the greatest harm of all, one that nothing would make better. That morning I had gathered together the funeral service sheets of six Breast Friends members who had died when their cancer came back following operations by Paterson. I had taken them with me to the interview, and now I placed them down in front of Reverend Graham James and his team one by one, reading out their names as I did so. After each name, I said 'dead'. This was probably my best shot to get the inquiry to pay enough attention to the deaths to recommend inquests. I had to get my point across.

'All of these friends might still be here, but we will never know. What I do know is that they were not given a proper recall, and they believed everything they were told by the NHS and private sector at the time. When some of them started to ask questions, it was too late for them. Those of us who had immediate reconstructive surgery were told by Spire that we were left with just fatty tissue but also that the reconstruction meant there was no way to tell what tissue was left. That's a time bomb.'

James said, 'Why were they not told, recalled, investigated?'

I told him about the shambolic nature of Spire's recall, the conflicting letters and how patients were left to chase and ask questions rather than being given information proactively. I said how years later the NHS carried out risk assessments of Paterson patients and it was deemed that they were at higher risk of a reccurrence if, for example, they had an immediate reconstruction. NHS patients were given an individual treatment plan by the Trust to either remove the breast tissue or get regular yearly monitoring. Spire offered no such monitoring, and seemed to lose or have accuracy issues with many patient records, including mine.

I knew about the criteria for that plan, and although I was treated privately I had attended all the NHS workshops and understood that the key to keeping safe if you couldn't have the breast tissue removed was to have regular monitoring, and the best diagnostic tool for identifying breast tissue after reconstruction was an MRI scan. I had had to advocate for myself, and I was lucky that Ingle knew the protocol. I was transferred to the NHS, where my monitoring is ongoing.

Harrowing asked me to clarify about the poor record-keeping that had featured so heavily in Paterson's trial.

'My understanding was it was the responsibility of the hospital to look after our medical records and keep them secure and safe.' I told them about Paterson's claim that the six lever-arch files of MDT notes that were found by Ruth Walker were never in his office and that he didn't even have an office. He had insinuated that Spire had lost all his MDT notes, conveniently for him. I described the appalling lack of internal procedure, how the records handler had testified, 'Sometimes we scan them, sometimes we don't. Sometimes we file them, sometimes we don't. Then some of them get back to us, and some of them don't.'

If there was any hope of the inquiry making a real difference, it was imperative for the team to recommend changes not just to culture but to the seemingly mundane yet crucial elements of patient care. Record-keeping, data monitoring, inter-hospital communications. Something as small as an improperly handled letter could have huge repercussions later down the line.

42

Unsurprisingly, a lot of key players refused to speak to the inquiry, and there was no legal way to compel them, but 200 patients and over a hundred medical professionals gave evidence.

In a phone call, James had said to me that once the inquiry was closed, Paterson patients would have no formal support. This was bothering me, so I called Paul Stonebrook at the Department of Health and Social Care. He had been at the first meeting I had with Philip Dunne, and I knew he was now working for Nadine Dorries, who was the under-health secretary reporting to Matt Hancock. I asked him what support we would have going forward and who we could contact for help if we needed it. He said he would get back to me and he arranged a call with me a few weeks later.

There were three people on the call. Paul, his boss Helen Causley, and a private secretary. I got the impression none of them knew what was going on. They asked me what I needed from the inquiry, and I said that patient safety needed to be at the heart of it, that Paterson patients would experience repercussions for the rest of their lives and many had still not yet come forward or been identified. When they did, there wasn't anywhere for them to go, so they were coming to me. I explained that, for example, there was no contact phone number for people affected by Paterson, and no published proposal or timescale for a full recall. I left the call frustrated. They hadn't been able to offer anything, and seemed to know less than I did.

At the end of January 2020, after barely a few months of normalcy and hope, my daughter Jen developed a temperature and once again we found ourselves at A&E. I was now used to the song and dance of explaining her compromised immune system, but this time, while Jen waited in the car, I also had to explain to the nurses that she'd recently had a stem cell transplant. Eventually, she was given a bed and blood tests. Nurses had the usual struggle to find her veins. One completely gave up and handed over to a colleague to try while Jen sat patiently, ignoring the pain. But this visit, something was different.

'Have you travelled abroad recently?' the nurse asked, before taking a swab of Jen's nose and throat. We weren't told what this was for and we had not yet heard the word that would dominate everyone's lives within weeks: Covid.

Jen was admitted to a ward and a few days later had a CT scan on her chest. The doctors wanted to do a lung biopsy, and said they could see enlarged lymph nodes. This could have been a simple infection, or …

I told Jen I was getting a coffee and followed the consultant. I stopped her in the corridor and asked what she thought. She said everything was pointing to the Hodgkin's lymphoma coming back. With a lump in my throat I went to get drinks, composed myself, put on my bravest face and went back to Jen, praying the whole time that she would be alright.

The tests that would confirm if the cancer was back were scheduled for 4 February 2020, the same day the Ian Paterson Inquiry report would be published. The timing could not have been worse. My thoughts were conflicted, confused and complicated. I had to be at the inquiry press conference, it was something we'd all worked so hard for. It was a matter of justice for all of Paterson's victims. But I could think of little other than Jen. Would it be good news, or had the stem cell treatment failed and the cancer returned? Scott took the day off to be with her, and his mother had the kids so I could attend the event.

By this time I was a regular media face for the Paterson story. The journalist Darragh MacIntyre had filmed me for a BBC *Panorama* special called 'How Safe is Your Operation?', about the lack of governance in private hospitals. One segment was about Paterson, and when he called me the day after it aired to ask what I thought, I said, 'You missed a trick, the whole programme should have been about Paterson and the crimes he committed.' 'Then write a book, Deb,' he laughed.

The morning of 4 February 2020 was terrifying on several counts. Alison Millar had stayed over at my house so she could film me all day for *Bodies of Evidence*. She had the camera rolling as soon as I emerged, having barely slept. She asked how I felt about the day finally being here, meaning the inquiry, but I was worried to death about Jen's results. Bob drove us into Birmingham city centre, the car loaded with Ali's equipment. We parked up and she filmed me walking through Digbeth, along the canal past the beautiful old Victorian and Edwardian buildings, and into the Zellig building where the inquiry was being held.

I had a TV interview lined up with Victoria Derbyshire, but the producer didn't call until 10am, just as people started to file into the meeting room. I answered questions live on air, via Zoom, as best as I could, but eventually had to say, 'Sorry, I have to go!'

The room was huge, with white-painted brick walls, exposed steels and high ceilings betraying its industrial history. It was freezing. Around eighty people – mostly Paterson patients who had given evidence to the inquiry – made their way towards the large round tables.

It was appropriate that an inquiry affecting the people of Birmingham should be held in the heart of the city, but I did wish it was somewhere a little warmer. I saw Rebecca Chaloner across the room and she smiled at me encouragingly. Graham James was concerned with the room set-up and the temperature, and eventually the heating was switched on. There was a sound like a small aircraft engine from a huge fan on the wall which started blowing out dry heat. It got warmer, but it also became more difficult to hear what was being said. The mood in the room was sombre and nervous. I took my seat at a table near the front next to Bob, my friend and fellow campaigner Jane Smith, and her sister. We were each handed an A4 purple booklet entitled 'The Report of the Independent Inquiry into the Issues raised by Paterson'. This was it, the culmination of years of work. I quickly flicked through, trying to find the recommendations, then the room fell silent as Reverend James began to speak.

His opening statement began:

'This report is not simply a story about a rogue surgeon. It would be tragic enough if that was the case, given the thousands of people whom Ian Paterson treated. But it is far worse. It is the story of a healthcare system which proved itself dysfunctional at almost every level when it came to keeping patients safe, and where those who were the victims of Paterson's malpractice were let down time and time again.'

Reverend James went on to describe the myriad ways we had been let down. By Paterson himself, by the NHS and Spire, by the 'wholly inadequate' recall procedures, by regulators and by the Medical Defence Union who, he acknowledged, 'used its discretion to avoid giving compensation to Paterson patients once it was clear his malpractice was criminal'.

'Even today, many patients, especially those treated within Spire hospitals, have no individual care plan. Thousands of people are still living with the consequences of what happened. It is wishful thinking that this could not happen again,' he said, and I felt a strange surge of validation that he was acknowledging this was not just an isolated rogue surgeon, but a whole series of failures by multiple parties that could – and would – lead to more injustices.

'The inquiry team were told by regulators and other witnesses that procedures and processes had tightened up considerably in the past decade,' he continued. 'We were informed that the regulatory system was more vigilant, and patient safety was now given a much higher priority so that another Paterson would be unlikely. We acknowledge many areas of improvement in processes and procedures. But in Paterson's years of practice, there were many regulations and guidelines in place which were disregarded or simply ignored, and not just by him.'

This was the crux of the problem. Regulation is only useful if it is enforced, and quite often, it is not. This is not unique to the Paterson case, and is key to answering the question, 'how can we stop this happening again?' I did not want anyone else to be in the position I was in, scarred and traumatised, distrustful of doctors while relying on them for healthcare. So far, it sounded like Reverend James and the inquiry team weren't shying away from the issues. He spoke about the 'culture of avoidance and denial' as I nodded along, having butted my head against exactly that at every turn.

He then moved on to the subject of data, which is critical to the safety and accountability process. Reverend James rightly acknowledged that simply collecting data is not enough, and that members of the medical community – particularly managers and those charged with governance – are not always good at understanding or using it. 'Instead,' he said, '[they] seem to look for patterns which reassure rather than disturb.'

Aerospace, like healthcare, is a safety-critical industry. While an infinitely complex body of flesh and blood is not the same as an aeroplane, many if not most of the same basic safety procedures should apply. For example, where in the process might human error occur? Which parts of a process would – if they failed – cause catastrophe? In surgery, that could mean injury, death or malpractice, and in aerospace it could mean a plane crash. Data is not the whole story, but it does help to paint a picture. For example, let's say that nationally, patients presenting with a breast lump are given one breast scan a year. Patients who are being sent for five breast scans in a year by the same consultant warrant further investigation, simply by merit of the data. But if no one collects or looks at that data as routine, as quality assurance or patient safety, then of course that consultant will continue unimpeded. If the mean average for a breast cancer operation is six hours, and one surgeon is consistently doing it in three hours, something is clearly happening, but only if someone looks at the data and then goes to investigate.

My job was to investigate failures that happened due to a supply chain issue. Aircraft parts are rigorously tested to emulate conditions in service. Here's an example: data was showing that a sensor in a mechanical part wasn't performing properly. This seemed to be an issue across multiple batches rather than a one-off, and we isolated the failure to a glass diode. I was duly dispatched to the manufacturer to audit their assembly process. After checking out various aspects of the production, I sat with a woman on the manufacturing production line, chatting to her as she did her job. As she relaxed and got used to my presence, I noticed that after she had dipped the small glass rods in solder, she then placed them carefully into a small mesh basket to go through a wash process. At the end of the wash cycle she used her first and middle finger to deftly pick up each diode … and then casually flicked them onto her work bench where they would clink against each other. This was causing tiny, almost invisible cracks in the glass. I asked her supervisor why he hadn't picked up on this and he said when he observed her, she didn't do it. So the system allowed for error in two critical places: the control of process itself, and in the way the operator was trained. This was discovered by first looking at the data, then tracing it all the way back along the line.

Once I'd found the problem, it wouldn't be enough to tell the woman to stop. The operator instructions needed to be updated, all operators retrained and made aware of the fragility of the components they were handling. The supplier also added a more vigorous test to try to identify potential faults before the parts left their warehouse. This is how you stop it happening again, but also how you make a team aware that the wrong things can be normalised.

There was no suggestion in the diode story that anyone involved was deliberately looking the other way, although that can happen when profit is involved and is in part why jobs like mine exist. In Paterson's case, though, Reverend James called it 'wilful blindness, illustrated by the way in which Paterson's behaviour and aberrant clinical practice was excused or even favoured. Many simply avoided or worked around him. Some could have known, while others should have known, and a few must have known'. Wilful blindness – exactly the right phrase. All of those who 'could/should/must have known' what Paterson was doing for so long had completely ignored the harm he was inflicting on innocent patients, and the trust that he (and by association, they) were breaching. Little Aston, for example, only had three operating theatres. He shared a theatre with the same people over and over, collaborated with favoured colleagues for years, was the subject of internal complaints, investigations and reports, all of which were ignored. As the bishop talked I thought about how many people had blood on their hands, and, of course, why.

Reverend James went on to acknowledge the difficulty of whistleblowing. 'At the very least a great deal more curiosity was needed, and a broader sense of responsibility for safety in the wider healthcare system by both clinicians and managers alike. However, some seem to have been inhibited from complaining because they had seen colleagues appearing to get nowhere by doing so (and in some cases finding themselves under investigation).' He described those who did try to raise concerns about Paterson as 'poorly served by those to whom they reported, [and who] have themselves been traumatised'.

'Some who should have acted now live with the guilt. Others are in a state of denial. Many patients felt that some of those who worked closely with Paterson should answer for their actions or negligence,' he said. I nodded vehemently. This was a drum I had been banging for years. While I do believe the silence of some staff was a 'chilling effect' from fear (of Paterson himself, or of professional reprisals), it does not explain it all. Senior, highly intelligent colleagues earning a lot of money had excellent motives for looking the other way.

I was relieved to hear James say, 'In conducting this inquiry, I have reported five health professionals to either the General Medical Council or the Nursing and Midwifery Council and referred one matter for investigation by the West Midlands Police.' This was something. Action, not words. But what of the other main concerns: why Paterson was able to receive legal aid, and – most importantly – what about those Paterson patients who had since died? When I was giving evidence to the inquiry meeting I had read out the names of six deceased women. After each name I reiterated, 'dead'. I had nagged and nagged every step of the way. I was the only one who met with Kevin Bolger, Caroline Williamson and Martin Lee to demand an investigation into the deaths, and many meetings became tense because I kept raising it. I wanted an investigation into the possibility that those patients would not have died had they received the correct treatment from Paterson. I had heard from someone on the inquiry team that that was likely to be included today, but I wanted to hear James say it.

He continued:

'There are two other issues that concern some patients and their families, and which other agencies have the legal competence to pursue. The first relates to those Paterson patients who have died and whose families are left wondering if they would not have done so if treated by another surgeon. This is a task for the coroner. The inquiry team did not have the authority to pursue individual cases, but we engaged with the Birmingham and Solihull coroner on this question. I am confident this serious and distressing matter will be rigorously pursued.'

This was it. A promise, or so it sounded, that the coroner would look into it.

I didn't know what justice looked like for the dead women. I didn't even truly know there was a case to answer, whether there was any legal wrongdoing. That would require inquests, the involvement of the Crown Prosecution Service and the courts.

239

But as yet no one had looked into the deaths at all, and I wouldn't rest until they did.

So that just left the legal aid question. Everyone I'd ever spoken to about Paterson's legal aid, from solicitors to police to family, patients and friends, had been disgusted. Everyone is entitled to a fair trial, but not everyone is entitled to hundreds of thousands of pounds of taxpayer cash. The idea that Paterson didn't have money of his own was laughable.

The inquiry team seemed to agree.

'The second matter raised with us concerned the belief among patients that at his criminal trial, Paterson was in receipt of legal aid, despite his high earnings over many years. I have reported this claim to the Legal Aid Agency and asked that it is investigated.'

I had no idea whether the Legal Aid Agency listened to bishops or non-statutory inquiries, but this was still great news on top of everything else. Reverend James finished his introduction by thanking the campaigners:

'This tragic story would not have been told in its fullness were it not for a relatively small number of Paterson patients who were determined to prevent other people suffering as they had done, and who pressed for an inquiry. I pay tribute to their brave and resolute determination. If patients in the future are safer in both the NHS and the independent sector as a result of this report, it will be due largely to their efforts, and to the many patients who gave such detailed and frequently harrowing testimonies. Their courage and nobility in the face of so much suffering has been an inspiration. It is to them and their families that this report is dedicated.'

I exchanged a small smile with Jane, as if to say, 'We've all fought for this for so long, but now they are finally listening.'

43

I desperately hoped the team had understood the scope of the problems. James announced that the inquiry was making fifteen recommendations, which can be read in full in the inquiry report online. They included suggestions for a single database that tracks and compares consultant procedures, better and more direct communication with patients, and more transparency around the limitations of private healthcare, including the lack of ICU facilities if something goes wrong. For example, in 2018, routine liposuction was carried out at Spire Little Aston on a middle-aged mother who then went into cardiac arrest on the operating table. There were no ICU facilities, so the woman was blue-lighted to the nearest NHS hospital some miles away, where she died.

He also recommended a review of the patient consent process, suggesting a 'cooldown' period between giving consent for a surgical procedure and the operation itself, to reflect on diagnosis and research treatment options. He suggested the GMC monitor this as part of good practice. I struggled to understand how this would help. Why would an average patient distrust their surgeon, and where would they go in any case? I could have googled my symptoms, but I had been told I had cancer so all I wanted to do was trust my surgeon and get treated as quickly as possible. Putting the onus on the patient to ensure they didn't have a Paterson on their hands seemed misguided, although if there had been an available public database I could at least have made a more informed decision.

James recommended better monitoring and compliance in the matter of MDTs, the all-important but sometimes neglected meetings where a patient's case is supposed to be discussed by clinicians of different disciplines, and better patient complaints procedures in the NHS and the private sector, including the right to an independent resolution of complaints.

Several recommendations related to the recall, with James strongly suggesting that all 11,000 Paterson patients have their cases reviewed and for national recall guidelines to be drawn up in the event something like this happens again.

Next, James called for urgent government reform of clinical indemnity. 'The Medical Defence Union used its discretion to withdraw cover since Paterson's activity was criminal. This left patients without cover,' he said. The current system is unregulated, which is massively disadvantageous to patients.

He also called for the government to better regulate and facilitate collaboration between regulators, essential given so many identified failings by the CQC, the Quality Audit team, the GMC and internal management, and for any healthcare professional under investigation to be suspended when the investigation includes a potential risk to patient safety. If the healthcare professional also works at another healthcare provider, any concerns about them should be communicated to that provider. It still blows my mind that this wasn't already the case.

The next recommendation was a call for the government to urgently address the gap in corporate responsibility and liability. 'In the NHS, consultants are employees and the NHS hospital is responsible for their management, and accepts liability when things go wrong,' he points out. This is not the case with private hospitals, which in my experience is not something patients are aware of.

Then he simply asked that when things go wrong, hospital boards should apologise as early as possible. In the case of HEFT and Spire, that did not happen, adding to our anxiety and mistrust of management in both the private sector and the NHS.

The final recommendation was that all of the above be applied across the whole of the independent sector (private and NHS funded) in order for private hospitals to qualify for NHS contracts. Given the billions of NHS contracts awarded to the private sector, including and increasingly to Spire, it is extraordinary that these very basic monitoring, safety and regulatory processes are not already in place.

It was the first time I had heard a few of the details, and James had not minced his words when it came to the failings of everyone involved, but I couldn't help think there was nothing groundbreaking here. It had largely all been covered in the Kennedy and Verita reports already, and – as strong as the recommendations were – there was nothing to force the government to implement any of them, let alone all.

I knew I would be heading into the press scrum as soon as I came out of the meeting and that they expected me to say something. My stomach was churning, half because of the meeting and half because I was thinking about Jen and her impending results. I'd been trying to put it out of mind like she had asked me to, but a presentation about cancer is not the most distracting environment when you're waiting to hear if your daughter's lymphoma has returned. I badly wanted to be with her, but she had been adamant I should see the inquiry through. As I left the hall, my phone rang. It was Jen's husband Scott to say that she was going for the scan now and that the results would be today but could be hours away. 'Send her our love, we're thinking of her,' I said, trying to disguise the pain in my voice. I walked down the passageway to be greeted by a bank of journalists and cameras. With no time to really digest the inquiry findings or prepare, I took a deep breath and answered their questions.

I was asked what I thought about the inquiry findings and replied that we, the victims, had fought for this and welcomed the report, but that I was shocked to learn that up to 11,000 patients might be affected. As I always did in interviews, I reiterated the risk of recurrence and pleaded for patients to be followed up and monitored, in the hopes that any Paterson patient watching who hadn't yet come forward might do so.

'The fight goes on until legislation is changed, we don't want somebody from the government paying us lip service by saying "lessons will be learned"; lessons aren't learned unless legislation is changed. It's something we must live with daily. All the people affected, those people at home wondering if he harmed them.' I also talked about the deaths and the need for inquests, and how the fifteen inquiry recommendations must be implemented if we had any hope of real change.

I was interviewed by one journalist after another, saying the same thing over and over.

Then Bob, Jane, Jane's sister, Alison Millar and I walked to the local pub, where I gave more interviews in a quiet corner. I had noticed a tall dark-haired woman following closely behind us and wondered if she was with the press, or perhaps a solicitor I hadn't met yet. We sat down in the back room of the pub and ordered coffees and sandwiches. It had been a long cold morning. The woman sat at a table on her own near us; she kept looking over. I said, 'Hello, are you okay? I saw you after the inquiry briefing.' She said, 'Yes, I was a Paterson patient.' I went and sat down with her and she told me how she had believed everything he had said. 'I ended up having five operations that I didn't need, and chemotherapy that I didn't need. At one point he told me I'd got secondary cancer and I hadn't. My children were eight and ten at the time and he was doing all this while holding my hand and befriending me. At one of the surgeries that I didn't need he stood at the bottom of the bed and told me he was proud of me. I was really pleased that he'd told me I'd been brave.' I felt for her so strongly. Her words were carefully measured, I could see she'd gone over what he'd done to her before. I recognised the look, the clenched jaw and the little laugh that comes when you're relating to people how stupid you must have been to believe him, because what else can you do when someone you trusted implicitly has butchered you?

I was due to appear on the BBC *Six O'Clock News* and also *Newsnight* that same evening, but couldn't get Jen's impending results off my mind. If it was bad news, I would cancel all media appearances. I didn't think I could do any more anyway, I was so drained and scared. I whispered to Bob that I wanted to leave, so we said goodbye to everyone and made our way home to wait for a phone call.

We'd been home for a while but still hadn't heard anything. I thought maybe Jen and Scott didn't want to call in case I was doing press, but I was going mad waiting so I called her mobile.

She picked up. 'How did you get on, Jen?'

She was still in hospital. Her voice was shaking. 'Scott's just gone to get me a drink,' she whispered. 'He'll be back in a bit to explain.'

'Just tell me, Jen,' I said gently, although I already knew. Her cancer had come back.

44

I woke up the next day not knowing what to do. The inquiry had gone completely from my mind. I'd been getting media calls and requests for interviews all evening but had turned them all down. All I could think about was Jen. I certainly couldn't focus on medical malpractice and an evil cancer surgeon when my own daughter's life was back in the hands of doctors. I had to trust them. Jen's consultant Ram Malladi told her that, thankfully, she had options, but that she needed a stem cell transplant immediately.

Anthony Nolan is a charity that links people who need a stem cell donation with potential donors. It was set up in 1974 by Shirley Nolan, whose son Anthony had a rare blood disease. No donor could be found, and Anthony died in 1979 aged seven, but Shirley continued her work in his memory and the charity now has over 700,000 potential donors registered. Over 20,000 patients have received a transplant. I looked at the Anthony Nolan register, recruited family members to sign up and do a swab test, and threw myself into research. One of

Jen's friends from the hospital had received a transplant from her own brother, so we hoped that Rob or Will would be a match. Jen was started on immunotherapy treatment and discharged from hospital. While the work continued to find her a potential donor, she would need to keep herself as healthy as possible, away from contagions and viruses. Even a simple cold could kill her.

March 2020 was the last time I'd hug Jen, Scott and the girls for a very long time. The government announced a nationwide lockdown due to Covid-19. While families were able to create a 'bubble', we couldn't be in theirs as my son Rob was living with us while he studied to be a teacher. Jen's hospital appointments became a gauntlet of risk, car rides with windows open, masks on, fingers crossed. The pandemic dominated the news, inescapable, and suddenly the whole country had to adjust.

Towards the end of June, Jen had an appointment with Malladi. None of the family had been a match, and the hospital had been searching hard. She wanted me to attend as an extra pair of ears and a calm presence, someone who was good at asking questions. We went in separate cars, sat apart from each other in the room, not even close enough to hold hands, both wearing masks. Scott was on speakerphone. Malladi gave us the news. They had found a stem cell donor.

This should have been good news, but receiving a transplant meant time in hospital and the near destruction of her immune system during a global pandemic. The transplant had a 50 per cent chance of working, and I was terrified it wasn't worth the risk. Was it worth the risk of dying of coronavirus for a chance to end her cancer for ever? 'The treatment she's on now isn't curative,' Malladi explained, meaning that she would just be kicking the can down the road. 'She is at the right point to accept another stem cell transplant, and currently there is capacity in the ICU if there is a problem.'

It was Jen's decision to make. She went home, talked it through with Scott, and decided that the risk was worth taking.

The alternative was worse. The donor was a thirty-nine-year-old man from Frankfurt, Germany. I wondered what sort of person he was, whether he had a family, what he did for a living. Jen wasn't allowed to request contact with him for two years, and even then he might refuse. Jen was admitted to hospital and the stem cell transplant process began.

A few days after the inquiry report, I got a call from the whistle-blower, Hemant Ingle. I hadn't heard from him for a while. 'Hello Debbie,' he said, almost sheepishly, 'I need your help.' Given everything he had done and sacrificed to draw attention to Paterson's wrongdoing, he could have any help he wanted, but I was still shocked to hear him ask. My head wasn't in a Paterson space, I was entirely focused on Jen. But I always had time for Ingle.

He told me that he had been suspended by Spire because he had chosen not to give evidence to the inquiry. This is something we had talked about at the time. He had told me he couldn't cope with the thought of going through it all again. The strain on him and his family had been too much. This is a common problem when people whistleblow. The backlash can be horrendous, people are driven out of their jobs or made to work in hostile conditions. Ingle had been pushed out of Solihull Hospital and he felt like he had been the one under investigation. I was disappointed, but there is only so much a person can take, and if he was at his limit, he was at his limit. I understood, but I had also made it clear to him that anyone not giving evidence would be named and shamed in the inquiry, and I had thought he'd decided to do it. He told me at the time that his colleagues had said he'd be mad to give evidence, but later it turned out they themselves had. I wondered if he'd been stitched up. I found out that CC Kat had also been suspended for not giving evidence.

I had to put my disappointment in Ingle aside. He had already done more than most to try to bring Paterson to justice, and I didn't think it was fair he'd been suspended. He was also a victim of Paterson. I called a journalist who had been covering the Paterson case, Alison Stacey.

The next day a story in the *Birmingham Post* read:

HEALTH CHIEFS SUSPEND MEDIC WHO EXPOSED ROGUE SURGEON

[...] Mr Hemant Ingle, who alerted hospital bosses to Paterson's malpractice, is one of two surgeons suspended by Spire Healthcare. The other doctor suspended was plastic surgeon Mrs Chien C. Kat, who carried out reconstructive surgery on Paterson's breast cancer patients. Both have been suspended after they declined to give evidence to the Paterson Inquiry led by the Rt Rev Graham James, retired Bishop of Norwich.

The medics, who were both colleagues of Paterson at the former Heart of NHS England Trust, were not legally obliged to give evidence. Nor is there any suggestion that they harmed patients or acted in anything other than good faith.

But, according to the inquiry report: 'Individuals who were in breach of their professional code of conduct by not cooperating with the inquiry have been reported to their professional regulator.'

[...] Deborah Douglas, who was instrumental in convincing the government to launch the Paterson Inquiry, spoke out in support of Mr Ingle.

'Mr Ingle is a good man,' she told the Birmingham Post. *'I was disappointed that he didn't give evidence, but I understand. Paterson put him through hell.'*

The article detailed exactly what sort of hell Paterson put Ingle through, and the collapse of the MDTs leading to Ingle's relocation to Good Hope Hospital to resolve the conflict with Paterson. It made me so angry to think of Ingle being sidelined this way while Paterson got to carry on working as though nothing was wrong. My only consolation was that one of those men was now in prison, but I worried the cost to Ingle had been too great. Spire said, 'We fully support all the recommendations made by the Inquiry. In its report, the Inquiry team expressed concern about individuals who did not give evidence or cooperate with the Inquiry and indicated that they had been reported to their professional regulators. As a result, we have taken appropriate action and two people are currently suspended, pending investigations.'

The story was picked up by patients who were furious on his behalf. Ingle was reinstated by Spire soon after.

My life stopped while I waited for Jen to come out of hospital. I'm good in a crisis. I spring into action, do my homework, ask the tough questions and push for answers. I have been through a lot, and I hold up well. But not being able to see my family except through a video screen almost broke me. I looked at her poor swollen face through the screen, pink from the effects of the drugs, her tongue puffy and covered in a white film. She had had a reaction to the platelet transfusion and been put on strong antihistamines, but otherwise the transplant had apparently gone well.

I resumed my Paterson campaigning. In mid-July 2020, I called Spire's Head of Communications, Paul Lehmann, to find out what actions he was taking post-inquiry. I told him, 'You'd better come clean about how many are dead, or the coroner will drag the numbers out of Spire.' I didn't actually know if the coroner was yet investigating, but I didn't plan on stopping until there were inquests. The same day Jen texted me from hospital to say her friend's dad had received a letter telling him that in 1999 he had been operated on by Paterson. He wanted advice. I was pleased to see proof that the NHS and private sectors had started writing to all 11,000 Paterson patients, some progress that surely was the result of the inquiry.

In mid-July Bob and I took Scott's birthday presents round and stood at the back door, socially distanced. Bella was in her highchair and Sophia knew she couldn't step out of the sliding glass door boundary to their kitchen. Scott was doing so well looking after the girls, taking every precaution to keep them safe. I wanted to hug them or pick them up like I'd been able to every day before the pandemic. Shortly after it was Sophia's fourth birthday, and Jen was determined to come home for it. I was allowed to collect her from the hospital, masks on and car windows open, but I couldn't go into the house with her. Scott and the girls had made a 'welcome home Mum' banner. He opened the front door to welcome her in, and she shuffled inside, so happy to be home.

Jen and Scott told Sophia her birthday was actually a day later, so Jen would be strong enough to celebrate (a ruse that worked perfectly). The next day Bob and I turned up to sing happy birthday to Sophia from the patio. We watched from outside as she opened her presents and jumped about in delight as baby Bella looked on from her highchair. I could see Jen was trying very hard to join in but was so ill and exhausted. She had a long way still to go.

A few days later her temperature spiked, and Jen was readmitted to hospital. There have been many deaths throughout my story, cancer taking friends and family alike. It does not discriminate. But Jen was not destined to be one of them. The hospital staff got on top of the situation quickly. They had been incredible throughout her entire treatment, during the extraordinary and unprecedented horrors of the pandemic, and I will be grateful to them for the rest of my life. After an initial worrying blip, Jen's strength began to come back and she improved rapidly. She could be discharged with annual follow-ups for the rest of her life. By the end of July 2020, she was back home for good.

I almost can't describe my feelings about the thirty-nine-year-old stranger from Germany who saved my daughter's life. As

Jen was discharged from hospital for the final time, I remarked that I hoped to buy him a beer someday.

45

The recall process is still ongoing. When I gave evidence to the inquiry, I was asked about it at length. I had seen it from many sides, been tangled up in its administrative errors, and campaigned publicly and behind the scenes for progress, but I still can't fully comprehend the degree of incompetence involved.

During the last NHS 'recall' (which was no such thing) back in 2017, a plastic surgeon from HEFT was invited to talk at our monthly Breast Friends meeting about recent changes to the Trust. After speaking on that topic, he then produced slides about the new oncology unit at Spire Parkway. It was clearly a sales pitch for private sector services. I had to be diplomatic, but if he was going to bring Spire into the room then I was going to take my opportunity. I stood up.

At that time I was attending the NHS support group for Paterson patients, because private patients weren't getting any help or information at all. HEFT's head of the recall activity, Richard Brown, had worked on the recall protocol for the NHS which involved a 'virtual' review of patient records by a supra-MDT. At the support meetings he presented a lot of data including statistics showing how many Paterson patients had died. I knew the NHS had been rolling out partial recalls, but Spire had not, and I knew that patients might die if they didn't get checked.

'Sorry, I know you're our guest, but what is Spire doing about the recall?' He looked confused, then a woman who I hadn't noticed and who turned out to be a breast care nurse at Spire piped up with, 'Oh, you just phone up,' in a tone which suggested everyone obviously knew this. What I actually knew was that patients in the private sector hadn't been properly recalled at that point, and she was talking nonsense.

Still, I was prepared to put it to the test. A few days later I called Spire saying I was a Paterson patient who had been harmed and I understood I should be recalled. The receptionist replied, 'We don't just recall anybody, you know.'

I had to argue with her. Eventually someone called me back and offered me a recall, and I wondered how much of that was because they recognised my name as a troublemaker. It boded poorly for the robustness of the so-called recall.

I had been pressuring Ingle to find out what was happening. He was still my doctor at the time, and he had promised to go to the director of Spire Parkway, and to raise the issue of recalls at the next management meeting, which he duly did. 'In the meantime,' he had said at the time, 'if you know anyone that you think needs a review, give them my name and I will see them.'

That was an incredibly generous offer, and I quickly sent out a bulletin to Breast Friends members saying that Spire Paterson patients could call them to arrange a recall review with Ingle. But Ingle and I had jumped the gun. A few weeks later I called his breast care nurse, Paula Loveland, because I couldn't get hold of him, and asked her what was happening. She told me that the recall process hadn't been agreed or rolled out, and she didn't know what was going on. One committee member from Breast Friends had called Spire and they did arrange to review her case, but by then it was too late. She died two years later.

If patients weren't prepared to be proactive and approach Spire themselves, assuming they even knew to do so, then they would simply fall through the cracks. It disgusted me that Spire wasn't doing everything in its power to identify, contact and recall Paterson patients.

It took until February 2020, when the inquiry report was published, for Spire to finally agree to a proper recall. While the NHS gives Paterson patients a risk assessment and annual monitoring, to this day there has not been a treatment or care plan offered by Spire to Paterson patients.

No one understands why Paterson undertook unnecessary surgeries on the NHS. There was no profit in it for him, and if the patient did not need the operation then it wasn't helping waiting lists to give them one anyway. Following the inquiry, the NHS extended its recall to include Paterson's general surgery patients as well as his breast surgery patients. In early March 2020, days before the first government lockdown, I was invited to a meeting with Kevin Bolger, Interim Deputy Chief Executive of UHB (formerly HEFT), along with Gillian Waterhouse, two women from the board of HEFT, and several other Paterson campaigners. The meeting was to discuss the recall and how best to communicate it to patients. We all crammed into a tiny meeting room in a Birmingham hotel, and Bolger read out a draft of the recall letter. He had been incredibly helpful, and I got the impression he genuinely cared and was being as transparent as he could.

Following the meeting, the NHS set up a dedicated recall team which contacted 4,394 patients between May and August 2020. Of these, 355 patients responded and had their cases reviewed by either an independent breast consultant, or a general consultant for those who had had hernia repairs or varicose vein or other treatment. He emailed to say that the unfolding pandemic would delay things, but that he would share the NHS's recall plans with Spire. He signed his email 'Keep safe'.

The NHS's recall did proceed despite the pandemic, although there were hitches. In early May 2020, Bolger wrote to say that there had been problems with the letter sent to those who had had a breast procedure, over 2,500 patients, some of whom had not in fact been treated by Paterson and whose breast treatment had been necessary after all. These patients were understandably distressed at the confusion, but there was nothing to be done other than an apology. I felt very bad for those patients for their distress, however temporary.

Spire, on the other hand, had not yet formally started their recall despite agreeing to it. I had regular calls with the Department of Health and Social Care and kept asking the same questions, 'What is Spire doing about the recall and where is their plan for implementation of the recommendations from the Paterson Inquiry?' Each time it felt like the DHSC were just paying lip service to me. There was never any concrete progress and often it was me that was updating the DHSC on the NHS recall because I was talking regularly to Kevin Bolger and Caroline Williams, head of the NHS recall. I also kept pestering Paul Lehmann. In October 2020 he emailed:

'Our progress in implementing this recommendation of the Paterson Inquiry has been held back by the pandemic, which has seen all our hospitals and clinicians tied up in providing urgent care to NHS patients to relieve pressure on NHS hospitals. However, in the next few weeks, we will be contacting all known patients of Mr Paterson as far back as we have records for. Our aim will be to make sure that all patients have had their records carefully reviewed, that the outcome of the reviews has been fully communicated to them and that, if required, they are getting the support and care that they need.'

He offered for me to meet with the group clinical director, Alison Dickinson and Liz Monaghan, their corporate concerns officer, in November 2019. I asked how many of the identified 6,500 Paterson/Spire breast cancer patients are now deceased, and Monaghan replied that around a thousand had died. None of the surviving patients had yet been contacted. I grilled them on how many patients had been risk-assessed and whether anyone had been given an ongoing treatment plan, particularly those who had had cleavage-sparing mastectomies, but I was fobbed off with vague assurances that each patient would be considered individually.

I also wanted answers about unnecessary chemotherapy by Latief, and whether that was being included in their review, whether any other colleagues of Paterson were being investigated, and whether ongoing treatment for Paterson patients would be free. They said they'd get back to me on those questions, and eventually I realised the answer – to all of them – was no.

I was invited to a further call with them in December, and said that I wanted other Paterson campaigners involved. I contacted Gillian Waterhouse and Anne Butler of the NHS breast cancer support group, and Sarah Jane Downing, who had set up a Paterson patient support group. I asked them to email their databases to ensure as many patients as possible could be invited to attend.

It was reassuring to know that Liz Monaghan and Alison Dickinson hadn't worked for Spire when Paterson was there, so they weren't party to any of his influence. Dickinson apologised on behalf of Spire, which some people on the call found quite an emotional moment, while Liz Monaghan reassured us that they would do everything in their power to carry out a robust and proper recall. I reserved judgement on that commitment as we had been let down so badly for years. Only time would tell. Paterson patients were mentally scarred as well as physically. I asked if there was mental health support in place and if it could be extended to close family members of affected patients, and Spire confirmed they would provide this as long as it was through their in-house counsellor, not a third party.

I asked to see what Spire's care plan looked like. I wanted to see a template. I was told there wouldn't be one as every patient would be assessed based on their own clinical circumstances. I was assured the recall team would liaise closely with HEFT to ensure that Spire's approach dovetailed with theirs, but I had seen detailed templates, risk assessments and care plans from HEFT and couldn't understand why Spire was so resistant to doing the same.

Patients who later received recall letters were told there was a follow-up care plan, but there simply wasn't.

I also requested a booking code for Paterson patients so that they did not have to go through the humiliation and upset of explaining at reception that their recall appointments were free, and to Spire's credit they did implement this.

Spire finally started sending out recall letters in December 2020 and almost immediately I was contacted by recipients. It was a trickle at first, but then I was getting calls every week from Spire patients who had seen me on the news and either tracked me down from the Breast Friends Solihull website or via Liz Monaghan. I had given her permission to pass my contact details on to anyone who asked. I was also getting requests through Gillian Waterhouse. If there were patients who had later used the private sector she would ask if they could speak to me as I was 'better placed to respond'.

The patients that contacted me had no trust in Spire, so they wanted my take on what they had been told, or they wanted to know how they could access services. Many were in shock as they had fallen for Paterson's lies and believed they had dodged a cancer bullet. Now they were being recalled and told they had had unnecessary surgery. They were devastated. They wanted clear answers, emotional and medical support, acknowledgement for the harm that had been caused, and many were rightly looking for compensation.

When I finally saw Spire's recall letter, I was struck by a box that said 'delete applicable'. Under it was a list of the many operations Paterson had carried out, whether he had practising privileges or not: breasts, varicose veins, colonoscopy, gastroscopy, hernia and a blank box to add 'other'. There currently isn't a full record of all the different types of operations Paterson performed, but it seems there was little if any limit on his appetite for surgery. I have even heard from a source that their mother's leg was amputated by Paterson.

Paul Lehmann was calling me regularly, sometimes a few times a week. He would ask me who he should be contacting and how to keep patients informed. I was also in regular contact with Liz Monaghan. She mentioned that Spire had around 200 letters 'returned to sender'. Obviously it was essential that these patients were tracked down. I asked if we could publicise the recall in the media, and suggested a media strategy. Spire agreed to put out a statement to the press drawing attention to the recall, the support available, and the helpline number. I thought it would help find the missing patients. Spire agreed to work with local media to do this the following January, when the inquiry recommendations were due to be published.

But of course they never did. I called Paul Lehmann to chase, reminding him that 200 patients never received a recall letter. He said that Spire had changed their mind, preferring instead for patients to contact them rather than the other way around.

I was livid. I immediately called my press network. Stacey Foster of ITV called Paul to quiz him about the patients Spire hadn't managed to contact. He called me back immediately. 'Did you talk to Stacey Foster?' 'Of course I did! You've gone back on your word to go to the press to try to trace these people.' That evening I appeared on local ITV and BBC news talking about the 200 missing patients, and recommending that anyone who was a Paterson patient get in touch with their hospital for a medical review.

During lockdown I had been invited to sit in on three different patients' associations' forums, including one for the Independent Sector Complaints Adjudication Service (ISCAS) on the complaints procedure in the private sector. It was clear to me that patients did not know how to make effective complaints about Spire, so I asked that the recommendations from the inquiry be embedded in the complaints' procedure. ISCAS responded that provided the government agreed to implement the recommendations, then they would include them. This should have been a win, but the government has not yet done what the inquiry recommended.

46

I had been fighting for an investigation into the deaths of Paterson patients for over fourteen years, making it the focal point of media appearances and my evidence to the inquiry, but I don't know if I believed it would ever actually happen. At times it had felt like authorities wanted to draw a line under everything. Paterson was in prison, compensation had been paid, the inquiry was concluded, but to me that was by no means the end of the story. The inquiry recommendations had yet to be implemented, the legal and regulatory loopholes in private medicine had not been addressed, there was no culture change to ensure this couldn't happen again, Spire still hadn't put a care and monitoring package in place, and hundreds of Paterson patients who had had cleavage-sparing mastectomies had died at a rate far above average.

On 23 January 2020, I got a phone call out of the blue from Jane Pawson, engagement lead to the inquiry, to say that the coroner was going to be in touch. She couldn't tell me why, but she did say it was good news about something I'd been fighting for. My stomach was in knots when I got off the phone. Oh my God, I thought, they must be looking at the people who had died. This was huge news.

The next day I received an email from the coroner's office:

'West Midlands Police have asked the Birmingham and Solihull Coroner to review a number of cases where patients have died from breast cancer and who were previously treated by Mr Paterson.'

The statement went on to say that the senior coroner Mrs Louise Hunt and the area coroner Ms Emma Brown were jointly carrying out a preliminary investigation into twenty-three test cases. These cases had been selected at random from Paterson's deceased patients to work out whether the required legal threshold for inquests had been met and identify whether there is evidence to suggest unnatural deaths as a result of potentially substandard treatment. They concluded the statement by saying:

'We understand that this will cause anxiety for a lot of families, and we would ask at this stage that families do not contact us.'

A website (coronerspatersoninvestigation.org) had been set up with preliminary information, and a firm of solicitors, Higgs & Sons, were appointed to assist with the investigation and field enquiries.

I was so relieved. Finally, those victims who died would have a voice. This was something I'd fought for, but it was more than I'd expected. I texted Jane Smith, 'OMG they're investigating the deaths.' She texted back, 'OMG Deb, you made them listen!'

At last things were moving forward. My mind was racing. I wondered if some of the friends who had died were on the list of the first twenty-three. I thought about all the families out there who had lost loved ones and how they would be feeling at this news.

The investigation into the twenty-three patient deaths used the following criteria:

'First, to identify whether there appears to have been any culpable human failing or system failing in the medical management of a person's breast cancer, and secondly, whether, on the balance of probabilities, that failing has more than minimally, trivially or negligibly contributed to death.'

In other words, did Paterson's cleavage-sparing mastectomies mean that cancer recurred when otherwise it would not have?

I checked the website every day for updates, but there was very little information. I got in touch with Higgs to try to find out what was happening, but to no avail. Eventually I started checking the general Birmingham coroner's website rather than the Paterson-specific one, as it had all newly announced inquests listed. I saw four names: Deborah Hynes, Yvonne Cordon, Shionagh Gough and Marie Pinfield. I knew Marie Pinfield.

These must be inquests into Paterson patients. Eventually this information was confirmed via the dedicated Paterson website, and the four inquests were opened on 6 July 2020.

I couldn't attend the coroner's court in person every day, but I had been sent a link so that I could dial in for audio access. This had to be applied for in advance so the court would know who was present. Over the crackly phone line the court official asked for everyone to confirm their name, and I introduced myself.

In her opening address, the coroner Louise Hunt said the inquests would examine whether there were systemic failings at Spire Little Aston and Parkway Hospitals in responding to concerns about Ian Paterson, and that the court would also speak to representatives from the NHS. It was a solemn occasion as she read out the names of the four deceased before announcing that the inquests would be adjourned to a date to be confirmed once the preliminary investigations were concluded.

In an earlier chapter I mentioned Marie Pinfield, a child protection officer with West Midlands Police, who had died when her cancer returned following a cleavage-sparing mastectomy. Hers had been one of the cases the whistleblower Hemant Ingle had tried to draw attention to.

I met Marie's sister, Shirley Moroney, during the Paterson trial and we struck up a friendship. She was still mourning the loss of her sister, and now she had to deal with the stress of an inquest, knowing it could be years before she got a definitive answer. 'My sister was my life and my enrichment. My life will never be the same. I'm eternally grateful to have had her,' she told me. She's currently in limbo waiting for the outcome of the inquest, frustrated by what she perceives as a lack of compassion from the coroner's court. Birmingham is one of the only coroner's courts not to offer free counselling, so I lobbied Caroline Williams, Head of Recall, to ensure families had access to help. She was able to secure funding for six free counselling sessions for each of those affected. I also petitioned Spire to offer the same, which they did.

On 22 July 2020, a further three inquests were opened in respect of Lindsey Phipps, Christine Gould and Judith Bruce. All of their deaths were deemed to be unnatural and the primary cause was recorded as breast cancer.

The coroner's office announced that while they were anxious that the investigations into the deaths should proceed as quickly as possible, it was a huge undertaking involving hundreds of patients, interested persons and medical experts, and thousands of documents. The work, they said, was being managed alongside the normal work of the senior coroner and area coroner, who have also been occupied with the consequence to the service of the Covid-19 pandemic, the latter affecting the availability of medical experts. Realistically, it was going to take years.

Almost two years later, on 28 October 2022, inquests were opened into the deaths of thirteen former Paterson patients and were adjourned at Birmingham Coroner's Court on the same day.

One of them was for my friend Catherine Coyne, a retired data protection officer. She died of breast cancer aged fifty-one in 2008, at home in Solihull. I got to know Cathy when we both attended Breast Friends; she was a lovely woman and the first person I met there. She was just a few months ahead of me with her chemotherapy treatment. On our first meeting she asked me if my nails had been affected by the chemo, as hers had. We were close in age, and like me she was married with children, so we bonded. Around the time she died she had been attending a counselling course funded by Breast Friends so she could volunteer to help other cancer patients at Solihull Hospital. I have a beautiful photo of her at our Christmas party, raising her glass and smiling.

Future inquests would consider any failings in the supervision of Paterson, including by clinical colleagues and whether they should have informed the appropriate authorities. The evidence would also examine whether there were 'systemic failings by hospital management ... in addressing and responding to concerns raised about Mr Paterson ... any inaction or failure of supervision by the regulatory agencies ... any failings in the culture at the hospitals where Mr Paterson worked (and) ... any failings in the recall system of patients.'

By June 2023, reviews had been completed into 417 former Paterson patients where breast cancer was listed as a cause of death in part one of their death certificates, and a further 130 cases were under review where breast cancer was included as a cause of death in part two. Bafflingly, the coroner's team has been unable to locate the death certificates of some deceased Paterson patients.

All of the inquests so far had immediately been adjourned pending the review of other cases. It's standard procedure to open an inquest – which is basically an admin process – and then immediately adjourn it while data and statements are gathered, but the delays were excruciating. The pandemic delayed everything and for two years there was no progress. I began to be contacted by other families. They all had very little or no information as to why their loved ones were chosen to be investigated by the coroner other than that their deaths were deemed to be unnatural and that their primary cause of death was recorded as breast cancer. By now I had a routine for dealing with this. I gave them the contact details of the relevant person in either the NHS or Spire to ask for the medical records of the deceased person and to schedule a meeting (usually over Zoom) to discuss. Most of them would then come back to me to ask me to take a look at their records, as they didn't trust the official line. I'd help them draft a list of questions to ask based on what I read, then I'd talk it through with them so they understood the medical jargon in advance of their meeting.

On 24 March 2023, seven more inquests were opened. Due to an administrative error these were not announced by the solicitor for the Coroner and I only found out when a press contact called the coroner's office for an update. The new names were Veronica Padget, Shena Mason, Melanie Chalkden, Shareen Cartwright, Margaret Shine, Patricia Smith and Janet Pay.

I saw Shena Mason's name and felt so sad for my friend, who had died in January 2014. I had quoted her words to the press after the trial, and I wondered what she would say now if she knew that finally there was a proper investigation into the deaths of Paterson patients. I knew the court had been struggling to contact some of the next of kin, and I worried that was true for Shena as her husband and son both had recently died, and her adult daughter had moved away.

I called Gillian Waterhouse. Although she had stepped back from her formal role of supporting Paterson patients, I knew she had kept in touch with Shena's family. The following day I was contacted by a BBC reporter asking for my reaction to the new inquests and if I knew any of the names on the list. I declined to talk about Shena as I didn't know if her family knew, but immediately contacted Gillian again to let her know the press would be covering it so she could tell Shena's family before they saw it in the media.

Paterson's mastectomy patients had a less than 56 per cent chance of survival, far below the national average (patients aged between fifty and sixty should have a 90 per cent chance of survival). I knew from Martin Lee's 2008 report that as many as 675 Paterson patients had died, and a source told me that these were being looked into as part of the coroner's investigation. I had been trying to get media coverage of the deaths for years, and I called the *Sunday Times* journalist Shaun Lintern. I had often given him information for stories and his coverage of the Paterson story had been some of the most detailed. He wrote an investigation in April 2023, which made the front page.

47

It quickly became clear that the size and scope of the inquests was greater than originally anticipated, and that same month His Honour Richard Foster, a former circuit judge, was nominated by the Lord Chief Justice to take over. Unsurprisingly, Paterson did not take any of this well. He had not been charged with any crime relating to the deaths, and no one was on trial, but nonetheless he did not want to appear as a witness in the coroner's court to give his side of the stories. Of course, it would be very difficult, if not impossible, to investigate without his testimony, but he attempted to use the same claim of poor mental health that he had used to delay his criminal trial, with the addition of complaints about the difficulty of working from a prison environment. This only worked for so long, and eventually Higgs, the solicitors for the coroners, applied for a Schedule 5 Notice, which would compel Paterson to give evidence to the coroner's court. After hearing from Paterson's solicitor and his psychologist (whose main qualification turned out to be in zoology), the coroner rejected Paterson's delay tactics and at the end of October 2024 granted the Schedule 5 Notice, saying:

'All witnesses have had to sacrifice aspects of their daily lives in order to give evidence, no doubt to considerable inconvenience to themselves and their families. Many witnesses are long since retired. In the same way it is not unreasonable to expect Mr Paterson to sacrifice aspects of his settled prison regime in order to provide evidence.'

It was within Foster's powers to fine Paterson up to £1,000 or even refer him for prosecution or contempt of court if he continued to refuse. He would have to appear in court via video from prison once a week, having been given access to relevant notes and time to prepare. Of course, the Paterson who eventually appeared on camera showed no signs of the symptoms his psychologist had described, as was also the case with his criminal trial. Instead, he was his usual arrogant, confident self. I sat in the Birmingham coroner's court and watched as the screen flickered into life and his face appeared. I hadn't seen him since the trial. He had lost a lot of weight, looked gaunt and tired, but if I hadn't known he was appearing from prison I wouldn't have been able to tell. He was in a nondescript office-looking room, wearing a shirt and holding a pencil. This time he was appearing as a witness rather than a defendant, but his attitude was the same as at the trial, that of an eminent surgeon who had somehow found himself the victim of a great miscarriage of justice. He seemed irritated at his medical expertise being questioned, and showed no sympathy for the dead women whose cases were being discussed, or their families.

Marie Pinfield's sister, Shirley Moroney, said, 'His participation, or lack of it, is just unacceptable. It's like water torture, like a dripping tap in your brain, with all these delays. Now, at the eleventh hour, he's putting in another obstacle. It's atrocious. He's had plenty of opportunity to prepare. It feels like, why are we even considering these requests?'

BUTCHER SURGEON IAN PATERSON'S EXTRAORDINARY OUTBURST OVER 50 WOMEN PATIENTS WHO DIED

A rogue breast surgeon jailed for 20 years had an outburst during a coroner's hearing, ahead of an 11-month-long inquest into the deaths of more than 50 of his patients.

Ian Paterson, who subjected more than 1,000 patients to unnecessary and damaging operations over 14 years, raised his voice and made demands as he insisted his preparations for the case were being hampered by his prison sentence. In the forthright torrent he also claimed coroner Judge Richard Foster had pre-judged him and moaned that he was being denied access to a laptop that contained files he claimed to

need for the inquest. He also said he wanted to be
transferred to an open prison.

The *Mirror* story summed up the situation well. Paterson couldn't keep his temper under control and was adamant that the whole thing was deeply unfair, particularly as he no longer had enough money for the sort of legal representation he'd previously enjoyed (his vast assets having been transferred elsewhere following his divorce). In front of the press and public – including me and another of his victims, Tracy King – he said:

'I'm being denied access to the materials currently on the basis of regime problems that occur at the prison and that – I can't see a way round that, although I am due to be decategorised. It has come the time in this unjust sentence that I am decategorised and should move to an open prison very soon and that may improve … the security situation which would presumably allow me more access to technology to become better prepared.'

If Paterson was being moved to an open prison, I wasn't aware of it. How could that possibly be acceptable when he had only served nine years and was currently the key witness in the inquests of the deaths of his patients following alleged cleavage-sparing mastectomies? New inquests were being opened regularly, surely now was not the time to give Paterson brand new privileges and access to the outside world?

I would have to worry about that later. Paterson was fighting his corner, claiming not to have access to documents or a laptop.

'I have nothing in my possession. I'm not allowed anything in my possession. The laptop upon which it is meant to have been uploaded, I haven't had access to for months, despite regular requests to the wing staff for that to be the case. I've been told there's no ability staffing levels and regime-wise for me to have access to it in a supervised capacity in a wing office. That's happened, I think, once or maybe twice since I actually had the laptop in my possession in the cell. Now, during that time of

three or four months where there wasn't a single incident, BCL [Paterson's legal advisors] *have pointed this out to the prison and to your representatives, and during that time I have produced more than 200 pages of submissions on the ridiculously embarrassing evidence that your experts have provided to you. So I think my participation is important. I'm willing to participate. I think my participation is important because nobody has actually heard from me. All of the submissions I sent to James's little inquiry were ignored completely and I haven't really been heard. I do think there's been a conflation between the current sentence I'm serving and what's happening in your court, and you've assumed guilt before innocence and that is – really that's a legal principle that we're all entitled to, is innocence until proven guilty, yet you seem to have decided that the first part has been proven, because you've already started collecting documents for the second part.'*

Of course, I hadn't previously had any insight into what Paterson thought of Bishop Graham James's inquiry, but his reference to it as 'James's little inquiry' told me everything I needed to know. Contempt, superiority and complete refusal to admit wrongdoing despite overwhelming evidence and the rather more unavoidably damning position of being in prison. He had referred to his existing convictions as 'unjust' but was clearly terrified of further charges relating to the deaths under investigation.

'I need an infrastructure that you have, that I don't have. There isn't a level playing field here. It's all you and your apparatus against me with no access, no representation and no funding. That doesn't seem like a fair representation of the British legal system to me.'

Judge Foster rebuffed the accusations of bias, responding:

'All that's happened so far is the doctors advising me have raised issues which give rise to an inquest being triggered, but no more and no less than that. Whether or not any or all of those deaths are what are called in the coronial law process an unnat-

ural death is a matter for me to decide and I sit there to decide that and I am also the investigator and not just the tribunal. But can I be quite clear that the infrastructure which I have is an infrastructure to look after your interests as well as the interests of everybody else. My job is to investigate fully, fairly and fearlessly and I underline for these purposes the word fairly. That's fairly to you and fairly to all the other interested persons as well.'

Foster asked John Burrell, the offender supervisor who was also on the call, to explain the logistics of Paterson's laptop situation. Burrell said that provision could be made to move Paterson to another wing. The unit he currently resided on did not lock cell doors, which meant that prisoners could access each other and therefore any laptop he had in his possession. Burrell proposed Paterson be relocated to a wing where the cell doors were locked in the evening, so he could have possession of the laptop during those hours. Paterson did not like this suggestion one bit.

'So what he's talking about is being transferred to a wing where the inmates are currently locked down for up to 23 hours per day, depending on regime and staffing levels. That is not something which I would be prepared to undertake for the sake of this process, particularly as I have the laptop in my cell for months after it was given to me by Mr Burgess ... and there wasn't a single incident. And you will see I'm actually sitting here with a tablet in front of me. This has been in my possession for the past year as I've been finishing off my Open University degree and it's not – it doesn't have any memory. It couldn't be used for the type of thing that we're talking about, but it is an electronic device which I have had in my cell for nearly a year with no incident. So the fact that they – the prison's solution to this problem is reversing my progression ... on a drug-infested, death-ridden, bang-up regime for most of the day is, I'm afraid, not an acceptable solution.'

It didn't sound like Paterson was having a very good time in prison, but nor should he be able to have access to a laptop where other prisoners could get it. Burrell disagreed with Paterson's claims, countering that the wing in question was not locked down for 23 hours a day and had better facilities, including toilets in cells (something Paterson currently did not have, which is why his cell was not locked at night). 'So from a prison point of view, we would not see that as a reversing of progression as was stated, and if Mr Paterson is due a categorisation review, that would not hinder that at all,' said Burrell.

This gave Paterson the opportunity to expose his true motive. He wanted to be moved to an open prison, and the inquests were giving him ammunition to try to expedite that.

'The problem is that when you come to Wymott, you start in G and H Wing and you progress to A or B, which are the more open, residential wings, or to J Wing, and thereafter to an open prison,' explained Paterson. 'I think that the solution here actually lies in the acceleration of my progression to open conditions, because my category window opened several weeks ago and my [inaudible] always promised me that I would move to a D Cat prison nearer to my family the minute that was available. So I'm due re-categorisation now, so I would suggest that that is the way forward.'

Most convenient. Open prisons are more relaxed, the final step in a detainee's journey through the system, but reserved only for those deemed to not be a risk (to staff, other prisoners, or of escape). In addition, prisoners may be allowed to come and go, even working at a local business or studying at college. Paterson's application would be considered based on his convictions, behavioural record and, of course, public interest. I had something to say about that.

48

In October 2024, the health secretary Wes Streeting took the very unusual decision to strip Paterson of his £1-million NHS pension following reporting by journalist Shaun Lintern and advice from Shaleel Kesavan, senior policy lead. It's rare, but in cases involving criminal, negligent or fraudulent acts that are particularly harmful to the public or the state, the government will sometimes intervene to strip perpetrators of their taxpayer-funded benefits. A similar decision was enacted in the case of Wayne Couzens, the murderer of Sarah Everard, who was stripped of his police pension in 2023. I talked to Kesavan on the phone, thanking him and asking if there could also be an investigation into the NHS pensions of other senior figures involved in the scandal, but he couldn't give me an answer.

That same month, Paterson's application to be moved to an open prison was approved. I found out when one of the victims from the trial contacted me. I was furious. It was practically the same as him being released. I spoke to the *Birmingham Mail*, telling them there was no way he should be released after serving half his sentence. Patient recalls were still ongoing, many former patients did not yet have answers about their treatment under Paterson, and many had not yet received compensation. Spire's database was at least 1,500 patients. 'This man is really evil,' I said.

Shirley Moroney said, 'It feels to me that if you had a thug that had gone to a pub and caused GBH to ten people we would never have given them any soft options … But because you are a manipulative surgeon you get a fast pass to getting out of prison. It is a scandal.'

To make things worse, many of the families and victims were not informed. I had to break the news to them so they didn't find out through the press first. I was asked to be interviewed the next morning by Mark Gough at the BBC, and I suggested Carol Johnson join me, who was one of the victims from the trial. At first she said no, as she had already done so much press and wanted to put it all behind her, but she turned up just before the journalist did, saying 'I couldn't let you face them on your own.'

The Prison Service, under pressure from the media, had to issue a statement:

'We apologise for this miscommunication and any distress it may have caused. Any decisions to move an offender to open conditions are made by prison governors after strict risk assessments. If they step out of line they face being returned to closed conditions immediately.'

I was also hearing from families involved in the inquests who did not believe Paterson should be moved at this stage of the investigations. So at the beginning of October 2024, I started a petition:

Paterson was sentenced to 20 years in prison for his heinous acts that resulted in significant harm to his patients. He has only served seven years of this sentence and has been given approval to move to an open Category D prison.

Transferring him to a lower-security facility would not only undermine the severity of his crimes but also silence the voices of the victims and their families who are still seeking justice and closure.

By signing this petition, we stand in solidarity with those who have suffered due to Paterson's actions. We urge you to take our concerns seriously and ensure that justice is upheld.

Petitions are useful for getting the attention of the press and politicians. Saqib Bhatti, the MP for Meriden and Solihull East, supported the petition and contacted the Ministry of Justice, telling the press:

'It is urgent that the decision to move Ian Paterson to a Category D prison is reviewed and reversed. His actions have caused unspeakable pain to so many people, and this move is

only increasing the anguish felt by the victims. I will continue to support my constituents and amplify their voices in objecting to this decision.'

It worked. I heard from two of the victims from the trial that they had been sent letters saying the move was now rejected. This felt like a big win. On 18 October 2024, the BBC reported:

FORMER BREAST SURGEON'S OPEN PRISON MOVE CANCELLED
A jailed former breast surgeon's move to an open prison has been cancelled following a risk assessment, the Ministry of Justice (MoJ) has confirmed.

Disgraced medic Ian Paterson, who was jailed for 20 years in 2017, was due to transfer from a Category C prison to a Category D prison.

The move had previously sparked outrage among his victims and their families, with one describing it as a 'kick in the guts'.

But a communication from the MoJ to one of Paterson's victims, seen by the BBC, said his Category D status had been rescinded following a review.

Confirming the update, a Prison Service spokesperson said: 'This move has been cancelled after a change in the prisoner's risk assessment.'

Despite his failed bid to be moved to an open prison, Paterson managed to cope with his weekly obligation to give evidence at the inquests. His first formal witness session was on 31 October 2024, at the inquest of Elaine Turbill. She had died in 2007 aged sixty-three, following a cleavage-sparing mastectomy by Paterson. He left behind 20 per cent of her breast tissue, and her cancer returned. At the inquest, Paterson claimed the cleavage-sparing mastectomy was an 'adaptation of a standard operation' and did not require separate consent. He even tried to put blame on the late Bethan Lloyd Owen.

'Most ladies know what a mastectomy is. I never went into great detail, it scares them and I don't think they hear it, they just hear the word cancer,' he said. 'This lady [Turbill] would have been taken into a separate room with a breast care nurse and would have discussed things in more detail.'

This seemed like deflection at best. One of the scariest things you can hear is that you have cancer. All you want is for the consultant to remove all the breast tissue and not leave any that might mean the cancer would return. Lloyd Owen explained the procedure to me but at no point did she mention that it would be an incomplete mastectomy, and nor did Paterson. Nor did they warn me how long and brutal my recovery would be.

During his evidence to the coroner Paterson tried to claim, 'It was frightening and [patients] didn't need to or want to know.' This is just not true. I can speak for myself, but I have also talked to hundreds of patients and they absolutely did want and of course needed to know. It is inconceivable that anyone would accept having breast tissue left behind if it could increase their risk of recurrence.

At the time of writing, sixty-three inquests have been opened, with new ones announced regularly. Two of them are from the list of six I read out at the inquiry. It is now one of the largest inquest investigations in British history, second only to the Hillsborough disaster.

49

In February 2019, the Royal College of Surgeons (RCS) published new guidance influenced by Paterson's wrongdoing, which recommended a strong framework for prioritising patient safety when developing and introducing surgical innovations. The guidance referenced the 'case of a breast surgeon single-handedly creating and applying a novel surgical procedure, the so-called cleavage-sparing mastectomy'.

But as of 2025, five years on from the inquiry, there is very little other progress. Many in the medical establishment badly want to file Paterson under 'one bad apple', forgetting that one bad apple spoils the rest. But he was never unique. There have been Patersons before, and there will be again if lessons are not learned and changes – systemic and cultural – are not priorities. For example, the spinal surgeon John Bradley Williamson has been found to have caused serious harm to patients and is currently the subject of a major investigation. He was allowed to continue operating even after concerns were raised, when a suspension could have saved patients from significant harm. Another case is that of bone surgeon Yaser Jabbar, a by-now all-too-familiar story of a bullying, toxic working culture in which a senior surgeon was undertaking harmful, unnecessary surgery on patients (in Jabbar's case, children). An investigation and lawsuits are underway, and a Royal College of Surgeons report into his conduct suggests hospital managers failed to act when staff raised concerns about Jabbar.

The NHS has always struggled with change, in part because it is not one cohesive, well-oiled machine but a legacy system comprised of multiple conflicting, neglected, often under-funded organisations, each of which has their own complicated way of doing things. Then, of course, there's the increasing reliance on private healthcare to provide NHS services, which can only make things worse. Paterson was able to thrive in part because private medicine is not regulated properly, has little to no over-sight, and prioritises profits over patients. In the NHS, he was lauded for getting the waiting lists down (something else that private hospitals are being used for), which blinded manage-ment to the problems.

But, of course, the inquiry was meant to address all this. On paper, it looks like progress, but in between the buzzwords and government-speak of the updates (of which there have been very few), nowhere near enough has actually happened.

Only one inquiry update has been formally published, in December 2022. In the introduction, the Conservative MP (at the time the party in power) Maria Caulfield said,

'Ian Paterson's patients were failed. Through the work of the inquiry, the campaigning of the patient representatives and all the organisations that have been part of implementing its findings, we hope that no one should ever find themselves in a similar position in the future.'

I can assure her that a great many patients are going to find themselves in a similar position in the future. Of course, there was subsequently a change of government, but that shouldn't have changed the remit of the taskforce. The 2022 update promised a lot, but in real terms it hasn't delivered.

At time of writing, ten of the recommendations or sub-recommendations have been accepted (that is, agreed as actionable and in theory put into practice), four have been 'accepted in principle', with little to no action actually being taken, and two were rejected outright.

For me, the most urgent concern is that a consultant can still rent a room in a private hospital and that hospital has no indemnity if the surgeon then commits a crime. Patients are simply not protected from wrongdoing. This is a loophole that needs to be closed, but it isn't being done.

One of the recommendations that is progressing is the creation of a database that tracks the number and outcome of consultant procedures. While not every doctor can be excellent, every doctor can, and should, be safe. There is currently a basic online database called the Private Healthcare Information Network (PHIN), mandated by the government but run by a private not-for-profit organisation, which gives patients topline information about their private consultant or hospital. In 2017, seven hospitals were criticised by the Competition and Markets Authority for not uploading data to PHIN.

Users can search by location or speciality type and find out how many of a particular procedure a consultant has done. There is even a section for patient reviews. Not all the data is complete or verified, but it is still a very useful tool for managers and patients to track and compare performance, as long as it is kept updated.

There is now also the National Consultant Information Programme (NCIP), an online database that managers and consultants can access to see and compare data. But it is not available to the public, so I met with Sir Norman Williams, the chair of NCIP, to ask why. He was incredibly sympathetic and helpful, and clearly distressed by the Paterson controversy. He told me that to roll out the NCIP to the public was a major IT project, firstly to integrate the data with PHIN to give a complete NHS and private overview of a consultant's practice, and then to make the interface and results user-friendly. I did get the impression he was serious about it, and he told me he wanted mandatory use of the data in consultant appraisals. It remains to be seen if this happens, but we have stayed in contact.

The second recommendation, that consultants write directly to patients in plain language, instead of using GPs as a middle-person, was put on hold by the last government, and the team disbanded. I met with Hugh Rayner, the medical director of HEFT, who assured me it's moving forward again, and there are some reports it's been rolled out in the West Midlands, but patients are still telling me it is not happening in their cases.

An extremely important recommendation that could save lives is that patients should have clarification on the care differences between the NHS and private medicine. The main one of these, of course, is the complete lack of emergency care and ICU in private hospitals should something go wrong. In addition, patients should know whether their consultant is truly independent (for example, do they own shares in the equipment being used for testing?) or whether they are covered by insurance. No one can give informed consent to a procedure in the private sector without this basic information. This information is not currently available on the websites of the private health-care providers I checked, including Spire. There's plenty of marketing blurb about the apparent benefits, but nothing about the risks or limitations compared to the NHS. The general public still does not know the downsides of going private, and nor will they unless providers are forced to be transparent.

The fourth recommendation is that patients should have time to reflect before consenting to a procedure. A cooling-off period, in essence. Of course, this is not always practical where the treatment is extremely urgent, but even in the case of cancer care, a few days does not usually make a clinical difference. While this recommendation was accepted, I do not believe it has been put into practice. I continue to hear from patients who were not asked for consent until the day of surgery, without proper time to reflect on the diagnosis or treatment options they were agreeing to. They did not know what they were consenting to until they signed, and in some cases it wasn't fully explained until afterwards, or at all.

The recommendation that MDTs be monitored for compliance is something that would have halted Paterson in his tracks. There are clear and strict guidelines, and the importance of multidisciplinary communication cannot be overstated. But I am concerned about the CQC's monitoring capabilities, especially as it has been beleaguered by delays to its auditing programmes (a recent public review by Dr Penny Dash was critical of the CQC). It is currently not clear how the CQC is measuring MDT compliance, and how patients are protected when non-compliance is found.

Another accepted recommendation is for clear communication to patients of the complaint procedures when something goes wrong. In the NHS, the PALS service is supposed to deal with this. It can work, but a lot of patients struggle to advocate for themselves, so they give up quickly. Most people don't know that the PALS service is staffed by volunteers, who can be unaware of issues or lack the authority to help, and I was concerned that Paterson patients were not getting the right advice. I received a letter from Paul Lehmann of Spire telling me that they were waiting for a response from PALS before sending recall letters out.

I spoke to Rachel Power, head of the Patients Association, and she told me that Spire had actually received that information just three days after requesting it.

I also discovered that the lead solicitors in the lawsuits, Thompsons and Slater and Gordon, along with thirty-eight smaller law firms, were no longer allowed to handle new Paterson cases. PALS gave me the name of three new firms of solicitors they said were handling it, so I called them. Two had not heard of Ian Paterson. I was horrified to learn that inexperienced law firms would be handling the new recall patients, so I emailed Rachel Power to complain. She replied to say she would advise the PALS helpline to refer Paterson patients to the Action against Medical Accidents charity rather than solicitors, and asked me for details of support groups for them to pass on. I also spoke to the journalist Shaun Lintern, who wrote a piece for the *Independent* outlining how Paterson patients were being blocked from justice by not having access to the right law firms. Eventually the restrictions on the original solicitors representing more Paterson patients were overturned in court.

In the private sector there is no standard complaints procedure at all. The Independent Sector Complaints Adjudication Service (ISCAS) – itself a private company – is supposed to handle it, but it's voluntary and many private providers have not signed up. Nor is there any pressure for those who have to comply. I had a meeting with an ISCAS board member to ask what they were doing about their sector's problems. It did not go well. We chatted a bit about Paterson. She then asked if I'd considered elocution lessons to address my Brummie accent. After, she cancelled the next meeting, saying they'd already dealt with the Paterson situation. Thankfully, she is no longer on the board, but I still see no progress or clarity on how complaints are monitored.

The next few accepted recommendations are about recalls. The ongoing Paterson recalls are the canary in the coalmine, with Spire identifying a further 1,500 patients from a 'legacy database' they had somehow missed. I still meet patients and families of deceased Paterson patients who have never been contacted and do not know it is not too late to have their case reviewed. There was never a care plan for private patients, and I have never been given an answer about what Paterson patients can expect if they have a problem in the same breast he removed. As far as I know there is no criteria for assessing this, but instead a case-by-case process that only really works for those like me) who can strongly advocate for ourselves. I was able to negotiate ongoing monitoring, but that is rare.

In the NHS there is now a national framework for recalls, originally written by Kevin Bolger. It is publicly available, but I find it piecemeal, perhaps because hospitals want to avoid recalling every patient of a known rogue surgeon even though, had they done that in the first place with Paterson, much of what unfolded could have been avoided.

One of the simpler recommendations is that hospital or Trust boards must apologise at the earliest stage when things go wrong. It took a long time to get apologies from the parties involved in the Paterson case. Of course, Paterson himself has never said sorry, and I highly doubt he ever will.

One of the rejected recommendations is that any healthcare professional under investigation should be suspended while the investigation is carried out. The problem is that suspensions are not consistently applied in healthcare but handed out on a case-by-case basis. It's difficult not to believe that, as in the case of Paterson, a surgeon who is getting the waiting lists down or who has a big personality might be given preferential treatment when it comes to deciding on suspension, regardless of the severity of the accusations or potential for damage. Many still see Paterson as a one-off rather than the product of a broken system, which makes it easier to avoid tough decisions about the culture of medicine. But, of course, he is not alone.

The final recommendation is that all of the recommendations that apply to the NHS should also apply to the private sector. This was rejected.

In reality, I am not clear that much, if anything, has actually changed.

On the five-year anniversary of the inquiry I briefed the press about how little had been done to implement the recommendations in the hopes it would embarrass the government into action. At the time, the committee had not met for over a year, and I was becoming incredibly frustrated at the lack of action, particularly as new rogue surgeon stories were popping up frequently. As the medical negligence lawyer Kashmir Uppal said, 'What is the point of having an inquiry when five years down the line so few of the recommendations have actually been implemented?' A government spokesperson told the ITV journalist Hannah Bechelet, 'We are working urgently to implement the remaining Paterson recommendations and will put patient safety at the heart of our 10 Year Plan for Health.'

I am now in communication with Baroness Gillian Merron, former MP for Lincoln and, as of July 2024, Parliamentary Under-Secretary of State for Women's Health and Mental Health. She's responsible for managing concerns relating to patient experience, complaints and safety. She told me the recommendations are moving along and once the inquests are concluded and there is news about whether any new criminal charges are being brought, things will proceed further. I can't say I have much faith, given it's been over five years since the inquiry. The can is being kicked along the road. There is nothing to stop the recommendations being implemented now other than a lack of political will, but I shall keep fighting.

In October 2022, the General Medical Council ruled on the tribunals of Mark Goldman and Ian Cunliffe. Both had been condemned by previous investigations, including the Kennedy Report and the James Inquiry, and the GMC spent eight years investigating the pair before bringing them in front of a medical practitioner tribunal to formally decide if they were guilty of failing to protect patients and of failing to report concerns about Paterson to the GMC. The hearings lasted several months and included evidence from previous investigations, including Kennedy's. Goldman's lawyer Mark Sutton argued that, 'The GMC cannot reasonably criticise Mr Goldman for not restricting Mr Paterson's practices when an Interim Orders Panel (IOP) didn't impose an order. What material did IOP have in front of it to justify imposing no restrictions?' The tribunal panel agreed, and none of the charges were found proved. In addition, Goldman and Cunliffe were awarded costs at a Medical Practitioners Tribunal Service tribunal after finding the GMC's conduct 'unreasonable', by failing to adhere to its own rules in pursuing the allegations, and 'unfair' to make a case against them when allegations were not supported by evidence and witnesses not prepared to give evidence.

The role of the NHS and potential systemic failures will be looked at by the Birmingham coroner. Goldman and Cunliffe are named as interested persons and have given evidence to the inquests.

Mark Goldman issued a statement during the James Inquiry regarding the events surrounding Paterson:

'I've not previously had an appropriate opportunity to speak out to the many patients of Ian Paterson who suffered at his hands. I recognise there's nothing I can say or do now to change what happened to them and, I acknowledge this and I'm profoundly regretful for that fact. And I also recognise that I can't alleviate the horrible physical consequences which they see daily, and it will forever serve as a long-term reminder to them of those events. And I recognise, I personally, cannot remove the physical and emotional burden from them which they will carry for ever. As the Chief Executive of Heart of England Foundation

Trust at the time of these events, I believe I made decisions in good faith, which were intended to ensure the safe practice of all the doctors and nurses within the Breast Service but, it is now clear that these were unsuccessful, and I would like to apologise to all the people who were affected during that period for the failure of those measures.

'*And I regard today as an opportunity for me to assist this inquiry and to learn the lessons beyond the work of Ian Kennedy. I gave evidence to Ian Kennedy in May 2013 and I stand by my comments at that time, which were actually made entirely from recollections because I'd already left the Trust, but it's some years later now and I think it's an opportunity for me to add further details which have emerged since and, particularly with reference to any misunderstanding or inaccuracies within the documented history. And I know and respect that many of Ian Paterson's victims will actually never be able to forgive me for the part I played and the failure to contain Ian Paterson's malpractice and his criminal activity and, frankly, I don't think I'll ever be able to forgive myself.*'

As of 2025 the plastic surgeon CC Kat is giving evidence to the coroner and denies knowledge of remaining breast tissue. At the inquest of Paterson patient Chloe Nikitas, who died aged forty-three in 2008 after her cancer returned following a cleavage-sparing mastectomy, the radiologist Dr Arpan Banerjee said the back tissue used for Nikitas' reconstruction made it impossible to tell whether there was breast tissue left behind, explaining, 'When you examine a reconstructed breast following a mastectomy you're not expecting to find left-behind breast tissue.'

At the same inquest, the BBC reported Kat as saying:

'*After a mastectomy it is very, very difficult for me to differentiate between what is just left behind subcutaneous tissue or even a thin layer of breast tissue, as it all looks the same.*'

She denied Paterson's claims that he had asked her to remove breast tissue he missed during his surgeries:

'Knowing what I know of Mr Paterson now, I'm not surprised that he has tried to extricate himself from this situation by putting forward these theories.'

The BBC reported that Kat told the inquest it was 'almost impossible' to expect 'absolutely no breast tissue' would be left behind following a mastectomy, but that 'one would hope that the breast tissue left behind is absolutely minimal'.

50

In March 2022, Bob, Jen, Rob and I dressed in our finest to attend the star-studded Pride of Birmingham Awards at the University of Birmingham's Great Hall (my artist son Will also came with us, but he chose to wear a T-shirt with my face on it). The beautiful high-ceilinged, wood-panelled room reminded me of Hogwarts, which was appropriate as one of the first celebrities we saw on the red carpet was David Bradley, who played Filch the caretaker in the Harry Potter films.

The event, a regional offshoot of Pride of Britain, was hosted by actress and presenter Kym Marsh. I had been on a camping holiday with Bob when I got a phone call saying I'd been nominated for a Special Recognition award for my campaigning, and now here we were, drinking champagne and eating a three-course meal among celebrities, a far cry from the tent I'd been in when I got the call. Alison Millar was following me around with a camera crew for her documentary It was surreal.

I sat nervously waiting for Kym Marsh to call my name. A video was played on the big screen detailing my work, including interviews with Bob and Jen, and then it was time for me to make my way onstage. The singer Beverley Knight and actor Don Gilet handed me a beautiful sculpture, a white figure with outstretched wings. I launched into a speech about how much still needed to be done, the changes needed in medicine and the justice not yet addressed for all victims. I was probably just supposed to say thank you and get off the stage, but I wasn't going to waste a good opportunity to campaign.

Afterwards, Bob and I mingled with the celebrity guests (I chatted to Black Sabbath legend Tony Iommi, knowing Bob wouldn't mind if we ran away together) and then I was interviewed by the press alongside Beverley Knight. She is an incredibly impressive charity campaigner, raising funds and awareness for causes including HIV, maternal mortality, poverty and disaster relief. She told the press:

'*I don't think I can find enough superlatives to describe Debbie Douglas and her tenacity. When you have a woman who has a mission and a fire in her belly, woe-betide anybody who stands in her way.*

'*Tomorrow is International Women's Day, and around the world, we will be celebrating the Debbie Douglases of this world who have fought bravely and tirelessly – and continue to fight – to make sure the voices of the unheard are lifted up. She's an absolutely incredible woman and she's from our area. I'm going to talk about her on* Loose Women *on Tuesday.*'

I couldn't believe what I was hearing. At that point it had been a battle largely fought from my front room, or in overheated meeting rooms with officials who didn't always want to listen. To hear such kind words from someone I admired so much was incredible. I reiterated to the press that I and the other campaigners are still fighting, that the inquiry recommendations had not yet been implemented, and that the inquests had only just begun.

Beverley Knight was as good as her word, appearing on the ITV show *Loose Women* to say:

'*I gave an award yesterday, a special recognition award to a woman called Debbie Douglas at the Pride of Birmingham awards, and she profoundly moved me with her fight to see the disgraced doctor Ian Paterson come to justice.*

She became the voice of women that had been butchered unnecessarily. An incredible woman who refused to give up on that fight.'

In June 2022, Alison Millar's ITV documentary was released. Titled *Bodies of Evidence: The Butcher Surgeon*, it featured an extensive interview with me. I had provided a great deal of evidence to the producers, and Millar had asked me if I would persuade Ingle to be interviewed on camera. He still felt bad about not giving evidence to the inquiry, so he agreed to appear on film. His testimony formed a crucial part of the story, along with that of Professor Wishart and others. The film won Highly Commended at the True Crime Awards, and afterwards I was contacted by patients from all over the country.

Campaigning has taken up the last fifteen years of my life. I'm retired now, and while I've had plenty of time to do all the usual things a retired woman does, I still spend hours every single day working on some aspect of the Ian Paterson story. The recommendations have still not been implemented, and I'm working with politicians and members of the House of Lords to try to fix that. There are patients who still don't have compensation, a care plan or a proper understanding of what happened to them. Then there are the families of those affected by the inquests, many of whom have little to no resources or understanding of the complex medical and legal detail they're being presented with. I'm often a go-between, translating information between the authorities and patients, or between two different sets of authorities (passing information from the NHS to the government, for example).

I am now Chair of Breast Friends Solihull following the death of our co-chair Claire, a Paterson patient whose death is being investigated by the coroner and who was one of the six names I gave to the inquiry. I continue to support breast cancer patients and their families alongside my campaigning work. In 2024, we created a community garden and allotment with time and resources kindly donated by local businesses. This gives patients somewhere to go, to gain a small respite from the daily stresses of their illness.

My own illness is at bay. I have regular monitoring through the NHS (Spire still won't monitor Paterson patients) and although it is difficult for scans to pick up signs of cancer because of the mess of reconstruction and breast tissue, so far my cancer does not seem to have come back. I still have health and mobility issues, and I can't know what state I'd be in had I not had an unnecessary mastectomy and chemotherapy in the first place, but I don't let anything stop me. I travel the UK talking to medical and patient groups, trying to ensure that change happens. I regularly talk to the media, and have appeared in multiple documentaries, on podcasts, in magazines and newspapers, and worldwide on broadcast news. I have a great deal to say.

Because Ian Paterson is not a one-off. He is a symptom of a system that not only allowed him to carry out his crimes but actively helped to cover them up. I am often asked for advice from solicitors or patients of other 'rogue' surgeons, and the patterns are always the same. Bullying, fear of speaking out, poor systems and lack of oversight, and pressure to deliver results that can compromise patient safety. One of the biggest contributing factors to Paterson's behaviour in the NHS and the main reason he got away with it for so long is because his surgery was so fast, he got the waiting list down. In July 2025, the government announced plans to link NHS pay to waiting lists. The health secretary Wes Streeting called it 'carrot and stick reforms' to 'boost productivity, tackle underperformance and drive up standards for patients'. The wider issues around Ian Paterson are a clear example of what repercussions and unintended consequences there can be when medical bosses are motivated by money and making spreadsheets look good. Without significant reforms and joined-up access to data (for example linking the NCIP and PHIN databases mentioned in the previous chapter), nothing will change. We are in the middle of a perfect storm for another Paterson.

When the motive is not money or data, there is no greater force for good than the NHS and the people who work in it. In April 2024, almost my whole family travelled to London to catch the train to Bruges. Me, Bob, my son Will, Will's partner Poonam, Jen and Scott, and their two girls, Bella and Sophia. We were excited and nervous the entire journey, the culmination of years of stress, fear, hope and, eventually, triumph.

We walked across from Brugge station to a beautiful cafe with outdoor seating and ordered drinks. The Douglas clan must have been a sight, three generations on a mission. We were not exactly tourists, though, as we were there to meet someone. Jen kept looking nervously at her phone for messages, then suddenly said, 'He's coming!'

We all looked across the square. A tall man was making his way over with his wife and two kids, who were about the same age as my grandkids. Jen got up and almost ran to meet them. I got out my phone and started filming, capturing the moment she and the man enveloped each other in a powerful hug. I watch the footage often. His name is Jorn, and he is Jen's stem cell donor.

Protocol for stranger donation is that after two years the recipient can request to contact the donor, who can choose to accept or not. Jen had immediately done so, and Jorn replied straight away. They got to know each other over email over the next few years, discovering a mutual love of rock music and football. Jorn had a similar family to Jen, and they vowed to meet up when circumstances allowed.

Of course, Jen had to take the whole family. We'd supported her together, just like everyone had supported me when I had cancer. That same year we'd all taken part in the British Transplant Games to raise money for the Anthony Nolan Trust. We do so much as a family because we're all so glad to be together. When she first had the transplant and it worked, I had said that one day, if possible, I would buy the donor a beer. Now I had my chance. As Jorn came over, I stood up and hugged him for a long time. 'Thank you for everything you've done,' I said through my tears. It was incredible to hug the man who had saved my daughter's life. I looked at him, wondering if I'd somehow recognise something in him that suggested he'd be a perfect stem cell match for Jen. He told me had grown up in a small village in Germany and that twenty years ago, a local boy had needed a stem cell transplant for leukaemia. Jorn had signed up to the register in the hopes he might be a match, but he was not. Two decades later, he was contacted to say he had matched with someone.

We all spent the day together. Despite the language barrier, the kids got on famously, almost feeling like blood relations. I chatted to Jorn's wife Vera, a lovely woman who seemed as moved as I was. We went out for dinner and Jen handed over the presents she had bought for Jorn: British goodies from Marks and Spencer, and an Aston Villa shirt. Jorn is a Werder Bremen fan, but he promised to wear the Villa shirt in secret.

A year later, Jorn and his family came to visit us in Birmingham. Bob and I made them a traditional afternoon tea and we all sat and laughed like we were one big family. Without Jorn, mine would not be complete. But he is not the only person I owe my gratitude to. Jen's medical team saved her life. Everyone involved in her care, during a global pandemic no less, was incredible. The medical research and the transplant registers that match patients with donors are a global effort, showcasing medicine at its very best. The NHS, for all its faults, for every criticism levelled at it in this book and the investigations that identified major shortcomings, is still the most extraordinary and precious resource we have, and it deserves protection. Its staff save lives every single day.

2025 was the year of Jen's fortieth birthday. She planned months of events to celebrate the milestone she thought she'd never see. I was finalising some bits of research in June 2025 when my phone pinged. It was Jen sending me photos She had just climbed Mount Snowdon to mark her birthday, and was pictured triumphant and glowing, surrounded by friends, beaming in the sunshine, a picture of health. 'Top of the world!' said the caption. I smiled and sent back a love heart before returning to my work.

Acknowledgements

To my husband Bob – my rock, my friend and my guide – thank you for your constant love and support, for believing in me, for telling me to slow down when I do too much, for looking after me, and for walking beside me through every chapter of this journey.

Thanks to our wonderful, inspiring children Robert, Jenny and Will and their partners, Mary, Scott and Poonam. I'm grateful for your love, patience and encouragement. You remind me every day of what truly matters.

And to my two beautiful grandchildren, Sophia and Bella, whose laughter and love have helped balance the harder moments in this book. You bring endless joy, hope and light to my life.

My deepest thanks to my mum and dad, who taught me the importance of truth and integrity. You showed me that there is never a reason to fear anything when you are right, to fight for what you believe in and to always be the best you can at whatever you do. You taught me to think for myself, to always meet life with courage, compassion and conviction, and to never give up. The values you lived by are the foundation of who I am.

To my brother John, who always had my back growing up, and his wife Jackie: thank you for your support, humour and for always being there.

Thank you to Tracy King for reaching out to me and allowing yourself to be part of this book. I appreciate your knowledge, understanding, humour and generosity of spirit. I've learned so much from you about how to construct, weave and tell my story. You also introduced me to my wonderful agent, Will Francis, who championed this project so enthusiastically.

Thanks to Joel Simons, my publisher, and the team at HarperNonFiction for believing in this story and giving me the opportunity to tell it.

I would like to thank Jane Smith for her unwavering support throughout the trial and inquiry. My deepest gratitude also goes to the many victims who entrusted me with their stories, provided witness statements to the various inquiries, and bravely testified in court.

Thanks to all the journalists mentioned in this book, and all those who covered the story in the media.

Special thanks to Darragh Macintyre, who after I told him he'd missed a trick by not making Paterson the whole story on *Panorama* said, 'You know what to do: write a book!' and for introducing me to Alison Millar.

I'd like to thank all my friends and family for their support and encouragement on this journey, particularly my dear friend Mandy, who passed away before this book could be published. She always told me how proud she was of what I was doing, and that we'd drink champagne at my party when I became a bestseller.

Credits

HarperCollins
Joel Simons
Simon Gerratt
Gaurika Kumar
Megan Smith
Izzy Warner
Dean Russell
Alan Cracknell
Francesca Sidhu
Fionnuala Barrett
Sarah Allen-Sutter

Janklow & Nesbit
Will Francis
Corissa Hollonbec
Kirsty Gordon

Additional research
Alex Taylor